The Business Travel Survival Guide

Jack Cummings

John Wiley & Sons, Inc.

New York • Chichester • Brisbane
Toronto • Singapore

DO YOU WISH TO ADD TRAVEL TIPS—CHANGES—
UPDATES?

To ensure that future editions of this book are up to date and
filled with even more travel tips please send your suggestions
to the AUTHOR, Jack Cummings, 3111 NE 22nd Street, Fort
Lauderdale, FL 33305, or FAX: 305-563-4354.

Copyright © 1991 by Jack Cummings

Published by John Wiley & Sons, Inc.

Library of Congress Cataloging in Publication Data

Cummings, Jack, 1940–
    The business travel survival guide / by Jack Cummings.
    p.   cm.
    Includes bibliographical references.
    ISBN 0-471-53075-1 (paper)
    1. Business Travel.   I. Title.   II. Series.
G156.5.B86C86 1991
910'.2'02—dc20   91-8414

Printed in the United States of America
10 9 8 7 6 5 4 3 2 1

Contents

1	Surviving Business Travel	1
2	Before You Leave	9
3	Pack Light, Travel Right	37
4	How to Find and Keep a Super Travel Agent	49
5	How to Beat the Airlines at Their Own Game	67
6	Dealing with Overbooked Flights and Nightmares	117
7	The Ills of Travel and How to Avoid Them	129
8	Importance of Immunization & Vaccination	161
9	How to Survive In-Flight Calamities	169
10	How to Survive Political Unrest	191
11	When What Can Go Wrong, Does	199
12	How to Deal with Customs Officials	235
13	How to Survive Travelers Check Dilemmas	247
14	How to Survive the Rental Car Racket	263

15   Some Tips on Tipping   287

16   Using Tax Laws to Your
         Advantage   309

17   Information for 25 U.S.
         Metropolitan Areas   325

         Index   389

1
Surviving Business Travel

Travel is glamorous, exciting, and filled with experiences like those of the rich and famous. Beautiful people in exotic places—that *is* what traveling is all about, right? It is if you believe the airlines, travel agencies, and their advertisements. But if you've traveled on business with any regularity, you know better. And if you expect to be a frequent business traveler, you'll soon find out how little of that is true.

Traveling can be lonely. Frequent travel often means hardships saturated with disappointments as well as mental and physical burnout, and can often disrupt family harmony. As a business traveler, you can easily find yourself paying top dollar for airline tickets, hotel accommodations, meals, and just about any service that comes with a price tag. All business travelers eventually experience the frustration that results from being shuttled about like a badminton birdie—bumped from flights or rooms that were reserved weeks in advance and dealing with substandard accommodations, meals, and service. Doesn't sound like a glamorous way of life, does it?

It often isn't. But there are ways to make business travel less difficult and, most important, *less costly*. Your trips can at least be pleasant and affordable, if not exotic. And if you are willing to put forth the initial effort, you can bring a degree of excitement and adventure to each new trip.

Travel and the Bottom Line

You can begin by recognizing that the cost of doing business on the road has become a major overhead expense for many companies. Unless you take positive action, your travel expenses can eat deeply into company profits. Travel expense records submitted by you and your colleagues can represent the difference between a good year financially and the milestone year in which your company has to file for bankruptcy.

No kidding. Travel expenses can add up to plenty of red ink. You aren't going to win any friends or allies at the top levels of your company if you turn in travel vouchers that look more like winning lottery tickets. Likewise, if you are responsible for your own travel expenses, you certainly aren't going to be able to afford to travel much longer unless you discover some ways to save money. And you heard it here first: You *can* travel for less, and at greater comfort than you might otherwise expect.

That's what *The Business Travel Survival Guide* is all about. You'll learn not only how to survive the hazards of travel but also how to transform potentially personal and financial disasters into positive travel experiences. You'll discover that comfort and good service are available at a lower cost, and you'll see how to survive and prosper on the road.

The Business Traveler's Attitude Checklist

The three-step checklist described here deals with a sometimes ignored, yet important, part of travel—your attitude. You are a businessperson, probably a successful one. You know the importance of maintaining a positive attitude. It's one of the qualities that helped you rise to your current position. Have you ever paused to consider, though, how a positive attitude is developed and maintained? Probably not, because a good attitude comes fairly naturally to you. But think about it. You find it easy to maintain a good, positive attitude when you are confident—when you know you understand what is expected of you and when you feel in control of your situation. When you lose control, it becomes more difficult to maintain a positive outlook. So, confidence leads to a positive attitude. But what leads to confidence?

Organize, Organize, Organize

You are confident and feel in control when you know what to expect; when you recognize possible problems, alternatives, and benefits; and when you seize a strong position to act on this knowledge. In other words, confidence results from foresight and from careful planning.

In travel, like other business situations, the more carefully you plan, the greater will be your effectiveness. Sound, advanced travel planning leads to increased comfort and cost-efficiency on the road. To make successful plans, you need information. That's what you will find in this and later chapters of *The Business Travel Survival Guide.* You'll be given tips, checklists, warnings, helpful hints, casual advice, and specific examples all designed to explain what you should and what you should not do when making travel plans. In my experience, astute, advance travel planning leads to a level of confidence that you don't often see among business travelers (most of whom, quite frankly, tend to be focused almost solely on the specific business goals they hope to achieve during their trip).

If you don't want your business trip to be ruined by travel problems, it pays to develop what I call a *superattitude* toward business travel. A superattitude evolves from a conscious effort to plan all aspects of your trip. A superattitude goes beyond a typical positive attitude, because you feel certain that your business-trip objectives are no longer in any jeopardy: You have planned, as far as possible, for most potential travel problems. You know what to expect, because you have taken steps to avoid most of the unexpected situations that can arise during business travel. As a result, problems will be less frequent, and when they do occur, you'll be ready to deal with them effectively.

Don't Agonize Over Unorganized Travel Plans

When last-minute travel is inevitable, when your expected itinerary has fallen apart despite all plans you have tried to make, *go with the flow.* Don't worry about it—because *it won't do any good to fight it.*

Let me explain. A superattitude involves more than ideal planning. It also acknowledges that you've done all that you can do. Through conversations with thousands of business travelers, I've learned that the single most frustrating factor for all business travelers, at one time or another, is the legitimate inability to make effective travel arrangements. I know. I've already said this book is intended to help you organize future travel plans more easily, at a reduced cost. But accept the fact that there will be situations in which you have zero time to plan—you are called away on business, in essence, *yesterday*. In such situations, you might as well give in to Murphy's Law. (What *can* go wrong, *will* go wrong.) Why fight what you cannot control?

Enjoy Your Travel

This might sound simplistic. But, face it, travel involves an element of the unknown, the mystical, the exotic. For some, travel is a dream. To others, it's a chore. Most business travelers, although they might pretend to hate leaving town, deep down know that travel is the essence of escape. Maybe it all goes back to childhood, or when these businesspeople traveled for holidays or vacations. Maybe these travelers were smitten by game shows that offer trips to Paris, Caribbean cruises, or other fantasy destinations.

But remember the dose of reality offered at the start of this chapter: Travel can be lonely. You might come to despise what you once thought you would love. Somewhere between the first day on the job and that moment when travel begins to seem tedious, both the company and you will seem to have different goals. You foresaw some power and benefits in travel and now see only a work task. The company just wanted you to get the job done. Whenever this disparity occurs between expectations and reality, nobody benefits. As the business traveler, you are going to feel unhappy and burned out. Your company, in turn, is not going to benefit from a disillusioned employee.

The trick is to keep in mind the motivations that initially attracted you to a life that involves frequent travel, and to seek new ways to renew or enhance the mystique of travel. Although I've tried to suggest that glamour is an infrequent sensation of the business traveler, I'm not suggesting that enjoyment and even excitement are not possible. I remember reading, long ago, Somerset

Maugham's short stories about South Pacific travel on tramp steamers and remember what attracted me to those stories. The world was dreamlike, fantastic. Every page brought adventure and meetings with unusual people in unusual places.

At this point, with perhaps hundreds or thousands of miles of travel experience, you might wonder with a bit of cynicism how you are going to find adventure and excitement in your next seemingly mundane travel assignment, say Belle Glade, Florida. If your only interests are opera and museums, you may never find excitement in this farming town. But if you want to find out more about largemouth bass fishing, the winter migration patterns of North American birds, the geological phenomenon of sinkholes, early Southeastern Native American culture, or the sugar cane industry, then you couldn't be going to a more treasure-filled environment. Somerset Maugham might have envied you.

When you treat each new destination as a potential for learning, you certainly expand your knowledge and you might discover new interests. However, there are also practical reasons for learning more about your travel destinations. It makes sense to learn about the people of that area, and about their interests and life-styles. You can better deal with clients if you understand their attitudes, interests, and the manner in which they are likely to view *you*. Learning about an area in which you are going to transact business can also impress clients and help you build a strong working relationship with them. Simply put, the greater your knowledge of a country, region, or city, the more at home you can expect to be there, and the more *confidence* you can expect to feel. Of course, this kind of knowledge and confidence only serves to enhance your superattitude as a business traveler.

TIP

Try to find out where your client calls home. The cliche "When in Rome, do as the Romans do" may or may not be relevant to your business situation. For instance, you might be all geared up to do business with a Roman in Rome, and you may have studied about the city—its people, culture, and history. On your arrival in Rome, you find that your client is actually a homesick native of Houston and would much rather talk about the Oilers or Texas chili than Italian culture. You didn't do your homework! Try to learn as much about the people you are going to deal with as you learn about the area in which they live.

As You Travel Through This Book

One of my reasons for writing *The Business Travel Survival Guide* is to help business travelers increase their enjoyment of life on the road. This book should help you achieve the following three travel goals:

1. Maximize your travel comfort.
2. Minimize your travel expense.
3. Increase your ability to cope with potential problems, either by eliminating problems or by giving you the tools to deal with problems quickly and effectively.

Toward this end, each chapter offers ideas and specific techniques that can help you increase your travel enjoyment and your travel goals. A positive superattitude about travel benefits you, your family, and your company. Such an attitude actually increases your desire to visit new places. Read on, learn, and enjoy.

2

Before You Leave

One of the best ways to minimize your worries is to develop good pretravel habits. Perhaps you are the rare type of person who views traveling as a process as natural as taking a Sunday afternoon fishing trip. You feel confident in just throwing some clothes in a garment bag and then dashing out the door. If you are such a carefree spirit, then you are truly blessed. However, you are also inviting problems—problems that can be easily prevented with a little planning. By developing pretravel planning habits, traveling might actually become almost as stress-free as a Sunday afternoon fishing expedition. When you think ahead, you not only make your time away from home as comfortable as possible for yourself but also for the family members and business associates you leave behind.

The Checklist of Business Travel Preparations

As you prepare to take a trip, it should become second nature to prepare and refer to a checklist of things to do before you leave. The following checklist provides a good plan to follow. Of course, you can adjust this list to meet your specific travel or personal needs.

____ 1. Book flights and accommodations in a timely manner.

    ____ a. Order special meals.

    ____ b. Get boarding pass and seat selection.

    ____ c. Request smoking or nonsmoking hotel room.

    ____ d. Be sure your frequent flyer data is current.

____ 2. Make a business travel itinerary.

____ 3. Leave a file of important documents at home.

____ 4. Enter travel dates and purpose in a business expense diary.

____ 5. Check weather conditions and forecasts for your destinations.

____ 6. Have matching, inexpensive luggage.

____ 7. Pack frugally.

____ 8. Label your luggage—outside and inside—with your name, business address, and business phone number.

____ 9. Review and confirm your reservations.

____ 10. Be sure you have all needed items:

    ____ a. Tickets

_____ b. Registration and confirmation
numbers

_____ c. Needed medicine

_____ d. Prescriptions for medicine and
glasses

_____ e. Special travel conveniences

_____ 11. Hide a key to your car and home.

_____ 12. Make a copy of important items in
your wallet.

_____ 13. Have a phone number to cancel credit
cards if lost or stolen.

_____ 14. Make a note indicating where you
parked your car.

_____ 15. Have personal and auto insurance
data with you.

_____ 16. Wear a bracelet or chain with a
medallion indicating your allergies or
medical alert data.

_____ 17. Use a hotel safety box when available.

The remainder of this chapter explores each of
the checklist items in detail, concluding with special tips for preparing to fly for business reasons.

Book Flights and Accommodations in a Timely Manner

Even if you travel only occasionally, you probably know the importance of booking flights and accommodations in a timely manner. The farther in advance that you book arrangements, the more likely you will receive low fares, satisfactory seat selection, and desired hotel accommodations.

To arrange for special meals during flights, either for medical reasons or personal preferences, you should do so _at least_ 48 hours prior to each flight's departure. For some airlines and types of meals, you might have to make arrangements even farther in advance. If you are like most business travelers, you will have your travel agent make bookings and reservations for you. If so, be sure your agent knows the kind of meal service you desire. Make a practice of confirming any special meals 24 hours before your flight. Table 2–1 (on pages 14 and 15) summarizes the types of special meals available from many major airlines.

When possible, your travel agent should obtain seat selections for all segments of your flights and should include boarding passes with your tickets. This procedure helps you to avoid being bumped from an overbooked flight, but only if you check in before the flight becomes 100 percent full. Advance seat selection also increases your chances of getting the section of seating you prefer. Before you make a seat selection, keep the following points in mind:

☐ Window seats that are situated in front of an emergency exit row usually do not recline.

☐ Often a second exit row is behind the first. So, if you like to ask for an "exit row" seat, make sure you get the second one, because the first-row seats may not recline.

☐ Smoking areas on international airlines may not follow logical patterns. On some international carriers, it is possible to be seated next to a smoker, even within the nonsmoking section.

☐ On jets, the farther forward you sit, the quieter the plane will be.

☐ Seats next to prop or turboprop engines are very noisy.

☐ Avoid sitting next to bathrooms and galley service areas.

The provisions and restrictions of frequent flyer programs seem to change daily. Make sure that your travel agent has processed your bookings to ensure you maximum points or mileage for your frequent flyer status. To aid you in this, tell your travel agent that you expect to be kept abreast of any new items that might increase your frequent flyer bonus points. Hotels, rental car companies, airlines, and credit card companies all carry special promotions from time to time. When you take advantage of these promotions, you supplement your regular mileage points. However, information about these promotions often will not come to you directly, so it is a good idea to tap your travel agent's expertise for frequent flyer promotions and changes.

Make a Business Travel Itinerary

Have your travel agent or secretary create a detailed travel itinerary that will be useful to you as well as to your family and business associates. The itinerary should contain at least the following information:

☐ Date and departure and arrival times of each flight

☐ City and airport for departures and arrivals

☐ Airline and flight number

☐ Assigned seat (if available) for each flight

☐ A copy of each airline ticket

☐ Car rental data: company, confirmation number, means of payment, and car type

☐ Hotel data: address and confirmation number, means of payment, type of accommodation requested, hour to which the reservation is to be held, phone number (including area and country codes), and (optionally) which card used to guarantee the reservation

☐ Anticipated date and time of each appointment

Table 2-1 **Special Meals**

Airline	Children's	Diabetic	Diet	Gluten-free	Hypoglycemic	Low Cholesterol	Low Sodium	Kosher	Oriental	Seafood	Vegetarian (Strict)	Vegetarian (Lacto-ovo)	Other	Advance Notice To Guarantee
Air Canada	•	•	•	•	•	•	•	•			•		Nutri-Action	24 Hours
Alaska Airlines	•	•	•			•	•	•			•	•		24 Hours
American Airlines	•	•	•			•	•	•	•	•	•	•	Bland	6 Hours; 12 Hours—Kosher
American West		•				•		•			•			24 Hours
Canadian Airlines Int'l		•				•	•	•			•			3 Days
Continental	•	•	•	•	•	•	•	•		•	•	•		12 Hours
Delta	•	•	•		•	•	•	•		•	•	•	Bland	3 Hours; 8 Hours—Kosher
Hawaiian							•	•						48 Hours
Midway	•	•	•			•	•	•		•	•	•		48 Hours

14

Airline										Bland	Advance Notice
Midwest Express	•	•	•		•	•	•	•	•		24 Hours
Northwest	•	•		•	•		•	•	•	•	6 Hours
Pan Am	•	•			•	•	•		•	•	6 Hours
Piedmont									•		24 Hours
TWA	•	•		•	•	•	•	•	•		24 Hours
United	•	•	•	•	•	•	•		•		24 Hours
USAir	•	•	•	•	•	•	•	•	•		By 8 P.M. prev. day
Wardair	•				•	•	•	•	•		24 Hours
											48 Hours—Kosher

Note: Each airline may have different titles for its meals, and several of the above may actually be the same kind of food. For example, diet and low sodium and vegetarian may all be the same. Ask for specific meal offerings available for your flight.

☐ List of companies and persons you plan to visit, including their addresses and phone numbers

☐ Special messages and information for business or family members. Possible items might include:

— Important clients to contact
— Travelers check numbers
— Personal information

TIP

Never travel without a detailed business trip itinerary. Also, leave several copies of your itinerary at home, at your office, and with any other people who may need to reach you. Place a copy in each piece of luggage or carry-on bag to aid in the bag's speedy return should it be lost or stolen.

WARNING: Losing your airline ticket can be worse than losing cash. For instance, if you have a round-trip super saver from Miami to New York City, your actual cost for the ticket might be less than $200. If you lose the ticket and have to replace it at the check-in counter, you might be forced to pay full fare for the same round trip, possibly at triple the super saver fare. Although you might eventually receive a refund for the lost ticket, you will still lose money by paying for the higher-priced replacement ticket.

TIP

Make two copies of your ticket (all segments). Leave one copy at home and bring the other copy with you. If your ticket is stolen or lost, your copy can provide the airline with all the information required to get the refund process started. In some cases, on some airlines, the station manager may even allow you to board using the copy of the ticket.

Leave a File of Important Documents at Home

Before you leave home—regardless of whether you are single, married, or live alone or with someone else—it is a good idea to let someone at home know where to find important documents. Although many travelers do not like to think about disaster, legal and other documents should be accessible to someone in the unlikely event you do not make it back from a trip. Important documents could include any or all of the following items, along with any other documents that pertain to your personal circumstances:

☐ Your will

☐ Insurance policies and names and numbers for insurance agents

☐ Auto titles

☐ Deeds to real property

☐ Safe-deposit box keys

☐ Stocks and other certificates of liquid assets

☐ Mortgages and other documents of indebtedness

☐ Evidence of money owed to you

☐ Locations where other documents can be found

☐ Copies of important documents and identification that you carry in your wallet

☐ Spare home and auto keys

☐ Travelers check numbers

☐ Phone numbers and addresses for your lawyer, accountant, and physicians

Enter Travel Dates and Purpose in a Business Expense Diary

You should use a business travel diary to document your expenses in case of an IRS audit. A simple notebook with at least 183 pages (use one side for each day of the year) will do. Of course, more elaborate and expensive diaries are available in different forms and sizes. Make sure the diary you choose is small enough to carry with you throughout the day, so that you can periodically make entries.

Be aware of the increased probes the IRS has been making about business and travel deductions. Considerable limitations apply today to businesspeople who entertain and travel. Be aware of how important it is to record travel expenses in detail. Include your date of departure on an appropriate diary page, then use the following pages to mark the place you will spend each night of your trip (and date each page). Clearly mark your return date.

Attach a copy of your itinerary to the diary and, if you travel frequently, place a copy of your itinerary in your office in a special file marked "Business Travel." This helps your company document any of your business travel expenses should the need arise and also provides a convenient place to look up travel information in case you are audited by the IRS.

If you carry a business diary when you travel, make it a habit to write *all* your daily expenses while away from home. Put down *everything,* regardless of whether you believe the expense is for business purposes. That way, you can include items that your accountant later deems to be deductible.

Check Weather Conditions

Check the current and forecasted weather conditions for your travel destinations *before* you pack. If forecasts are for heavy rain showers, snow, or other harsh weather that can tie up traffic and make it difficult to get around, you can pack and make plans accordingly. Closely timed, back-to-back appointments probably should not be made, for example. Do not rely on general National Weather Service reports for definitive weather information in local areas. For instance, "morning TV weather" reports tend to combine conditions into broad regional blocks to save time, ignoring the fact that although one area is sunny and mild, 100 miles to the south a tropical storm is developing.

An obvious solution would be to call the client you are going to visit at your destination, ask him or her for a forecast, then plan your schedule based on this information. However, unless you know for certain that your client makes it a practice to keep up on developing weather conditions, this approach is not reliable. It is safer to use a more professional source. Here are six sources you can use to determine accurate weather conditions and forecasts:

☐ Call a local newspaper or television station in each city you plan to visit. Ask to speak with the weather forecaster.

☐ If you have an American Express Card, call 1-800-554-2639 or (202) 783-7474, collect, to obtain a weather report and three-day forecast for just about anywhere in the world.

☐ Airdata, Inc., at P.O. Box 7000, Dallas, TX 75209, provides current weather information for 250 major cities in the U.S.A. Airdata's phone number is 1-800-247-3282 or (214) 869-3035. Enter the local area code of the city for which you want information. Write for the complete list of cities serviced by Airdata. A nominal fee of 75 cents for the first minute and 50 cents for additional minutes will be charged only after you have entered the proper codes, as instructed.

☐ If you are visiting a coastal area, use directory assistance to obtain the local number for the Marine Weather Service and call for information.

☐ If you are visiting an area surrounded by mountains, call your airline's flight service number. (Use the number for your local area code, not the number for your destination city.) Tell the flight service agent which city you are flying to and ask for the two-day forecast.

Have Matching, Inexpensive Luggage

Sturdy, matching, inexpensive luggage is the right way to go if you travel frequently. The occasional traveler, who might have the time to keep close watch on his or her luggage, can afford to take a less economical approach. However, frequent travelers can count on the following adaptation of Murphy's law: Airline baggage handlers and their equipment will eventually destroy your luggage. If you fly frequently, substitute "repeatedly" for "eventually."

Keep in mind, though, that inexpensive luggage does not mean cheap luggage. Your bags should at least be strong enough to take some punishment without falling apart after only a few trips. The key is to avoid buying designer brands, because you pay more for the name than for durability.

If you really want to splurge on a piece of luggage, spend your money on a well-made, ultralight, carry-on garment bag. There are many such bags on the market, and it is not necessary to buy a designer name to get quality. Look for lightness, metal supports, a strong hanging hook and chain, fabric (which can be vinyl coated) rather than plain vinyl, the inclusion of several compartments, and (for a folding bag) make sure it is long enough for your clothes. Women need longer garment bags than men.

Never check such an expensive bag unless the airline check-in staff can place it in a box. However, not all airlines offer cardboard boxes for folding bags. If you do box your high-priced hanging bag, tie a ribbon to the box to mark it clearly as being exclusively yours.

WARNING: If you travel abroad, avoid calling attention to yourself as an American. Your dress, manners, and luggage all can attract unwanted attention. Your appearance should not broadcast the suggestion that you have something to steal. If your appearance does suggest this, it is almost certain that eventually something will be stolen. Be low-key in all that you do, wear, and say.

TIP

Always examine your checked bags carefully when you retrieve them from the baggage area. Any damage—cuts, marks, grease, dirt, and so forth—should be reported immediately to the baggage representative for your airline. The baggage rep will ask you to fill out a form and then will direct you to a location in your home or destination city where you can have your bags repaired and/or cleaned free of charge.

Pack Frugally

The importance of packing lightly is greatest when you know you are going to have to lug your own bags from place to place. On the other hand, many people feel, with good reason, that it is better to have something extra than to not have something you need. Clearly, travel needs vary from person to person. Women generally have more difficulty than men packing lightly when they stay in the same place for several days. Men can often get by wearing the same suit for several days, changing only their shirt and tie to maintain a fresh appearance.

Travel dress is such a personal issue that you need to practice—that is, you have to put forth a conscious effort to learn from your experience. Before your next trip, lay out on your bed all the clothes you plan to take. Make no extra effort at this point to eliminate anything, even if it's something you want to take "just in case."

If your trip will keep you in one hotel long enough to have some of your clothing washed or pressed (a good rule is to allow from noon until 5 P.M. the following evening), consider eliminating an item or two that duplicate other washable items—for example, eliminate one dress shirt if you know the other shirt can be washed and reused. If you plan to wash any items yourself, such as socks or underwear, make sure you will have enough time to do so and that conditions in the hotel will allow the items to dry. At this point, pack your bags.

While you are on your trip, make a conscious effort *not to wear* at least one set of clothes. If you can return with several items unused, make a mental note to eliminate these items on your next trip.

Label Your Luggage—Outside and Inside

It is absolutely critical to label your luggage properly. Failure to do so can target your bags for theft or, if your bags are misrouted by the airline, can cause them to disappear forever. If you observe the six important labeling steps provided here, you can avoid many lost-luggage problems and can aid the airline in returning your bags to you *during* your trip rather than after you return home:

☐ Firmly attach your name, an address, and your business phone number to the exterior of all bags (even carry-on bags). Never use your home address—you do not want to alert potential criminals that you are out of town. A stick-on tag that uses a water-activated glue will adhere to most hard and smooth surfaced bags. However, stick-on tags are not reliable on soft or fabric luggage. For these pieces, use tags with a strong vinyl or leather strap rather than the string or light-plastic snap-on tags that the airlines provide.

☐ Firmly attach your name, business address, and business phone number to the *inside* of each bag. Airlines open luggage that has been lost if no name tag can be found on the exterior.

☐ Place a copy of your business itinerary inside each bag, where it will be seen as soon as the bag is opened. With this information available, the airline can sometimes return your bags to you before you even notice they are missing.

☐ Put a luggage belt (or two) around all Pullman or folding-type luggage bags. This serves two purposes. First, the belts help protect your bags. Second, they uniquely identify your luggage, decreasing the chance that other travelers will mistakenly pick up your bags.

☐ Tie a ribbon to the handle or use a strong colored cloth that can serve as unique identification. The ribbon helps you spot your bags at a distance and discourages thieves, because they cannot claim to have picked up your bags by mistake.

☐ Make sure the check-in clerk labels your bags for the right flight. If you check your bags at the curb, be aware that baggage checkers are often harried and overworked. Don't leave the luggage check-in area until you *see* your bags properly tagged and on their way.

WARNING: Luggage thieves operate in most major airports around the world and are adept at

their trade. For instance, one ruse is to play the role of the friendly native. The thief offers to load your bags into the cab for you. When you arrive later at your hotel, you notice too late that some of your bags are missing. The final portion of your trip often represents the most opportune time for thieves. You are likely to be tired, especially if the flight was long. Combine fatigue with late night or early morning travel, or with a crowded airport, and your luggage can become an easy target for thieves. Watch your bags at all times.

Review and Confirm Your Reservations

If you are a "constant change" traveler—that is, one who routinely makes a dozen or so changes in your reservations and itinerary prior to departure—it is critical to make a final confirmation of your travel plans. In any event, make it a habit to review and confirm your reservations before each trip. If you feel you don't have time to do this, have your travel agent or secretary confirm your reservations.

Even if someone else confirms your reservations, you should make sure you understand your own itinerary. Airports can be stressful places. You certainly do not need the added frustration of arriving at the check-in counter only to discover you are at the wrong airport. I have heard travelers relate even worse horror stories, including boarding the wrong flight; flying to a city with the same name as the one on your ticket but in the wrong state; and changing flight schedule dates (same flight numbers, different dates) without realizing that a recent time change (such as from Eastern Standard to Daylight Saving Time) alters the scheduled departure and arrival times for the revised dates. The most common mistake is trying to check in at the wrong major chain hotel in a city that has several hotels of that chain.

TIP

To avoid missing flights or appointments, make sure you know when and where time changes take effect. In the United States, daylight saving time takes effect (you advance the clock one hour) the first Sunday in April and ends the last Sunday in October (you turn the clock back one hour). A few areas—Arizona for example—do not observe daylight saving time. Check in advance.

International daylight saving times are a mixed bag. In Western Europe, daylight saving time usually starts the last Sunday in March and ends on the last Sunday in September. This may vary for some countries. Also, some international areas set time according to a standard other than Greenwich mean time. Israel, for example, is generally two hours behind the Greenwich mean time standard for that time zone.

Ensuring That You Have All Needed Items

Have you ever left home on business only to discover on arrival at your destination that you neglected to bring an important document or item—something that might even put an end to a potentially productive trip? Some items are obvious "must haves." Other items are less obvious but still are necessary to ensure a successful, trouble-free business trip. The general categories of items to bring are provided in the checklist earlier in this chapter. However, you might find it helpful to have a more detailed list of necessary items. The following two lists are handy reminders; the first listing obvious items:

☐ Tickets

☐ Business itinerary

☐ Rental car confirmation number

☐ Driver's license

☐ Hotel address and confirmation number

☐ List of appointments—with names, phone numbers, and addresses

☐ *All* your luggage

☐ *All* your business papers

☐ *All* your needed identification

☐ Money, credit cards, and travelers checks

☐ Passport for international travel

Here's a list of some of the less obvious, yet important, items to bring on business trips:

☐ Directions to your appointment locations

☐ Visas, if needed

☐ Records of inoculations and vaccinations, where required

☐ Proof of auto insurance, with name of insurance company and insurance agent

☐ International driver's license, where needed

☐ Needed medicine, with backup prescriptions

☐ Extra prescription glasses and backup prescription

☐ Any special travel convenience items that you like or need

☐ Clothing sizes of family members or friends for whom you expect to buy gifts

☐ An electrical extension cord

Of these less obvious items, the first on the list (directions to appointments) is the most frequently overlooked yet typically the most important—especially if cab service is unavailable. If you cannot find your way to your business appointments, your trip might be wasted. It is important to obtain directions in advance, even if you have been in your destination city several times. For instance, your client might have moved to a new, unfamiliar address in the same city. Also, landmarks you once relied on might have been torn down and replaced, or street numbering systems might differ for various parts of town.

If you cannot obtain reliable directions in advance, build extra time into your itinerary in case you get lost or need more in-town travel time than you initially expected. Toward this end, one of the best and least expensive investments you can make is a detailed city map. Do not rely on the free maps provided at hotels and rental car counters. Buy a map that includes a street index and clearly marks all streets and traffic-flow directions. As you near your destination, you might find it helpful to ask a native for the best place to park.

I carry a 16-foot electrical extension cord with me whenever I travel and find it essential for use with several items, including hair dryer, iron, computer, and electric razor. If you are traveling outside the United States, you might also want to bring a 1600-watt converter so that your U.S. electrical appliances will function. Keep in mind, too, that the wall sockets around the world often do not conform with plugs for U.S. appliances. Bring an assortment of plug adapters to connect with local outlets. Do not rely on buying these adapters during your trip, because they might not be available or, even if you can find the appropriate adapters, the cost might be double or more than what you would pay at home.

TIP

Your company should arrange with its bank to provide free travelers checks to all employees. If the bank will not accommodate this request, your company should find another bank.

Four Small Items

You probably are aware of the importance of many of the travel items mentioned so far in this chapter. Here are four small items that you probably haven't considered taking, but should:

☐ Swiss army knife
☐ Spoon
☐ Eye drops
☐ Skin moisturizer

You don't need one of those knives that features everything from the kitchen sink to a full jungle survival kit. A knife that has perhaps a half-dozen accessories is sufficient—scissors, screwdrivers, knife, and file, for example. You never know when you will need to cut, pry, un-screw, loosen, tighten, or file some small or not-so-small object. In fact, I once used my Swiss knife to repair an airliner. A broken wheel housing door on a Bahamas Air flight was causing the delay, and the crew had been instructed to simply remove the darn thing. After watching them beat at the housing door with the flat of an axe for a few minutes, I decided to help. Using only my Swiss knife and a nail I found, I managed to remove the door and become the hero of the moment.

A spoon might seem like a strange item to include, but it can make sense if you like to snack in your room or "on the fly." The thin plastic spoons that snack bars and hotels tend to provide are more a nuisance than a help. It's aggravating to have your spoon snap in two in the middle of a snack or meal. Keep in mind that a sturdy spoon and your Swiss army knife can combine to make functional eating utensils.

Air travel, extreme differences in humidity between travel locations, overwork, and unusual lighting can easily take their toll on your eyes. A few drops of eyewash can mean the difference between looking tired and looking alert. (After all, even though you might *feel* tired, you don't want to *look* tired when you meet an important client or give a presentation you've been planning for months.)

Hot, cold, and dry weather can create problems for your skin. Air conditioning on planes and in hotels and meeting rooms can dry your skin. If you find yourself in a cold climate and your body hasn't had sufficient time to adjust, your lips can chap and even painfully crack. A good moisturizing cream can be a big help in these situations. I've found that a small tube or bottle of Vaseline Intensive Care does the trick—and it's easy to find and is inexpensive.

Seven Special Items

The following hints can help you minimize inconvenience at home while you're away.

Stash Your House and Car Keys: Hide a key to your home and car in a location that you can get to in an emergency. Keys are extremely easy to lose during travel—you can misplace them, leave them behind at your hotel, or place them in luggage that later is lost or stolen. Of course, the location you choose to hide your keys depends on your personal circumstances. In any case, I recommend that you attach a name tag to the keys, but write a fictitious name and address on the tag label. If someone happens to find your keys accidentally, it is unlikely that the keys can be used to gain entrance to your home or apartment.

If you cannot find a safe place near your home or apartment to hide a key to your residence (and assuming your car is not locked in your garage), hide a door key inside your car.

You can safely hide your car key by first making two spare keys—an ignition key and a car trunk key. Then, use some black electrical tape to hide the ignition key in an out-of-the-way place inside the trunk. Next, use a magnetic hide-a-key box (available at locksmith shops and hardware stores) to hide the trunk key in a difficult-to-reach external part of the car.

TIP

Note on paper the hidden location of your keys (or any other hidden items, for that matter) and file this note with other important documents. Memory can play funny tricks on the mind. A few months or a year after you hide your keys, you might find it impossible to recall where you placed them.

Copy Important Papers: Make copies of all papers and identification and credit cards that you carry in your wallet. Simply empty your wallet and spread all items across the glass surface of your office copy machine, then make two or three copies. You will find one or more copies to be extremely useful should you ever lose your wallet and need to replace its contents.

Place one copy of your wallet contents in a file with other important documents. You might want to place another copy among the business documents you plan to bring on your trip. You can use this copy if your wallet is lost or stolen during your trip. Be sure to make copies of other important, nonwallet items, too: include your passport, international driver's license, travelers check master number sheet, and so on.

List Lost Credit Card Phone Numbers: Be sure to include among the business documents you bring the phone numbers to call if your credit cards are stolen. Of course, you can subscribe to one of the many credit-card security services available. However, I recommend that you bring no more than two credit cards. This way, you will only need to call one or two numbers if your cards are lost or stolen.

Record Your Car's Location: Whenever you drive—either your own or a rental car—and then park, enter the parking location in your business diary. It is easy to become disoriented, and many a business traveler has spent an hour or more looking for his or her vehicle.

By the way, because most U.S. airport parking garages require you to pay as you exit the garage, many people are in the habit of leaving their parking ticket inside their vehicle. However, there are some good reasons to get out of this habit. Many parking garages within U.S. and European cities, even self-park garages, require you to pay prior to returning to your car. When you pay the attendant, you are then given a token that operates the exit gate. In these situations, of course, you *must* have your ticket with you before you can return to your car or before your car is returned to you. Second, banks, stores, and many offices that adjoin a parking garage often can validate your parking garage ticket with a stamp, allowing you to park free. If you keep your ticket with you, it may be possible to take advantage of these free parking opportunities.

Carry Auto Insurance Information: Always carry information about your personal auto insurance. When you rent a car, you probably will want to rely on your own liability insurance. If you have a credit card that provides you with collision coverage on rental cars, you may elect not to pay the rental agency's CDW (collision damage waiver). Keep your automobile insurance information in your wallet. I discuss CDW and other auto insurance issues in more detail later in the book.

WARNING: Your auto and liability insurance may provide you with little or no coverage outside the United States. At best, you may be covered only if a suit is filed against you in the United States. However, if you are in an accident in Mexico, Canada, or another country, lawsuits likely will be filed against you in that country. In fact, if you are fairly wealthy and cause an accident in, say, Munich, your victim might go to great lengths to keep your insurance company out of the picture. The idea is to force you to pay for your own defense in the hope that you will agree to a quick, out-of-court settlement.

TIP

Meet with your insurance agent to ask and get answers to the following questions:
- ☐ Is my coverage the same everywhere in the world for each policy I have? If not, what are the differences outside the United States? What are the limitations?
- ☐ How can I become fully insured wherever I travel?
- ☐ Does my medical insurance cover me worldwide?
- ☐ When I am in other countries, am I entitled to the same legal protection and defense from my insurance company as in the United States—regardless of whether a suit is filed against me within or outside the United States?

Display Medical Information: Wear a bracelet or medallion that indicates any allergies or medical problems that emergency and medical people need to know about in case of an emergency.

Store Your Valuables Outside Your Room: Make it a habit to use the hotel safe to store your valuables. Although some hotels provide small safes within rooms, I do not recommend putting your absolute trust in them. The hotel lobby safe is a far more secure location. However, if there is no lobby safe deposit box system, use the room safe; any safe is better than none.

Five Tips to Consider Before You Fly

Here are a final five tips that can help to make business flying more enjoyable.

Entertainment and Snacks

Bring your own entertainment and refreshments. If you are a work fiend, you might find it enough to bring paperwork that you can work on in flight. But if you like to relax during flights, do not rely on the in-flight entertainment or reading material. Above all, do not rely on the meal or beverage service to be satisfying.

Most sound systems on aircraft are of poor quality, and you can usually listen to all of the selections that appeal to you within an hour. Magazines, too, can be read quickly and, if you travel frequently, you can expect to have already read all of the print material provided on the aircraft. A good book or two can help pass the time.

A small tape player with headphones can be a good investment. With your own tape player, you can bring tapes for many hours of listening, at a better sound quality than the in-flight system. Be sure you bring extra batteries.

Despite all preparations you or your travel agent might make to ensure good meals, the airline might still disappoint you. One idea is to bring along some snack items. Fruit, a candy bar, a bag of nuts and dried fruit, or even a packaged lunch or dinner are all possibilities. A friend of mine has an interesting approach. He visits a gourmet store on his way to the airport and fills a picnic basket with everything from chilled lobster salad, a small thermos of carrot soup, and a cold plate of chicken and other meats to a dessert, a bottle of wine, several after-dinner miniatures, some fruit, cheese, port, and a box of chocolates.

Casual Dress for the Flight

Dress comfortably, which is often easier said than done. Many times you might plan to meet with some important people as soon as you depart the plane, so you need to look your best on arrival. One solution is to wear or bring a jogging suit on board. You can wear this outfit during your flight and leave your business clothes in the garment bag until you are about 30 minutes from your destination. Then, change back into your business self.

Prevention of Dehydration

Drink plenty of water several hours prior to boarding. Much has been written on the health hazard of becoming dehydrated during flights. You can become dehydrated even on short flights, because water evaporates from your skin and hair through respiration and body eliminations. You should build up a reserve of water in your body to maintain your normal level of fluids during the flight.

However, this can be next to impossible to do on long flights. Plan to hydrate your system continually by drinking water and juices throughout the flight.

Diet Restraint

Avoid eating gas-producing foods within 24 hours or so before departure. I discuss this touchy subject more in a later chapter, but for now keep in mind that anything that can upset your system under normal conditions can do so in a magnified way due to travel conditions.

Safeguarding Film

Pack film within lead-lined bags, which can be purchased at any camera store to shield your film against X rays. Never let your film be x-rayed, regardless of the message printed on the security

X-ray machine and despite anything you have
heard about these machines being film-safe. Although one X-ray dose might not affect your film,
why subject your film to a possibly faulty X-ray
machine or to several machines? Carry your film
with you through the metal detector at each security checkpoint. If the film sets off the buzzer,
let a security employee examine your film separately.

If you choose to pack your film, make sure
it is encased in a lead-lined bag. Many airports
now pass luggage through high-powered X-ray
machines that will cook your film unless it is
shielded.

TIP

Remove film from its box and place it in clear
plastic sandwich bags—no more than eight rolls
of film per bag. Put the plastic bags inside
lead-lined bags. If the local airport security
staff wants to see the film, it is better and
easier to remove a few plastic bags than to
have a dozen or more sealed film boxes fall out
and onto the floor.

The Benefits of Planning

All the tips, warnings, and items mentioned in
this chapter might seem to be a monumentally
long list to review before you leave for an overnight or two-day trip. However, keep in mind that
the items I've mentioned are simply things to
consider bringing—they might not be necessities.
You alone know what you need to bring with you
and what you need to leave behind. The idea,
though, is to start developing pretravel habits as
soon as possible. A comfortable and problem-free
trip usually is the result of good planning.

3
Pack Light, Travel Right

You can forget much of what you've heard and read elsewhere about packing and traveling light. Many of the "helpful hints" available in travel books and in magazine and newspaper travel sections are directed more toward the needs of the holiday traveler and fail to deal with the many realities of business travel.

Consider the holiday traveler for a moment. Mr. and Mrs. Getaway might be tempted to take more than they need on that trip to the Bahamas. But if they think intelligently, they can get by with perhaps a dozen pounds of clothing and toilet articles. After all, most of the Getaways' time will be spent at the beach, in casual restaurants, or sightseeing.

On the other hand, consider yourself—a savvy business traveler who wants to travel light but just can't ever seem to. That business presentation in Atlanta alone requires 40 pounds of material. And you have to take your clothing seriously in order to look sharp for perhaps a week or longer.

The point is that the business traveler, unlike the holiday traveler, has to pack to fit the occasion and the circumstances of the trip. Priorities are different. Whereas the chief priority for a holiday traveler is to have fun, the chief priority for a business traveler is to represent his or her company professionally. When you are acting as company ambassador, what you pack and wear can mean the difference between a signed contract and a wasted trip.

The bottom line is that each new business trip can dictate new travel requirements. Although I mentioned several important travel items in the previous chapter, I also recognize that specific needs vary from trip to trip. Perhaps more important, the subject of packing can be highly personal—different people need different things. For these reasons, it doesn't make sense for me to tell you which specific items you must or must not bring on a trip. What you can use, though, are some basic guidelines that will help you pack light, but travel right—for each new business trip you take.

When It Comes to Clothing, Know When to Say When

In Chapter 2 I mentioned that the best way to pack frugally is to make a conscious attempt to focus on what you bring and why. People often pack items out of habit, rather than necessity. In fact, I frequently observe both holiday and business travelers who have made the same packing "mistakes." I've seen both types of travelers burdened with an excess of luggage that is probably intended to increase their sense of security. In the end, excessive luggage adds nothing to the success of the trip and instead creates anxiety in trying to manage and keep track of too much.

On the other hand, I've known business men and women who go to such extraordinary means to pack light (no doubt with the intent to focus on the business at hand by avoiding the hassle of excess luggage) that they would practically freeze to death if the temperature dropped 20 degrees.

You can avoid both of these extremes by following some simple guidelines:

☐ Think light. Weigh your desire to bring everything you might need against the prudence of taking only what is adequate, with a minimum backup, *and nothing more.*

☐ Plan your events. Make a mental list of your planned activities—if you are good at making mental lists. Better yet, write down where you expect to be at different points in your trip and what you will wear at each place. You can even use your travel itinerary for this purpose. Ask yourself some questions about each activity. Will I need a separate change of clothes for the evening? Is this event formal? Will I meet with the same people on different days? (If not, you can often rewear items.) What will the weather and heating/air conditioning situation be?

You can (and should) answer most of these questions well in advance of the time you pack. Clothing might need to go to the cleaners or even to the tailor for an alteration.

☐ Time yourself as you pack. It helps to learn how long it takes, on average, for you to pack. If you make a conscious effort to time yourself, you can set aside ample packing time for later trips. A rushed packing job is likely to be a poor packing job. However, try to pack relatively close to your departure time. By doing so, you are more likely to pack for the appropriate weather conditions at your destination points.

☐ Take coordinated outfits only. Stick with clothing items that can be mixed. For men, a dark suitcoat with a lighter shade of slacks can transform a suit into a sportjacket-and-slacks look. And when you are trying to keep your luggage to a minimum, it doesn't matter that you look great in both your brown jacket and your light blue suit. Do not pack both for the same trip. Instead, count on mixing and matching your clothing.

Women can alter their look with one or two smart accessory changes. A change in scarf, belt, and/or necklace can make one outfit look like two or even three.

☐ Shoes should be kept to an absolute minimum. Shoes are heavy and tend to be cumbersome to pack. Most men need only the shoes they have on their feet while they travel. However, a pair of running or sport shoes can be handy if you like to exercise while on the road. Women will find that, if they are careful in selecting coordinated outfits, it is possible to pack only one or two changes of shoes.

☐ After your trip, make note of the items you brought but did not use or wear. I've said it before, but if you make this kind of conscious effort to evaluate your travel requirements, you'll pack lighter and smarter with each trip you take.

TIP

You are more likely to forget small toilet articles than main clothing items. In turn, it can be very annoying to unpack at your hotel only to find that the soap, shampoo, moisturizer, or shaving cream that you have grown accustomed to using isn't in your luggage. If you have forgotten to bring important medicine, this situation can even be dangerous to your health.

Don't count on buying these small articles at your destination. Stores in many cities and hotels will not stock the items or brand names that you need. Instead, make a checklist of the toilet items that you intend to bring on your trip. Make copies of the checklist for use on further trips. Then refer to the checklist as you are packing.

How to Pack

Knowing how to pack is as important as knowing what to pack. In the business world, first impressions do count. You need to pack so that your clothes remain clean and wrinkle free. Here are some tips to help you do just that:

☐ If you carry your bags on the plane, hang your shirts.

☐ If you plan to check your bags, fold your shirts. You'll find that folded shirts can endure the rigors of travel—if you fold them correctly. The key is to make a note of how your shirts are folded when you purchase them. Follow these same folds when you pack—without the pins, of course.

☐ Don't stuff items. You should use luggage that allows for a snug fit of all your items (so they won't shift about and become wrinkled). However, don't pack clothing so tightly that you force creases into it. Of course, if you learn how to travel light, you'll avoid the temptation to stuff more than you need into your bags.

☐ Pack heavy items off to one side and as much by themselves as possible. Ideally, your iron, shoes, hair dryer, and other heavy items should be placed in a separate compartment or even in a separate bag. Heavy items act as weights that can crease or even damage clothing—especially delicates.

☐ Pack noncritical items near the bottom, and important items near the top. This allows you to reach for important items quickly if necessary, with minimal digging through your bags. Also, your more delicate items should be packed near the top, where they are less likely to be wrinkled by the weight of other items.

☐ Unpack as quickly as you can. When you arrive at your destination, immediately unpack items that you can hang up. If your packed shirts are smooth and unwrinkled, place them loosely in dresser drawers. However, if shirts, slacks, or other items are wrinkled, hang them in the bathroom and start a hot shower to steam the room. You might need to keep the room steamy for an hour or two, but this technique can work miracles on wrinkled fabrics. The moisture is absorbed by the fabric, which then "relaxes" into a smoother appearance.

TIP

If you are taking an extended trip (four nights or longer), consider bringing along a small nylon bag that you can use to carry your dirty clothes. You won't always have enough time to get your clothes laundered or dry cleaned while you are traveling. And there is no sense in repacking dirty items that are going to make your clean clothes smell like an NFL locker room after a game. The nylon bag can also serve as a safe place to store gift items that you buy, since your dirty laundry will cushion fragile items against breakage.

Should You Carry On or Check Your Bags?

Travelers and their luggage should be together as much as possible, unless this togetherness will lead to a hernia. Beyond this rule of thumb, there are some constructive pros and cons for both carry on and checked luggage.

Reasons to Carry Your Bags On

Comedian Alan King once did a monologue describing a time when he flew to California to appear on a television program. Mr. King made it a point to travel light. But this one time, even though it was important to make a well-dressed appearance on TV, he relaxed his travel-light rule. Mr. King allowed the airline to place his garment bag into a cardboard box, which was then checked at the gate. You can guess what happened. The hanging bag went to Singapore or some such distant place, while King was deposited in California, without his tux.

Most frequent business travelers can identify with this story. The fact that airlines often lose and misroute luggage is the most obvious reason for carrying your bags with you at all times. Here are a few other good reasons:

☐ If you carry your own luggage you are inclined, or even forced, to pack light.

☐ Luggage will last longer if you keep it away from baggage handlers and airport luggage-moving machines.

☐ You save the time required to wait for checked luggage to appear in the airport baggage area.

Reasons to Check Your Bags

If you are on an extended business trip, the benefits of carrying on your luggage begin to fade as the weight of your bags increases. Add to this an international flight of several legs, several miles of airport corridors, and the constant threat of airport thieves, and you may decide to check those suitcases. Here are a few other arguments for checking your bags:

☐ It can be counterproductive to pack light solely to make sure you can carry on all your luggage. You might be tempted to leave behind clothing or other items that you really should take.

☐ The size of on-board stowaway areas is shrinking. In the interest of seating more passengers per plane, airlines have tended to reduce the space above and below seats used for stowing carry-on luggage. When you put your luggage in an overhead compartment, it can easily get squashed or damaged when your fellow travelers stuff their bags around yours.

☐ You might find that, after you have already boarded the plane, there is no available space for one or more of your bags. In this situation, a flight attendant may have to check your bags for you, and you won't be able to personally make sure your luggage is checked properly.

WARNING: In some foreign airports, you might be told that your luggage far exceeds the weight limit, and you must pay for the excess weight. Sometimes, your luggage will be loaded onto the plane before you are told about the excess weight. In these cases, you will be forced to pay the charge without seeing for yourself whether the charge is valid.

TIP

Recently, many airlines have chosen to purchase and use more jumbo jets for flights that tend to be long and crowded. With these jets, the weight of your checked luggage is less important than for smaller craft. It is not uncommon for check-in attendants to overlook some excess weight for jumbo jet flights.

TIP

If you think your luggage might be way over an airline's weight limit, call ahead to make sure. Excess weight charges can be expensive. If you are told that your luggage exceeds the weight limit, try to arrange to have some of your luggage shipped as "freight." This form of transport is much less expensive than paying for weight penalties, although it is still costly.

What to Do if Your Bags Are Lost or Damaged

If you do elect to check your bags, make sure you are prepared in the event they are lost or damaged. Chapter 2 offered some general precautions to help minimize the risk of lost or damaged luggage. But even the most carefully heeded precautions might not be enough to prevent mishaps. This section, then, provides some more detailed information about dealing with lost or damaged luggage.

WARNING: An airline's liability for lost or damaged luggage might be much less than the actual value of the luggage and its contents. For international flights, the liability limit was established in 1929 at the Warsaw Convention and has yet to be increased. The limit is $9.07 per pound of checked luggage, plus $400 per passenger for unchecked items (unless you increase the liability when you check in by paying a surcharge). If the maximum weight allowed for your class of travel is 20 kilograms, your total coverage would be $544.20, even though you might check in 10 times that value.

U.S. domestic flights provide added coverage, and there is a major push to increase the coverage further. The current coverage was last changed in 1984, and ranges from $750 to $1250 per passenger for any claim for damage, loss, or delay.

TIP

Travel by train and bus can involve even lower carrier liability. In these situations, it is a good idea to find out in advance what the carrier would have to pay if your luggage is lost or stolen. Most carriers are happy to sell you extra protection.

WARNING: Check your homeowners insurance policy to find out whether items are covered during travel and what you have to do to prove a loss. Most homeowners policies have limitations on some items, whereas no limitations may exist for other items. On one recent trip, my camera equipment was stolen. My insurance company used my detailed inventory list to replace every item at its new cost. It's a good idea to find out in advance whether your insurance company would be that generous.

If your luggage is lost:

☐ *Immediately* report the failure of your luggage to arrive. All airlines have a responsible person or department, at or near the baggage area, to handle such problems.

☐ Be able to accurately describe your luggage. A color photo of your luggage, with a yardstick in the photo to establish scale, will help.

☐ Be ready to describe the major or unique items in the luggage in the event you need to establish additional identification of the missing bags.

☐ Ask for replacement money to buy items you might need to tide you over until your luggage is returned to you. Most airlines will respond to any reasonable request, and many have toilet kits and vouchers for laundry and clothing purchases.

☐ Relax if you feel you are being properly attended to, but be ready to insist if the airline or the agent serving you appears to be lax or uncaring toward your problem.

☐ Immediately ask to see the station manager the moment you feel threatened or intimidated by any airline personnel.

TIP

At check-in time, you can increase the amount of airline liability by making a request of the airline representative. Most airlines will oblige with a charge of approximately one dollar for every hundred dollars of value over their liability limit.

If your luggage is damaged:

☐ Immediately take your damaged luggage to the baggage department (usually the same person or department responsible for lost luggage).

☐ Point out all the damage and/or scuff marks.

☐ Ask for a voucher or approval to have the luggage repaired and/or cleaned at the expense of the airline. Insist, if necessary.

☐ If the luggage is beyond repair, ask for a voucher for replacement of the luggage.

☐ Remember that you are entitled to have your luggage returned to you in the same condition it was in when you checked it. Do not let the agent try to "depreciate" your luggage by making an age versus value determination. You might point out that you didn't pay less for your ticket because you flew on a 15-year-old aircraft rather than a new one.

☐ Alert your own insurance company of the loss if your luggage has not been returned after a few days.

The final word, of course, is this: The less you bring, the less you have to lose. Try to strike a balance between what you would like to bring and what you would like to carry.

4

How to Find and Keep a Super Travel Agent

Good travel agents are committed to satisfying your travel needs. They'll make reliable travel arrangements at a reasonable cost. But frankly, you deserve better than good. If you travel frequently, you need the best service possible from your travel agent, and you want to count on this high level of service whenever you make travel arrangements. In other words, you want a *super travel agent*—someone who performs above and beyond the call of duty, repeatedly. Super travel agents do exist, and if you follow the advice in this chapter, you should be able to find and keep at least one such agent, and possibly more than one.

A super travel agent acquires a thorough knowledge of your travel requirements and satisfies these requirements consistently, from one trip to the next. But in order to find a super travel agent, you should first understand some basics about the job of the travel agent. If you know what problems a travel agent faces from day to day, you'll be in a better position to assess your agent's ability to solve common travel problems to your satisfaction.

The Travel Business Is Complicated and Frustrating

Travel agents serve as brokers, or intermediaries, between your travel requirements and available travel services, including airlines and other carriers, hotels, rental car companies, and more. Travel agents must function in a largely unregulated industry, where few standards exist and rules of the trade change almost daily.

For a given travel situation, the travel agent must review potentially dozens of prices for the same flight, dozens of hotels, and several different rental car companies and classes and makes of automobiles. Above all this is the patience required to remain on the phone when a company's toll-free telephone recording repeats, for several minutes or more, "Please do not hang up. All our agents are busy, but your call will be answered in the order it is received."

Super travel agents focus their work on the guidelines that you provide. They strive to match your specific wishes with the most appropriate services available. When the ideal situation is not possible, they try to find the best second-choice situation that meets the majority of your needs.

When you bought this book, its price was probably about the same as other books in the same class and of the same size. In the publishing business, like most businesses, prices are set with an eye toward the competition. In the travel industry, it is often difficult to determine exactly what or who determines prices. Not a week will pass without changes in prices, schedules, or both for hundreds of flights and car rental companies, and for thousands of hotels.

Consider hotels for a moment. Existing hotels occasionally burn down, new complexes are scheduled for grand openings or renovation, and changes in price structure often change literally on the basis of weather. Who can keep up with these changes? You expect your travel agent to.

Often, airlines, rental car agencies, and hotels offer lower prices for special events or special seasonal situations. Only the top, super agents track these and other opportunities that might be important to you.

Travel agents are inundated with mail and memos from the many travel services they represent. Each piece of mail, of course, promises the best for the travel agent's clients. Super travel agents know how to pick and choose—and they know which seminars are worth attending, which seminars will help them to service their best customers.

Selecting a Super Travel Agency

Travel agents are often bound by the procedures and tools that their agency provides for them. Even super travel agents will do a poor job if they are saddled with outdated procedures and equipment. On the other hand, it's generally true that you'll find super agents at super travel agencies. The best travel agents want to do a great job and naturally want to work for an agency that gives them the right resources.

A good place to start your search for a super travel agent, then, is to find a super travel agency.

The key to good service in just about any business is the ability and willingness to give personal attention to the needs of customers. For a travel agency to provide you with this personal attention, you must first understand what your own needs are. By knowing your own travel needs, you can better eliminate the agencies that cannot serve those needs.

Start by creating a synopsis of your business travel expenses for the past 12 months. You can use the divisions shown in Table 4–1.

When you meet with representatives of prospective travel agencies, give them a copy of your completed travel synopsis form. Review it with them and make sure they understand how they can use the synopsis to provide for your travel needs in the coming 12 months. If the agency representative doesn't seem to be interested in your synopsis, that agency probably isn't going to provide you with personal attention.

Also explain the method of payment you wish to use. This item is important to most agencies, because their margin of profit is quite small. The gross commission paid by airlines averages 10 percent. From this amount, the agency must calculate "lost" effort for refunds and cancellations for work done without compensation. However, because the travel agent does not pay the credit card discount for travel charged on a major card (for airline fares, car rentals, and hotel rates), you will find that agencies often prefer customers who pay by credit card for all their company travel. Most travel agencies must report and pay for all travel they book on a weekly basis. Cus-

Table 4–1 *Yearly Synopsis of Travel Expenses*

Type of Expense	12-month Budget	Average No. of Days	Total No. of Trips	Places Frequented
Nonair Travel				
Domestic Travel				
International Travel				
Auto Rentals				
Hotels				

tomers who request the agency to bill them or their company can create cash flow problems for an agency. So your method of payment can greatly affect the kind of service you will get from an agency.

Nine Items to Consider As You Select a Travel Agency

So you've evaluated several travel agencies and narrowed the field to a few that you believe can do a super job. Now what? As you narrow your focus, you can afford to examine a few agencies in more detail. A simple study made with the worksheet in Figure 4–1 will help you determine whether each agency you are considering can handle your business.

Check on Trade Association Approvals

Your travel agency should be currently approved by the International Air Transport Association (IATA). A bond is required to be a member. Airline Reporting Corporation (ARC) membership is also essential. ARC is the reporting organization that collects funds from travel agencies and regulates their day-to-day operations. Failure of an agency to belong to IATA or ARC means you are not dealing with a travel agency at all, but a booking agent, tour operator, or something worse.

Membership in other conferences and associations is not essential but can be helpful to an agency in obtaining up-to-date information and, in turn, in maintaining a strong position to meet your travel needs. Perhaps the most important of these groups is the American Society of Travel Agents (ASTA). This is the professional lobby and association that protects the welfare of the travel industry and offers continuing education,

---

Travel Agency Selection Worksheet

Date of Evaluation: _____

Name of Proposed Travel Agency: _____

Address: _____

	Yes	No
Agency's Trade Association Approvals: Are they current?	___	___
Automation: What computer system does the agency use? _____		
Owner Involvement: Is the owner active in the agency?	___	___
Level of Training: Does the staff undergo frequent training?	___	___
Convenience: Is the location convenient for you?	___	___
Staffing: Is the agency staffed well enough to serve you properly?	___	___
Is the agency willing to give you a discount and/or other travel benefits?	___	___

Agent Background: _____

Name of Agent Who Would Handle Your Account:

_____

What References Does the Agent Provide? _____

Figure 4–1 *Worksheet to Complete for Each Travel Agency Considered*

seminars, and publications directed toward the enhanced professionalism of travel agents.

Level of Automation

Automated travel booking is an absolute requirement for business travel arrangements. Don't waste your time dealing with a travel agency that is not automated. Each agent in the office should have an airline reservation computer terminal on his or her desk. Even more important, the agents must know how to *use* the computer system. Ask the agency representative what kind of computer training the agency provides for agents.

Also be sure to ask how long the agency has been using the current computer system. If the answer is, "Oh, this is a state-of-the art system— so new that it just arrived last week," you should let that agency practice on other clients.

Your agency's computerized reservation system should be able to do at least the following tasks:

☐ Book and ticket airline reservations

☐ Book hotel and rental car reservations

☐ Print boarding passes and flight itineraries

☐ Track your company's travel history and re-quirements

☐ Maintain personnel profiles (including the needs and preferences of individual employees)

What an agency's computer system can do is sometimes less important than *who* it is doing the work for. Many airlines own (or have a fi-nancial interest in) the computer systems that travel agencies use. When an agency sells a seat on a flight, the computer system's company charges a fee to the airline for handling the trans-action. The fee varies from company to company, but the fee is generally around $2 per booking. In other words, this is a direct transaction be-tween the airline and the computer center; the travel agency is not involved.

"So what?" you might ask. "Why should I care about some fee charged back to my airline for the use of a computer system?" Here's why. American Airlines, for example, owns the Saber computer system network. American Airlines would much rather be charged by a company that it owns (Sabre) than by a computer center owned by a competing airline. American Airlines will go to great lengths to assist travel agencies that operate a Saber reservation system.

If you know you will be flying frequently with a particular carrier, it might work to your advantage to use a travel agency that operates a computer system that's fully or partially owned by your carrier. For instance, TWA, Delta, and Northwest have mutual ownership in PARS; and American Airlines owns Saber. But keep in mind that not all airlines are directly connected financially with a computer system. If you fly Pan Am or USAir frequently, for instance, you only need to be sure your agency is automated and that its agents can operate the equipment effectively.

The Benefits of Owner-Operated Agencies

It might not be hard-and-fast, but it's a reliable rule nonetheless: If the owner is around, the business often runs smoother and better than does a company managed by a nonowner. Within the travel agency business, agents move frequently from one agency to another. It's fairly common for an agency's top employee to break off to start his or her own agency (taking along other top producers as well).

You want an agency that has some personnel stability. Because staff changes are frequent in the travel industry, an owner-operated agency offers at least one tenured person you can rely on— month in, month out. And, of course, the more qualified the owner, the better you can expect overall services to be and the lower the turnover rate of staff.

Staff Training

When you interview an agency representative, find out whether agents are encouraged to attend seminars and classes. Does the company make attendance at these updates mandatory or optional? Does the agency have a general philosophy regarding employee training?

You should expect an agency to require at least some ongoing training. The travel industry is highly volatile. Computer programs change, and there are weekly overhauls in prices, policies, and strategies by airlines, hotels, and rental car companies.

An agent who insists that he or she is too busy to attend classes that outline new policies and opportunities is an agent who will not be able to satisfy next month's customers. You can't be expected to know about all of the changes that take place in the travel industry, but your agent should. The subtle difference between a well-trained agent and one who functions by rote might not become apparent until you find yourself boarding a flight that requires six stops to get you to your destination—eight hours late.

I've watched and admired the super travel agent at work. Such agents love their job and seem to show genuine satisfaction when they've booked you in the best way possible at the most economical rates. These super agents read trade journals and keep up on incentives offered by rental car companies, hotels, and airlines. Don't be fooled by the agent who claims to have been in the business for a dozen or more years. What you should demand is an agent who knows what's happening in his or her industry *this week.*

Training also goes above and beyond the attendance of seminars. A super agent learns on his or her own. One top agent I know, Monica Martin, seems to get more done, in less time, than most other agents. She finds the time to document each client's trip, including everything from confirmation numbers to phone numbers for hotels and other carriers at destination cities. Her secret: She works at learning about her business. She's constantly reading travel material and following up on information by questioning people at the source—until she receives an answer that she feels will satisfy her clients. You shouldn't expect any less from your agent.

The bottom line: Take the time to get to know your agent. You might find through constant questioning that you need to switch agents. You might get lucky and find another Monica Martin immediately, but chances are you will have to work at interviewing and switching between several agents and agencies until you find the "right one." I'll have more on finding your super travel agent later.

Find Out Which Agent Will Handle Your Account

You know the old "bait-and-switch" game. Tell prospective customers that you've got something great to offer when they come in; but when they come, tell them that the "something great" has already been sold, so why not take a look at this "second-best" opportunity?

Bait-and-switch tactics occur in the travel industry, too. The owner of the agency impresses you with his or her poise, expertise, and knowledge of inside information. Then, after your account has been secured, the owner passes you off to an agent who has just entered the field. The owner of the agency isn't necessarily trying to be deceptive or malicious. This person is trying to run a business and probably has to hire inexperienced people from time to time. So it's your job to protect yourself from this layer of inexperience by imposing some demands.

Ask in advance which agent will be supervising your account and what that agent's level of experience and track record are. If you show concern at the onset, the owner or agency representative is more likely to acknowledge you as a demanding customer who requires a "proven pro." Get to know the agent who will be assigned to you. This might require little more than a 10-

minute phone interview asking about basic business philosophy and travel agency experience and approach. If you don't like what you hear, be tactful, but let the owner know you would appreciate an agent who is more experienced or up to date in meeting your particular travel requirements. If the owner or manager of the agency cannot accommodate your request, it's time to switch agencies.

Check an Agency's References

Unfortunately, the pace of business today means that references of prospective employees never get checked. We tend to rely too heavily on the interview, expecting that any lack of experience or skill will reveal itself as the prospect talks. Don't rely on a person's ability to promote him- or herself; expect the person to provide *proof* of past performance.

When you ask a travel agent for the names of past clients, realize that the agent is likely to provide you with names of customers who can be counted on to say positive things about the agency. Nobody is going to provide a list of references who might make negative comments. When you check references, then, it's your job to take a "hard line" of questioning. Ask previous customers whether they know about other customers of the travel agency. This approach can lead you quickly to the names of customers who were not put on the agency's "A" list of references. One or two statements from a dissatisfied customer can be far more informative than a litany of praise from satisfied customers.

Convenience of Location

Although I include this criterion, I should stress that it is less important than most other criteria. Just balance the ability and responsiveness of your agency in delivering tickets, itineraries, and other materials with the need for an agency that knows how to meet your travel needs economically and efficiently. Ideally, you want an agency that can provide service and information delivery. However, if you have to make a decision between two agencies—both of which are professional and competent, but only one of which provides delivery services or is close to your place of business—consider going with the agency that provides the convenience of location.

Ability to Serve Business and Leisure Travel Needs

A "business-only" travel agency might provide you with top-notch service in meeting your company travel needs. But unless you're a perennial workaholic, eventually you're going to take a vacation—or at least combine business and vacation into one trip. It makes sense to have an agent who can service all of your travel needs. Again, this isn't a "must-have" criterion. If 90 percent of your travel needs revolve around business, it is more important to have an agency that can devote itself to your business travel requirements rather than an agency that divides its time between business and pleasure travel services.

Willingness to Provide Discounts and Other Incentives

Business travelers represent volume business for a travel agency. The retired couple who has saved for decades to take that once-in-a-lifetime world cruise represents *good* business for an agency, but the business traveler who leaves town on a monthly or biweekly basis represents *steady* business. Ask yourself this question: Would you rather gamble on attracting occasional big-ticket customers, or would you rather have a flow of smaller-ticket, more frequent, and more reliable business travelers?

Any agency that prefers the leisure traveler is wrong for your business needs. And you can quickly separate the tour operators from the true business travel agencies by requesting a discount for volume business.

An agency should be willing to "bid" for your personal business or your company's travel needs. If you or your company represent volume business, the travel agency should be able to recognize the potential profit you represent and should be willing to offer a discount to secure your business.

However, you (or your company) need to weigh your value to a travel agency. You can't expect discount prices if you can't guarantee volume business. If your annual travel expenditures through a travel agency are modest, then the smaller agency will find you more attractive than will a commercial house that typically deals with large-volume clients.

Here are some simple guidelines you can follow in determining how to negotiate discounts with prospective travel agencies:

1. Use the synopsis in Figure 4–1 to show the volume and kind of business you can offer a travel agency.
2. Call the airline(s) you use most and ask for the travel agency marketing office. Explain that you are a major user of the carrier and wish to set your account with a single agency. Ask them to recommend two or more agencies with whom you can negotiate.
3. Send a letter to those recommended agencies, describing your annual travel requirements and requesting discounts for volume business. Also send this letter randomly to agencies nearest to your place of business or ones with whom you have had positive experiences. Make sure to state that the travel agency you select will receive all your business, and that

the agency will have an opportunity to solicit and secure leisure travel opportunities.
4. In reviewing agency-submitted bids, make sure you look at each agency's qualities in total, not just the amount of the discount that's offered. "Cheapest" is not necessarily the same as "best."

Finding Your Super Travel Agent

People often speak about their doctor, attorney, broker, and other professionals in service fields in a possessive way. "My broker recommends . . . ," "My doctor believes that . . . ," or "My lawyer says I should. . . ." Why do we do this? Certainly we don't feel like we own our doctor or lawyer, but for some reason, the best professionals make us feel as though we're their only customer.

A super travel agent is no different. You should expect your travel agent to have a strong understanding of your travel needs, your business, and even many of your personal needs. All agents are not alike. In fact, all super agents are not alike. You need to find not only a super travel agent, but *your* super travel agent. Here are six traits to look for in your super travel agent:

☐ Specializes in the kind of travel that you do

☐ Has experience dealing with the kinds of travel problems you encounter

☐ Keeps up with trends that could affect the kind of travel you do

☐ Understands and uses the most effective and efficient tools of the travel trade

☐ Quickly gets to know your needs and preferences

☐ Is compatible with your personality and temperament

Again, when you are selecting a travel agency, make sure you have an opportunity to interview the travel agent who will be assigned to you, either in person or by telephone. If your agent doesn't satisfy all six of the preceding criteria, don't hesitate to search for another agent.

How to Track the Effectiveness of Your Agent

Monitoring the results of your travel agent's work is largely a matter of keeping and reviewing records, and following up on any problems. In particular, follow these three guidelines:

☐ Maintain records of all company travel. Organize your records to keep track of costs.

☐ Keep records that describe any problems encountered that relate to the agency's level of service. Identify one person within your company to examine and resolve these problems.

☐ Give your travel agency the opportunity to resolve problems. Switching agencies without giving your current agency the chance to make amends is at the very least unfair and could lead you into a relationship with a new agency that cannot do any better, or that does worse.

WARNING: Problems in communication are the major cause of travel difficulties. To reduce the potential for these problems, make sure you communicate your travel needs in writing, cleanly typed, whenever possible. Do not assume your secretary, travel agent, or business associate understands your cryptic abbreviations, colloquial terms, or fragmented instructions. Unless your handwriting is impeccable, a request to "book flight to Frisco, Tue. night" can leave you with a seat on *a flight to Fresno, tonight.*

More on Communication Problems

The world is full of cities with identical names. Madrid exists on several continents. The words States, Granada, London, Washington, and Miami can all specify multiple destinations. If you want to go to London, Canada, make that clear to your travel agent.

The most common result of miscommunication is the wrong kind of ticket. Here's what happens: The agent notes all the flight information correctly but specifies the incorrect fare base. Because many different types of tickets and corresponding prices are available for a single flight, this kind of mistake is not hard to make.

However, the super agent will think to check the profile for your business travel, then double-check with you if you are booked on a first-class flight when you typically book coach. Again, you can prevent such problems by specifying your travel needs in writing, cleanly and clearly.

When You Have Problems

If you suspect that a problem that occurs during your travel is the result of unacceptable work on the part of your travel agency, it's best not to take your frustration out on the individual travel agent who made the booking. When you verbally assault your agent, you risk the chance of the agent becoming defensive or confused. Seek impartial high ground. I take my complaints to the top by telling the agency or owner, either by phone or, even better, in writing, precisely what the problem was. A simple statement like this one can be effective:

> Here are the problems I am having and the steps I would like taken to remedy them. [Describe problem(s).]
> If you believe these problems have been initiated by my company, please let me know and I will take steps to avoid the problems in the

future. However, if the problems are the result of actions taken by your travel agency, they must be corrected immediately or my firm will have to find another agency.

A good agency owner or manager will work swiftly to resolve problems. The most professional agencies will accept responsibility and take steps to ensure your future business. On the other hand, keep your eyes and ears open for this kind of reply:

> ... don't know how this could have happened. However, you know how airlines are, and hotels are even worse, and car agencies. . . .

Such buck-passing should send up a red flag telling you to find a new travel agency—immediately, if this is not the first time the problem has presented itself. However, resist the temptation to switch agencies if you feel you've received poor service in one particular instance. The travel business is complex, and even the best agents fall down at one time or another. The yardstick of a super travel agency should be whether its management responds to a complaint by providing a solution that satisfies you, a solution that annoys you, or a nonsolution. You should at least give your agency the opportunity to remedy a bad situation as a common business courtesy.

Your Travel Agency's Liability

Travel agents act as brokers for carriers; they can't expect to be held liable for mistakes made by a carrier. If your luggage is lost or you break a tooth on a stone buried in an in-flight meal, you shouldn't expect to collect damages from your travel agency. However, you do make specific requests of your travel agency, and if these requests are not satisfied, you might be able to file a claim.

For instance, if you have specified to your travel agency that you must have wheelchair assistance, and the agent books you on a flight that has no such assistance available (and consequently you miss a connecting flight), you might be able to claim negligence.

The key in assessing liability, of course, is determining who is responsible for a problem. Don't expect a travel agency to get your flight in the air on time, and don't expect the airline to reimburse you for an incorrectly written ticket.

How to Keep a Super Agent

I'll say it again: Personnel turnover at travel agencies is high. You think you've settled into a great relationship with a particular agent at a particular agency, and that agent moves or is reassigned.

Travel agents are like doctors, brokers, and other service professionals—they strive to be indispensable to their clients. When agents are reassigned or attempt to start their own business, it's natural for them to try to take their valued customers with them. Owners and managers know this and do their best to walk a tightrope, attempting to keep their top salespeople happy as they maintain the profile of the agency above the skills of any one agent.

If you find a super agent whom you believe you cannot do without, you might be headed for trouble. Agents will leave, and even agents who remain with your agency of choice will take time off to attend seminars and to assess vacation packages. You should never rely 100 percent on any one agent. Instead, find an agency that makes professionalism its goal, then build a relationship with several agents at the company.

5

How to Beat the Airlines at Their Own Game

Unfortunately, airlines have learned that the business traveler is willing to pay more for a seat than other travelers, as long as a seat is available on the right flight. The airlines know that many business travelers consider the price of tickets to be a tax-deductible expense or an expense that their employer will pick up. Even budget-minded business travelers can be maneuvered into paying top dollar for seats.

"Sorry," the ticket agent tells you. "If you had only called three weeks ago, we could have saved you some money." The agent knows you *must* be in Detroit, Boston, or Tokyo by tomorrow. So your tickets are being held hostage. Sounds a lot like scalping, doesn't it?

The airlines' ticket price structure is legal. But it's hardly fair to you. After all, you're paying perhaps 50 to 75 percent more for a ticket on the same plane, landing at the same destination, as the tourist who was able to book seats at least 14 to 30 days in advance or who called up yesterday and obtained a special promotion special.

On the other hand, you're a savvy business-person. You know that you're purchasing tickets only a few days or perhaps a few hours before the flight, and demand is the name of the game. Competition for seats drives the airlines' price structure, right? That's the nature of this business. You sigh. But *should* you have to pay full fare for the few in-demand seats left on the plane?

Consider another perspective. The so-called discount rate that airlines offer to vacation travelers or others who are able to make long-range plans is actually the "regular" rate. These travelers aren't getting any discount, just the basic ticket price. It's a lot like attending a performance at the theater. The basic ticket prices for attending a play or concert are the same, whether you purchase one week in advance or five weeks in advance. However, if you purchase your tickets at the door, you can expect to pay a premium.

But is the business traveler really "paying at the door"? No. Business travelers are the most frequent flyers on airlines—they are the airlines' bread and butter. They ought to be treated as preferred customers—subscription ticket holders, if you will. It doesn't matter when you buy; the fact that you fly frequently means that you're part of the airline industry's largest base of customers.

So you should get a price break for helping to subsidize the airline industry. But, as a business traveler, you don't get breaks from the airlines; instead you get taken advantage of. The game rules, in this case, are in the airlines' favor because they *make* the rules. And chances are that you've allowed the airlines to get away with these rules. But you ought to be angry. And you ought to be eager to change the rules.

That's what this chapter is about. I'll explore the airlines' price structure in depth so that you can understand what they're up to. You'll also learn how you can manipulate this price structure in your favor. Along the way, you'll get some inside information about little-known or little-understood bonus programs offered by some airlines.

How Do Business Fares Affect You?

Of all the hundreds of thousands of enterprises in the world, airlines top the list of companies who attempt to price their services more according to demand than to the service they render. I'll provide some specific examples of this later in the chapter. But for now, consider a general example that illustrates how easily and frequently the business traveler is ripped off.

A flight between New York and Paris (3636 air miles) has a one-way, "discount-fare" price of $489 (based on a round-trip ticket). This works out to about 13 cents per mile. So far, so good.

However, a flight from New York to Pittsburgh (381 air miles) can cost the business traveler $207 or more—about 55 cents per mile, or nearly five times the per-mile cost of the New York/Paris ticket.

What accounts for this discrepancy in fares? Nothing. Your friendly neighborhood airline is taking advantage of the perceived demand for its flights. The airline gauges fares based on what it believes you, the business traveler, can be trapped into paying. Airlines claim to be competitive and frequently give the impression that they will go head-to-head with their competition to match or beat prices. This is pretty much an illusion, and you ought to know how the airline pricing "magicians" operate.

TIP

Need to complain to someone about an airline's service? Follow these steps:

1. Write down the details of the problem.

2. Include dates, flight number, and a copy of the ticket, if possible.
3. Indicate how you would like to see the complaint resolved (terminate or reprimand an employee, provide a free ticket or free upgrade for you, and so on).
4. Send one copy of your complaint directly to the airline, then send another copy to:

> U.S. Department of Transportation
> Office of Consumer Affairs
> 400 Seventh Street, S.W.
> Washington, DC 20590
> (202) 366-2220

The Loss Leader: Miami to New York for Only $99

It's a full page ad in the business section of the morning newspaper. In extra-large type, blazoned across the top of the page, is the hook: *Miami to New York: $99.* Sounds good, doesn't it? It might be, if you are, in fact, lucky enough to actually book one of these cheap seats.

Most airlines have several prices for the same route, and the $99 seats might represent only a fraction of the seats available on each flight. This is especially true when other airlines quickly jump in to match a competitor's bargain fares. Because there is no regulation that dictates an airline must assign a minimum percentage of seats at an advertised price, an airline can easily match a competitor's fare by providing one or two seats of that price on some flights over the same route.

Advertising agencies call this kind of cheap seat a *loss leader*. More often than not, seats at the loss leader price will be sold out by the time you call, or you won't be able to satisfy all the restrictions. These superreduced, loss-leader fares are the carrots that airlines dangle in order to get you to call or to keep you from calling a competitor.

Whenever possible, try to take advantage of a loss leader, because it is usually a genuine bargain. However, if the advertised fare is not available, don't let yourself become a victim of this bait-and-switch tactic by being conned into booking a higher-priced seat on the same flight.

One way to increase your chances of cashing in on loss leaders (and in stretching your travel dollar, in general) is to develop an aggressive and creative approach to travel. I'll provide several specific strategies in this and other chapters. Basically, though, you will need to be flexible in your travel planning—making advanced planning the rule rather than the exception. You should also develop a "travel team" approach in which you and your travel agency develop a creative game plan to beat the airlines at their own game.

TIP

Airline price structures change daily. When one airline announces a special promotion, it is often matched by other carriers but without fanfare (often because the other carriers haven't had time to develop a full-blown ad campaign like the original carrier's). If you know about a super-low fare that's offered by an airline you'd rather not fly or whose flights are sold out, try the airline's competitors. Ask a competitor's reservation agent (or your travel agent) whether your preferred airline will match the fare offered by the other carrier. They often will!

Why Competition Doesn't Always Work in Your Favor

Two supermarkets in the same neighborhood sell the same items at basically the same prices. Competition tends to keep prices down, benefiting you, the consumer. It should work the same way with airlines, right?

Unfortunately, no.

No two airlines go head-to-head in all of their markets. True, with *maxiroutes* like Miami to New York, Los Angeles or San Francisco to New York, and other heavily traveled corridors, competition can get pretty keen. Each airline that travels these routes tries to fill a few more seats than the other carriers by offering special fares from time to time. But a large number of routes are flown by only a few carriers. Because there is less competition, the same airline that provides you with a bargain for its maxiroutes might make up the loss by charging double or triple for the miles flown on its other routes. You, the business traveler, get nailed for the loss.

Government control of fares within the United States used to provide a more stable price structure for both the passengers and for the travel agents who book and ticket the majority of all airline travel. But since the industry has been deregulated within the United States, airlines take advantage of open pricing by creating fare structures that are designed to confuse and take advantage of the frequent flyer.

As a consumer, keep this fact constantly in mind: *The airlines need to fill seats in order to stay in the air.* In the end, this basic truth can work to your advantage. Even on many moderately traveled routes, there usually is competition between at least two airlines, and probably more. For instance, three airlines fly nonstop between the Fort Lauderdale/Miami and the New York City area, and at least five airlines fly this route with stops or plane changes en route. All of these airlines are competing for your business—a situation that can pay off for you, but only if you or your travel agent are willing to work for that payoff.

TIP

If you live in an area served by several airports—such as New York City, South Florida, Chicago, or Los Angeles—check the flights from each airport to your desired destination. Sometimes, you will find a sizable difference in fares between one airport and another. It might be worth traveling a few extra miles to another airport in order to save big.

TIP

Flights to cities that are close to where you want to go may be much less expensive than flying directly to your destination city. In some instances, a neighboring city's airport might actually be no farther away from your final destination (in time, distance, or both) than the airport you originally thought to book for. Make sure your travel agent has checked into these possibilities.

WARNING: Wait lists are getting longer each year in order for the airlines to make up for increased no-shows. There are several ways to beat the wait-list wait. Try the following:

☐ **Insist that your travel agent go directly to the airline sales office to try to get you cleared from the list.**

☐ **On a domestic trip, try to book your flights so that you make connections beyond your actual destination on an international flight. This will give you top priority to clear the wait list; then, drop the international part of the itinerary.**

☐ **Use your frequent flyer account number to increase your odds of clearing the wait list.**

Airlines and Their Levels of Service

It isn't too difficult to arrange a trip that saves you time, saves you money, or provides you with the comfort you are looking for. But try getting all three at once. With airline travel, you probably can't save time, save money, *and* obtain extra comfort each time you fly. However, you can achieve some balance or at least ensure that the most important of these three desires is achieved. Again, the trick is careful and creative planning and knowing about the levels of service that airlines offer.

First-Class Service

First-class service usually lives up to its name, and with good reason. On most carriers, the price for first-class seats has risen more than that for any other seat type. As a result, first-class seats have become a genuine perk for frequent flyers. A first-class seat promises better food, free drinks, free movies (when available), separate check-in area, priority luggage handling (often), and better in-flight service from flight attendants.

First-class seating usually appears as an *F* fare type on your ticket (but can also be a *J* or *P*). An *F* fare will ensure that you get the best seat on a flight that you expect to be crowded and generally uncomfortable. For flights after 9 P.M., the fare type is usually specified as *FN*. First-class seats on night domestic flights are generally less expensive than their daytime counterparts.

The most obvious way to fly first class is to pay full price for a first-class seat. However, you can often fly first class at coach fares or slightly more. Because first-class seats are such a desirable perk, airlines often provide them to their frequent flyers as an award. It isn't unusual for the first-class section of a flight to be filled entirely with people who did not pay the first-class fare. They have all received upgrades or other special deals.

Delta Airlines, for example, offers frequent flyer passengers special first-class fares that are only slightly more expensive than the regular coach seat. TWA has a unique relationship in which its frequent flyer members can get upgrades when they buy coach seats—depending on the availability of seats on the day of the flight or at check-in time. Other airlines offer frequent flyer upgrade coupons when passengers have logged a certain number of miles with the airline.

It can't do any harm to sign up for frequent flyer programs that you think you might use. If you end up not using a particular frequent flyer program, there is no penalty to you. The airline simply removes your account from its enrollment file after a certain period of time elapses without any account activity from you. I'll tell you more about frequent flyer programs later.

Figure 5–1 (on pages 76 and 77) lists first-class services on transatlantic flights.

Discounts on First-Class Tickets from Your Travel Agent

A less obvious way to receive a deal on first-class seats is to use your travel agent's influence. Your agent might have a certain amount of "pull" with the staff of a particular airline. This is also a good reason for using a travel agent who uses the "airline computer" for the airline you frequent most. Experienced agents who work closely with their airline representatives can make these strategies work for you on a continuing basis.

Before deregulation, about 10 percent of flyers purchased first-class tickets. Today, about the same percentage of flyers represent the total for combined first-class and *business-class* seats (which I'll discuss later). Airlines know they can count on this percentage, even though the cost

MEAL SERVICE table (page 76)

Airline	Aircraft Types	No. First-Class Seats	Configuration	Pitch (Inches)	Width (Inches)	Type of Seat	Recline (Degrees)	Available on All Flights	Available Systemwide	Advance Seat Selection	Advance Boarding Passes	Airport Transfers	Separate Check-in	Priority Baggage	Priority Boarding	Separate Departure Lounge	Number of Courses	Number of Entree Choices	Cold Entree Available	Seatside Food Preparation	Toiletry/Shaving Kit	Other Gift	Frequent Flyer Program	Mileage Bonus
American	B767	14	2×1×2	56	20.5	B	60	•	•	•	•		•	•	•	S	5	4	S		•	•	•	50%
Austrian Airlines	DC-10	28	2×2×2	57	22	B	60	•		•	•	•	•	•	•	•	5	3	S	•	•	S	•	
British Airways	A310-300	12	2×2×2	60	18	C	NA	•	•	•	•	•	•	•	•	•	6	4	•	•	•		•	150%
Canadian	B747	18	2×2	62	21	C	60	•	•	•	•		•	•	•	•	3	3	S	•	•	•	•	50%
Canadian	B767	10	2×1×2	59	20.5	B	42																	
Continental	DC-10	12	2×2×2	57	20.2	B	60	•	•	•	•	•	•	•	•	•	9	3	•	•	•	•	•	50%
Continental	B747	16	2×2	60	20.5	C	60																	
Delta	DC-10	16	2×2×2	60	20	C	53	•	•	•	•	•	•	•	•	•	5	3		•	•	•	•	100%
Delta	L1011-250	12	2×2×2	55	20	B	49																	
Delta	L1011-500	12	2×2×2	55	NA	B	49																	
EgyptAir	B747	18	2×2	62	22	B	90	•	S	•	•	S	•	•	•	•	4	6	•	•	•	•	•	
El Al	B747	10	2×2	48	21.5	B	45	•	•	•	•	E	•	•	•	•	5	3	S	•	•	•	•	
Finnair	DC-10	12	2×2×2	58	21	B	60	•		•			•	•	•	•	3	3		•	•	•	•	•
Gulf Air	L1011	24	2×2×2	60		A	45	•	•	•	•		•	•	•	•	7	3	•	•	•	•	•	•

76

Airline	Aircraft		Config			Seat																		%
Iberia	B747	12	2×2	62	20	A	60	•	•			S		•	•	•	4	3	•	•	•	•	•	150%
	DC-10	16	2×2×2	56	20	A	60	•	•	•				•	•	•	6	5			•	•	•	50%
KLM Royal Dutch	B747	18	2×2	62	20.5	B	90	•	•	•	•	S		•	•	•	5	4		•	•	•	•	
Kuwait Airways	B747	34	2×2	39.5	26	B	63		•	•		•		•	•	•	3	3	S			•	•	•
Lufthansa	B747-200	21	2×2	55	24	B	60		•					•	•	•	6	3	•		•	•	•	50%
	DC-10	22	2×2×2	60	28.5	B	60		•	•	S			•	•	•								
	B747	18	2×2	62	21.5	B	50	•	•		•	•		•	•	•								
Northwest																								
Pakistan International	B747	16	2×2	NA	NA	NA	NA	•				S		•	•	•	5	2	•	S	S	•	•	50%
Pan Am	B747	21	2×2	55	20.5	B	45	•	•	•	S			•	S	•	5	5	S	S	S	S	•	
	A310	12	2×2×2	55	19.5	B	45	•	•	•				•	•	•								
Royal Air Maroc	B747	12	2×2	NA	NA	B	60	•	•		S	S		•	•	•	5	3	•	•	•	•	•	200%
Royal Jordanian	L1011	18	2×2×2	56	25	A	60	•	•	S	•	•		•	•	•	6	3		•	•	•	•	150%
Sabena	B747	16	2×2	62	21.5	A	51	S	•		•	NA		•	•	•	8	4				•	•	
	DC-10	16	2×2	62	NA	A	60		•	•														
Saudia	B747	36	2×2	60	26	A	75	•	•		•		S	•	•	•	5	4				•	•	50%
SAS	DC-10	10	2×2	62	24	A	60	•	•	•	•	•	•	•	•	•	5	3	•	•	•	•	•	
Swissair	B747	24	2×2	62	28.1	A	60	•	•		•		•	•	•	•	6	3	•	•	•	•	•	
	DC-10	22	2×2×2	62	28.7	A	60	•	•	•	•													
TWA	B747	21	2×2	57	18.75	B	60	•	•		•	S		S	•	•	5	5	•	•	•	•	•	50%
	L1011	18	2×2×2	57	20.75		60	•	•	•	•													
	B767	15	2×1×2	55	18.75		60	•	•	•	•			•	•	•								
UTA French	DC-10	12	2×2×2	62	21	B	56	•	•	•	•	•		•	•	•	4	3	•	•	•	•	•	
Zambia	DC-10	22	2×2×2	60	NA	C	60	•	•	•	•	•		•	•	•	4	3	•	•	•	•	•	

Type of Seat: A—Sleeper Seat, electronically controlled legrest; B—Sleeper Seat, fold-out legrest; C—Sleeper Seat, lever-controlled legrest; D—Standard first class seat; S—Sometimes; E—Extra Charge; NA—Information not available. NOTE: As the carriers take delivery of ordered aircraft, configuration, seat models, and amenities will change.

Figure 5-1 Guide to Transatlantic First-Class Air Service

for first-class seats has risen far more than the cost for coach seating. In fact, you might be able to buy an entire row of seats in coach (then stretch out and sleep) for the same price as a first-class ticket.

Take a look at the price chart in Figure 5–2. You can quickly see that an upgrade from coach to business class or from business class to first class is a worthwhile perk. Also notice that four seats at a 14-day advance coach fare make a nice bed and beat the business-class fare by over $2000.

Buying First-Class Seats from a Consolidator

A good way to beat the high cost of first- and business-class seats is to book through a ticket consolidator. A consolidator either resells broker-discounted seats, which airlines sell to them in bulk, or sells frequent flyer upgrade coupons. Consolidators can offer great savings on first- and business-class seats, and even occasionally have deals on bulk coach seats.

Buying from a consolidator can be risky, though, even if you know the rules of their game and have confidence in a specific consolidator. A ticket obtained through an upgrade coupon from a frequent flyer program might have restrictions unfavorable to your travel plans. Worse, many airlines are attempting to stop the sale of their

Class of Service	Round-Trip Price	Restrictions
First Class	$6572.00	Valid for 12 months
Business Class	3822.00	Valid for 12 months
21-Day Advance Coach	937.00	7-day minimum stay*

*Fares for 21-day advance seats may have additional restrictions, such as refundability limitations.

Figure 5–2 *Miami to London Round-Trip on British Airways*

frequent flyer awards and might confiscate your ticket at check-in.

To reduce your overall risk in purchasing tickets from a consolidator, you should do it through your own travel agent. Most of the consolidators listed in Figure 5–3 (on pages 80 and 81) work through travel agents.

If your travel agency does not deal at all with a consolidator, suggest that the agency contact one on the list. Ask your agent to screen the consolidator to ensure its quality and reliability, then let the agency act as your booking agent in dealing with that consolidator.

TIP

When you purchase a ticket issued through a consolidator, do so with a major credit card if possible. Some consolidators do not accept credit cards for late bookings; some accept no credit cards at all. In these cases, attempt to have your travel agency accept your credit card, even if you have to pay a fee that is charged to the vendor on such transactions. By using your credit card, you can refuse payment if something turns out badly.

Business-Class Service

Business-class service is increasingly available on most international flights, although it is not available on many domestic flights. As you might expect, business-class service is better than coach (free drinks, free movies, better food, and better service), but not as good as first class. The specific features vary widely from airline to airline. On some transatlantic flights, I have had coach seats that were more comfortable than business-class seats of other airlines.

In turn, the business-class seats on some airlines are more comfortable than the first-class seats on other airlines. Your own experience can

Name	Address	Phone	Specialty
Access International	250 W. 57th St. New York, NY 10107	212-333-7280 800-333-7280	Europe
Airdeal	P.O. Box 77437 San Francisco, CA 94107	415-543-4683 800-247-3325	Hawaii, Europe packages
Airkit	1125 W. Sixth St. Los Angeles, CA 90017	213-482-8778	Europe
All American Reservations	200 Convention Center Dr. Las Vegas, NV 89101	800-634-3466	Nevada, Southern California, Hawaii
American Travel Corp.	1800 K St. Washington, DC 20006	202-835-0099 800-634-0704	Europe, Middle East
A.P. Tours	41 E. 42nd St. No. 1515 New York, NY 10017	212-490-2972	Middle East, India
Asensio Tours	445 Fifth Ave. New York, NY 10016	212-213-4310	South America
Brazilian American Travel	5777 W. Century Blvd. Los Angeles, CA 90045	213-670-9347	Brazil, South America
Brazilian Travel Service	55 W. 46th St. New York, NY 10036	212-840-3733 800-342-3746	South America
C.L. Thompson	560 Sutter, Suite 400 San Francisco, CA 94102	415-398-2535	General
Costa Azul Travel	955 S. Vermont Ave. Suite N Los Angeles, CA 90006	213-384-7200	South America
Council Travel Services	5500 Atherton St. Suite 212 Long Beach, CA 90815	213-598-3338	Student Travel
Coupon Bank	5666 La Jolla Blvd. La Jolla, CA 92037	800-292-9250 800-331-1076	Europe, Hawaii, South Pacific
Destinations Unlimited	400 Madison Ave. New York, NY 10017	212-980-8220	Europe, Hawaii, South America
Diplomat Tours	527 Munroe St. Sacramento, CA 95825	800-727-8687	Europe, Orient, South America
DKL Group	1001 N.W. 42nd Ave. Miami, FL 33126	305-642-6160	General
Express Discount Travel	5945 Mission Gorge Rd. San Diego, CA 92120	619-283-6324	Mexico, Hawaii, Europe, Orient
Fast Lane Travel	4200 Wilson Blvd. Suite 410 Arlington, VA 22203	703-284-5222 800-522-0414	Europe
Flight Coordinators	1150 Yale St. #8 Santa Monica, CA 90403	213-453-1396	Europe, South Pacific
The Flyer's Edge	626 Green Bay Rd. Kenilworth, IL 60043	312-256-8200 800-345-2525	General
Flytime Tours	45 W. 34th St. New York, NY 10001	212-760-3737	General
French Experience	171 Madison Ave. New York, NY 10016	212-683-2445	France
Getaway Travel	1105 Ponce de Leon Coral Gables, FL 33134	305-446-7855 800-334-1923	General—Foreign
International Travel Center	275 Post, Union Square San Francisco, CA 94108	415-398-8462	Round the World, Asia
ITClub Travel	150 S.E. Second Ave. Miami, FL 33131	800-248-2582	South America, Europe

Name	Address	Phone	Specialty
Jetset Tours (NA)	8383 Wilshire Blvd. Suite 450 Beverly Hills, CA 90211	800-453-8738	Australia, New Zealand, Orient, Circle Pacific, Around the World
Katy Van Tours	16526 Park Rd. West Houston, TX 77084	713-492-7032 800-528-9826	South America, Central America, Europe
M & H Travel	16 E. 41st St. New York, NY 10017	212-689-1313 800-356-9648	Europe
McTravel	130 S. Jefferson Chicago, IL 60606	312-876-1116 800-333-3335	General
MIT Travel	551 Fifth Ave. New York, NY 10017	212-986-8210	Europe, Orient
Overseas Tours	475 El Camino Real Suite 206 Millbrook, CA 94030	800-222-5292	Orient, South Pacific
STA Travel	2500 Wilshire Blvd. Los Angeles, CA 90057	213-937-6274 212-986-9470	Students, S. Pacific, Europe, Scandinavia
Step Tourism	681 Lexington Ave. New York, NY 10022	212-308-4000 800-234-7837	France, French West Indies
Swan Travel	400 Madison Ave. New York, NY 10017	212-421-1010	General
TFI Tours International	34 W. 32nd St. New York, NY 10001	212-736-1140 800-223-6363	Europe, Orient, Domestic
Travel Associates	2025 Eye St. N.W. Suite 613 Washington, DC 20006	202-452-0999 800-452-0999	Africa
Travel Broker	393 Broadway New York, NY 10013	212-219-0612	General, Orient, Europe
Travel Center	38 W. 32nd St. New York, NY 10001	212-947-6670	South America, Far East, Europe, Asia
Traveler's Choice	141 E. 44th St. New York, NY 10017	212-983-8900 800-458-6278	First and Business Class— Europe, Orient, Hawaii
Travel Leaders	540 Biltmore Way Coral Gables, FL 33134	305-443-7755 800-432-4347 800-323-3218	Europe, Orient, South America
Travel Magic	576 Fifth Ave. New York, NY 10036	212-764-3520 800-543-0003	Europe
Travel Wholesalers	5201 Leesburg Pike Falls Church, VA 22041	800-572-1717 800-446-2424	South America, Europe, Orient
Trilogical Travel Service	547 W. 110th St. New York, NY 10025	212-749-7674 800-327-6765	Europe, South America
U-Travel	1140 S. Dixie Highway Coral Gables, FL 33146	305-662-1053 800-233-4466	Europe, Orient, South America
Up and Away Travel	141 E. 44th St. New York, NY 10017	212-972-2345 800-876-2929	South America, Europe, Domestic

Figure 5–3 *Ticket Consolidators*

help you determine whether business-class service is worthwhile. Figure 5-4 (on pages 84–88) lists the first- and business-class services of more than 50 airlines. But keep in mind that airlines frequently change the configuration of their aircraft to satisfy new marketing needs. The quality of services also may improve or degrade (without a corresponding change in price) in order to compete.

Airlines that provide business-class seating on international flights but not on domestic connections usually upgrade the business-class traveler to first class for the domestic portion. This might be something for your travel agent to consider when booking you from New York to Japan, for example. You could ride first class from New York to Los Angeles, then switch to business class for the flight to Japan, at the same price you would pay to fly business class nonstop from New York to Japan. You might have to spend some extra time en route, but the added comfort at a reduced cost can be worth it.

Here's an additional perk that often comes with first- and business-class tickets for international flights: special lounges to pamper you while you await the departure of the flight.

All of the techniques that I mentioned for getting first-class seats at bargain rates also apply to most business-class programs. Business-class seating is usually denoted as a *B* fare, but the actual letter differs among airlines.

Coach-Class Service

Coach is really a catch-all term for "the back of the plane," and is often called the *Y* fare. Unlike first- and business-class seats, however, several different fares can be charged for the same coach seat. Here's the distinction: First class is a type of seat and service on a specific aircraft; business class is a smaller seat, with somewhat less service, on that same aircraft; coach is a *price,* based on a set of restrictions, for a specific seat. The in-flight service is the same for all coach seats on a flight, although the price charged for different coach passengers can vary widely.

If you are planning to fly coach and you expect to pay one of the higher prices for a coach seat, check the business- and first-class fares before you purchase your ticket. You might find that, for only a slight increase, you can move to the front of the plane and fly in style. USAir, for example, once had upgrade prices of $20, $40, and $60 to move from Y to first class, depending on the distance you were flying.

Discount Fares

Virtually all discount fares apply to the coach section of the plane. These discounts are so numerous that I would probably confuse rather than help you if I tried to list and explain them all. Discount fares go by such designations as *Apex, B fare, Q fare, K fare, M fare, BY10 fare,* and so on, all of which have separate restrictions and prices. To add to the confusion, two or more airlines might use the same fare code with different restrictions.

In any event, the coach section makes up the majority of the seating space on any flight. Filling coach seats is a critical part of the airline business. For many airlines, each body, on each flight, represents one step closer to profitability. As a result, one of the easiest ways for an airline to increase profits is to add a few seats. The experienced business traveler can tell immediately when an airline is packing rows together to make up for lower fares. If you are looking for the savings that usually come with a coach-class seat, expect to pay for it in lack of comfort.

How to Buy a Superdiscounted Fare That Is "Sold Out"

You'll probably never find a flight where all seats—or even a majority of the seats—are priced at the lowest possible fare. In fact, the actual

	AMERICA WEST Business Class	AMERICAN Business Class	CONTINENTAL Silver Service	DELTA Medallion Class	JET AMERICA	NORTHWEST Business Class / Exec. Class; Exec. Suite
FLIGHT AMENITIES						
ELECTRONIC HEADSETS	•	•	•	•		•
CHOICE OF MEAL ENTREES	•	•	•	•	•	•
FREE DRINKS	•	•	•	•		•
WIDER-THAN-ECONOMY SEATS	•	•	•	•	•	•
EXTRA CARRY-ON SPACE	•	•	•	•	•	•
LAVATORY IN CABIN	•	•	•	•	•	•
PERMANENT SEPARATE CABIN	•	•	•	•		•
SEPARATE OR LATE BOARDING		•	•	•		•
SEAT PITCH	36	37 / 40	37	36	34–38	40 / 62
SEATS ABREAST	4	6 / 6	7	8	5(MD80)	4 or 8 / 4
BUSINESS CLASS AVAILABILITY	757; Phoenix/Las Vegas-CHI/NYC/BWI	Transatlantic / Transpacific	Honolulu, South Pacific, London	Transatlantic, transpacific, Honolulu	Systemwide	Transpacific, transatlantic
LAND AMENITIES						
PRIVATE AIRPORT LOUNGES	•	•	•	•		•
PRIORITY BAGGAGE HANDLING		•	•	•		•
EXTRA BAGGAGE ALLOWANCE				•		•
SEPARATE CHECK-IN		•	•	•	•	•
ADVANCE BOARDING CARD		•	•	•		•
FREQUENT FLYER PROGRAM	•	•	•	•	•	•
HELICOPTER				•		•
LIMOUSINE	•					
TICKET CODE	B	B	B F	B	V	B F

	Code	Name of Service	Routes	Seats Abreast	Seat Pitch
PAN AMERICAN					
Clipper Class	F	All widebody		6	34–38
TWA					
Ambassador Class	B	All widebody		6	38
UNITED					
Business Class	B	Transpacific and intra-Asia		8	37–38
FOREIGN CARRIERS					
Name of Service					
AER LINGUS					
Super Executive Class	F	Transatlantic		6	39
AERO ARGENTINAS					
Executive Class	B	U.S.–South America		4	38
AEROMEXICO	YR.	New York (DC-10), Miami, Madrid, Paris		8	35
Silver Class	F				
AIR AFRIQUE		All DC-10 and Airbus		7	NA
Business Class	F				
AIR CANADA		Transatlantic, transcon, domestic 767 and 727		6	38
Executive Class	F				
AIR FRANCE		Transatlantic; Paris to Asia, Latin America		8	36
Le Club	B				
AIR INDIA		New York–London/India and all 747		4 or 6	38–40
Executive Cabin	F				
AIR NEW ZEALAND		All international		4	40
Pacific Class	F				
ALITALIA		Transatlantic, Europe, Asia, Africa, all 747		4	35
Prima Business Class	F				
ALL NIPPON		Transpacific		4 or 6	40
Super Executive Class	F				
AVIANCA		New York/Miami–Bogota; Bogota–San Juan/Europe		4	32
El Colombian	F				

continued

	BRITISH AIRWAYS (Super Club)	BRIT. CALEDONIAN (Super Executive)	CAAC (Business Class)	CANADIAN INT'L (Empress, Royal Can.)	CATHAY PACIFIC (Marco Polo Class)	CHINA AIRLINES (Dynasty Class)	EL AL	FINNAIR (Business Class / Executive Class)
FLIGHT AMENITIES								
ELECTRONIC HEADSETS	•	•			•	•	•	•
CHOICE OF MEAL ENTREES	•	•			•	•	•	•
FREE DRINKS	•	•	•	•		•	•	•
WIDER-THAN-ECONOMY SEATS		•	•			•	•	•
EXTRA CARRY-ON SPACE		•	•			•	•	•
LAVATORY IN CABIN		•	•		•	•	•	•
PERMANENT SEPARATE CABIN	•	•	•	•		•	•	•
SEPARATE OR LATE BOARDING	•	•	•			•	•	•
SEAT PITCH	36	38(DC-10) 40(747)	38	34, 37–38	38	42	40	42
SEATS ABREAST	6	7	6	9–10, 4–6	8	4	4	7
BUSINESS CLASS AVAILABILITY	All international (Club Class in Europe)	All international (Executive Class in Europe)	Transpacific	Domestic, international	Systemwide	Transpacific, 747, and most international	All except Cairo	Transatlantic, Far East, intra-Europe (DC-9)
LAND AMENITIES								
PRIVATE AIRPORT LOUNGES		•	•	•		•	•	•
PRIORITY BAGGAGE HANDLING	•	•	•	•	•	•	•	•
EXTRA BAGGAGE ALLOWANCE	•	•	•	•	•	•		•
SEPARATE CHECK-IN	•	•	•	•	•	•	•	•
ADVANCE BOARDING CARD							•	
FREQUENT FLYER PROGRAM	•	•		•	•	•	•	•
HELICOPTER	•	•					•	•
LIMOUSINE		•						•
TICKET CODE	F	F	B	B F	B	B	B	B

GARUDA INDONESIA Executive Class	B						•		•	Transpacific	6	42		•	•		•	•	•	•
HIGHLAND EXPRESS Business Class Plus	F	•	•	•		•	•	•	•	Transatlantic	4	60	•	•	•	•	•	•	•	•
IBERIA Preference Class	B		•			•	•	•	•	Transatlantic, some intra-Europe	4 or 6	36	•	•	•	•	•	•	•	•
ICELANDAIR Saga Class	B					•			•	Transatlantic, Iceland-UK/Scandinavia	6	34	•	•	•			•	•	
JAPAN AIR LINES Executive Class	B			•		•			•	International	8	37		•	•	•	•	•	•	•
KLM Business Class	B	•	•	•		•	•	•	•	Most routes	4(747), 7(DC-10) 6(A300)	38,37 37	•	•	•	•	•	•	•	•
KOREAN AIR Prestige Class	B		•	•		•	•	•	•	Transpacific, Korea-Asia/Middle East	4 6(747-300)	41 41	•	•	•	•	•	•	•	•
LAN-CHILE Business Class	B		•			•		•	•	South America	6	36	•	•	•		•	•	•	•
LUFTHANSA Business Class	B		•	•		•	•	•		All widebody intercontinental	8(747, DC-10) 7(A300)	37 37		•	•		•	•	•	•
MALAYSIAN Golden Club Class	B B			•		•		•	•	Transpacific, 747-300 upper cabin; other routes 747, DC-10	2/4(747), 2(DC-10) 2(A300)	36–38, 30 30	•	•	•		•	•	•	•
OLYMPIC Olympian Class	F		•	•		•	•	•	•	Transatlantic, Athens-Singapore/Australia	4	42	•	•	•	•	•	•	•	
PHILIPPINE Mabuhay Class	B			•		•	•	•	•	Transpacific, Europe	8	37	•	•	•	•	•	•	•	•
QANTAS Business Class	F			•		•	•	•	•	Systemwide	8(747) 6(767), 4(747-SP & -300)	38	•	•	•	•	•	•	•	•
SABENA Business Class	B		•	•	•	•	•	•	•	Systemwide	4 or 7	36	•	•	•	•	•	•	•	•
SAS First Business Class	B	•	•	•	•	•	•	•	•	All widebody international	7(DC-10)	38	•	•	•	•	•	•	•	•

Figure 5-4 Business and First-Class Services for Many Airlines

	SAUDI / Horizon Class	SINGAPORE / Business Class	SWISSAIR / Business Class	TAP-AIR PORTUGAL / Navigator Class	THAI INTERNATIONAL / Royal Executive	UTA / Galaxy Class	VARIG / Executive Class	VIRGIN ATLANTIC / Upper Class
ELECTRONIC HEADSETS	•	•	•		•	•	•	•
CHOICE OF MEAL ENTREES	•	•	•	•	•	•	•	•
FREE DRINKS	•	•	•		•	•	•	•
WIDER-THAN-ECONOMY SEATS	•	•	•	•	•	•	•	•
EXTRA CARRY-ON SPACE	•	•	•		•	•	•	•
LAVATORY IN CABIN	•	•	•	•	•	•	•	•
PERMANENT SEPARATE CABIN	•	•	•	•	•	•	•	•
SEPARATE OR LATE BOARDING	•	•	•	•	•	•	•	•
SEAT PITCH	40	38	38		45(747) 39(A300)	38	40	55
SEATS ABREAST	4	4	8(DC-10), 5(DC-9)	7	4	7(747), 6(DC-10), 6(747-300)	8(747), 7(DC-10)	4
BUSINESS CLASS AVAILABILITY	Transatlantic	Transpacific, all widebody	Systemwide, except Lagos and some domestic	International	All widebody	San Francisco-Tahiti, Paris-Tahiti/Africa/Far East	U.S.-Brazil, U.S.-Japan, most international	Transatlantic
PRIVATE AIRPORT LOUNGES	•	•	•	•	•	•	•	
PRIORITY BAGGAGE HANDLING	•	•			•	•	•	•
EXTRA BAGGAGE ALLOWANCE	•	•		•	•	•	•	•
SEPARATE CHECK-IN	•	•	•	•	•	•	•	•
ADVANCE BOARDING CARD						•		•
FREQUENT FLYER PROGRAM		•	•	•	•	•		•
HELICOPTER	•		•	•			•	
LIMOUSINE								•
TICKET CODE	F	F	B	B	F	F	B	F

number of discounted seats available on a flight for just about any airline is a trade secret—devised perhaps by some vengeful computer program or maybe to meet competition through an obscure PFA (plucked from air) approach.

Because the airlines are so secretive (can you guess which class of traveler they're hiding the information from?), it is possible to "find" a discounted seat even when none is publicly offered. Sometimes, an aggressive travel agent with the right connections can call an airline's sales office and plead your case for a better fare.

Even if you have a super travel agent, you can't count on this approach working too often—especially if a flight is fully or nearly booked. There isn't much of an incentive for an airline sales rep to grant a travel agent's favor if doing so means less profit. Nevertheless, this strategy is worth a try. Your travel agent has more influence with the airline than you do, so let your agent do the dealing. The trick might lie in knowing what restrictions an airline is looking for you to satisfy. These restrictions can be anything from "stay over a weekend," to "travel on Wednesdays and Thursdays only."

The point is that the rules of air travel are about as stable as a glider in a thunderstorm. Keeping up with the voluminous and constantly changing regulations of dozens of airlines can drive anyone in the travel industry or anyone who travels just a little bit mad. If you expect your travel agent to find you a superdiscounted fare, you need to provide as much information as possible about the restrictions you can and cannot afford to live with. This kind of information gives your travel agent greater bargaining leverage.

But make sure your agent doesn't become overenthusiastic and take liberties with this leverage. It's very frustrating to learn that, although your agent has managed to book you on the flight you want, you are restricted on your return, forcing you to miss important business at either end or forcing you to stay a weekend in a city that you wouldn't wish on an enemy.

TIP

Whenever possible, charge your airline tickets with a credit card that offers you specific flight benefits. These benefits can include free travel insurance, frequent flyer mileage, and protection in case a problem occurs—such as the ability to refuse payment on a ticket when you are denied boarding for some reason.

Playing the Crisscross Game

One of the best ways to beat the airlines at their own game is to use the "crisscross" technique. This approach exploits an airline's "super saver" fares and allows you to purchase two round-trip super saver tickets for less than the price of one round-trip coach fare.

Super savers are a form of loss leader advertisements for airlines. On any given flight, a few seats probably are designated for this fare. You can get them if you plan far enough in advance—but with a catch. Most super saver tickets require the traveler to spend a Saturday night in the destination city and often require a minimum length of stay.

What could be more antibusiness traveler than this ploy? If you plan to travel to Chicago for a Thursday afternoon meeting, you might be willing to leave Thursday morning and return Friday night. But do you really want to stay over Saturday night? Probably not. So, the super saver fare is not, in theory, available for most business travelers.

Or is it?

Consider the savings offered on super saver fares. Take a look at Figure 5–5. As you can see, two round-trip super saver fares are lower than

First Class	$1308
Coach Class	$ 838
Super Saver (14-day advance)	$ 319

Figure 5–5 *Round-trip fares, New York/*
Chicago (American Airlines)
(3/14/91)

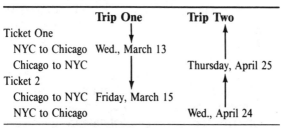

Figure 5–6 *Round-trip Super Saver tickets with*
overlapping dates

the cost of a basic coach round-trip fare, March 13, 1991.

The solution: Book two round-trip tickets, but use only one coupon from each. Assume you want to depart on Wednesday and return the following Friday. By using two round-trip super saver tickets that have overlapping dates, you can save at least $90 over the coach fare. Figure 5–6 shows how this crisscross strategy can work.

The price for these two tickets is $638, which is $200 less than the price for a single coach ticket ($838). By booking two separate discount tickets you have discovered one way to beat the system.

The key to using this system is to follow simple rules:

1. Each ticket must follow the airline rules, which in this case include staying over a Saturday night. Don't worry about the Saturday night, because you will use the other ticket for your actual return.

2. Before you call to book the flight, think through the entire mechanics of when you actually want to fly for the first trip. Because you are also setting up a possible second trip (at no extra real cost), you may want to plan ahead for a second journey to Chicago. For example, you may want to plan a quick trip to Chicago for April 24 with a return April 25.

3. On a paper show the two separate travel itineraries. Start at the top with Ticket One: This is the trip from New York to Chicago. Show a column headed Trip One and write in the travel date of March 13.

4. Skip down half a page and show Ticket Two: This begins with your actual return from Chicago to New York. Under the same column of Trip One, put the travel date from Chicago to New York of March 15.

5. Now return to the top section and put a second column to the right of Trip One, and label this column Trip Two. For the portion of Ticket One that covers travel from Chicago to New York you put the actual date you want to return from the second trip. This date is April 25 in this example and will be placed in the column labeled Trip Two.

   NOTE: This meets the Saturday stayover for Ticket One.

6. Go to Ticket Two and fill in the date of actual departure for Trip Two from New York to Chicago which is April 24. Because Ticket Two also spans a Saturday that regulation has been met.

   NOTE: It is critical for you to understand that for the second trip to function properly, the return date on Ticket Two must actually be the start of the second trip (New York to Chicago). You will read the itinerary much like a train schedule going from top to bottom on Trip One and from bottom to top on Trip Two. Once you are set on these dates, call and book the flight.

Getting Two Round-Trip Tickets for the Price of One

As Figure 5–6 shows, if you depart on Wednesday, March 13, and return on Friday, March 15, you can use the coupons shown in the Trip One column. If you depart on Wednesday, April 24, and return on Thursday, April 25, you can use the coupons in the Trip Two column.

If you have two business meetings scheduled in a city on different dates, you could book your super saver tickets so that you use all four coupons. Under this approach, you use two super-saver tickets—at less than the price of one round-trip coach ticket—without staying over on a Saturday. In Figure 5–3, for instance, you could use all four coupons.

If you had booked two separate coach tickets to accomplish the same results (because each of the two trips did not have a Saturday stayover) you would have paid $1676. Using my "beat them at their own game" plan, you pay only $638 and save a nice $1038. Because the airline allows you to make a change in the return portion of each of these two tickets at a charge of $75, you can actually make a complete change of the itinerary (within the other rules and restrictions, of course) at a cost of no more than $150. This is your safety valve should you have no immediate plans for a second trip to Chicago or need to adjust for a longer stay.

Obviously, most travel agents would rather sell you two coach tickets rather than trouble themselves with the effort required to make the most of crisscross strategies. However, if you have a hard-working travel agent and if you are insistent, you should be able to make the most of these bargain fares.

Using the Nonrefundable Ticket

The nonrefundable ticket is the newest twist to the airline game. The idea is that somebody gambles whenever a ticket is purchased. In the past, the biggest gambler has been the airline, because "no-shows" can cut heavily into an airline's profits. The airline industry's solution to no-shows has tended to lie in taking an even bigger gamble—overbooking. Overbooking seems to be a growing problem rather than a shrinking one.

The nonrefundable ticket is the airline's latest strategy to reduce the potential for no-shows and the problems that come with overbooking flights. The idea is simple: Let the traveler take the gamble. Offer a prize, in the form of a discount, to travelers who are willing to take the greatest risk. Unfortunately, this is a difficult risk to take if your flight plans tend to change more often than they stay the same. But with some creative and careful advance planning, the nonrefundable ticket game can work to your advantage. It's all a matter of playing the odds and using your frequently flying status to your advantage.

If, for example, you fly five times a year, round-trip between two particular cities, and you feel that your itinerary is fairly stable, it might be worthwhile to gamble on nonrefundable tickets. Say the round-trip nonrefundable fare is $150, a 50-percent savings over the two-day advance purchase price of $300. If you were to book all five tickets at the two-day advance price, your total cost would be $1500. If you plan carefully and pay the nonrefundable price for all tickets, you pay $750. If you have to cancel one of the five trips, you still pay $450 less for the year (again, $750) than you would if you had paid the full two-day advance price for four tickets

($1200). And if you have to cancel and reschedule one of the tickets at the two-day advance price, your total outlay for the year is $1050—you again save $450 over the total for the two-day advance tickets.

See how this works? Of course, constantly changing ticket prices mean the mathematics of a real example won't be quite as tidy as mine. And you have to be realistic about your odds of winning. If your travel schedule changes on a weekly basis, the nonrefundable ticket might never pay off for you. However, if your schedule is fairly stable, the nonrefundable ticket can represent substantial savings.

Why Advance Bookings Generally Mean Lower Prices

All airlines have at least one kind of advance ticket purchase fare, which allows you to pay less than if you buy your ticket at the gate. Like the nonrefundable ticket, the advance booking might come with some restrictions, and almost always has an advance-payment deadline. The level of savings depends on the number of days in which you must reserve and/or pay for your ticket, plus the types of restrictions that are attached. Advance ticket purchases won't save you nearly as much as nonrefundable tickets. But they do represent a good compromise if you want to save and can't afford the risk of nonrefundable ticket purchases.

It's All in the Destination

The enigma of air travel lies in the fact that you can pay more (even with discount fares) to fly between Fort Lauderdale and Atlanta than you can to fly between Fort Lauderdale and New York City. It's even more distressing to learn that you can book a flight on several different airlines— such as Delta or USAir—from Fort Lauderdale to New York, at a heavily discounted fare and stop in Atlanta along the way. It's clear that supply and demand is at work here, except the people who provide the supply—business travelers—aren't demanding enough.

When you begin to realize that the best way to get from point A to point B is to book a seat on a flight from point A to point C with a stopover at point B, you are on your way to really beating the airlines at their own game. To paraphrase Vince Lombardi: *Destination isn't everything, it's the only thing.*

Discrepancies in fares between relatively close travel distances and those farther can be even worse on the international scene. Travel between two cities of the same country often has a much higher per-mile cost than travel between two countries.

Making the Most of the Around-the-World Fare

One of the more interesting "special" fares available to international travelers is the "around-the-world" fare. Many of the special fares offered by international carriers involve agreements with connecting carriers that enable a traveler to literally fly around the world at a bargain rate. As an example, British Airways quoted me the around-the-world price structure shown in Figure 5–7.

If you refer back to Figure 5–2, you'll note that the British Airways first-class Miami-to-London round-trip price is $2268 over the around-the-world fares. In other words, you can go first-class from Miami to London, to Amsterdam, to Copenhagen, to Moscow, to Bangkok, to Shanghai, to Seoul, to Tokyo, to San Francisco, to Chicago, and back to Miami—all for less than the first-class seat from Miami to London and back.

Miami to Miami, Eastbound Round the World
(based on British Airways North-of-the-Equator routes)

First Class	$4605
Business Class	3319
Economy	2358

(Note: By checking with other international airlines, you will find a substantial difference in around-the-world prices. British Airways was one of the more expensive prices that I found. For instance, economy on a TWA/Singapore Airline around-the-world ticket was priced at just over $2099, whereas the airlines' normal prices were comparable to the British Airways rates.)

Figure 5–7 *British Airways Around-the-World Pricing, March 1991*

The around-the-world ticket has some limitations. You must remain headed in the same globe-traversing direction. Except for rare situations (such as necessary connections that cannot be made without retracing your route to some degree), you cannot backtrack. However, if you think on your feet, you can easily come up with a combination of around-the-world tickets that can get you to several interesting places at a fraction of the cost of direct flights.

For example, many international around-the-world tickets accommodate tourists by allowing for changes in schedules, called *open segments*. These are coupons for particular flights but can be used on any date, provided the entire ticket is used within the maximum time limit—which can be as long as 12 months. If your business takes you to many different international cities, you might find that two around-the-world tickets can get you to all of your destinations, and more, at bargain prices. Booking two sets of tickets—say, one that begins at Miami headed eastbound around the world, and another that goes westbound—could ultimately provide you with multiple round-trip tickets between several cities around the world at enormous savings.

How to Save by Booking Beyond Your Destination

Much of the information I've given in this chapter so far requires you to plan ahead. For instance, buying nonrefundable tickets involves some degree of confidence that your plans can be made in advance and will not change.

In business, that kind of planning is often just not possible. By now, you should be starting to realize that bargains are often achieved not by where you are traveling, but by where you *say* you are traveling. If you are called away on business suddenly, you are going to have to rely on every trick in the book in order to avoid the "scalper" fares that airlines charge the last-minute business traveler.

The name of the game here is to book to a "phantom destination," sometimes called booking to a "hidden city destination," because it involves a city beyond your actual destination. Airlines frown on this practice (hmmm, I wonder why) and discourage travel agencies from making phantom bookings.

However, more than one airline agent has told me that, "If the client knows enough to ask for a hidden destination booking and knows which flights will work for a particular trip, I book them." It seems that the rule travel agents try to avoid breaking is to *offer* phantom destination bookings. But it's okay to sell tickets for phantom destinations if the customer knows this insider move and is willing to set the itinerary.

Phantom destination bookings work because you use the airline's own routes and pricing structures to your advantage. Remember, many routes are so competitive that airlines offer special fares to entice you into booking with them. At the same time, prices between cities of lesser travel demand can be much higher, because the competition is usually minimal. So, distance does not play much of a role here.

Atlanta provides a classic example. With some airlines, you can fly from your home town to New York for less than a flight to Atlanta. However, it is quite possible to buy a ticket for a flight from your home town to New York—on Delta, USAir, TWA, and other airlines—that either stops or requires you to change planes in Atlanta. In this situation, you can book on the flight to New York, then simply deplane in Atlanta without making the continuing segment to New York.

You will find it fairly easy to take advantage of phantom destination bookings if you know the major *hub cities* (where airlines base their operations or coordinate a majority of their connecting flights). Hub cities include Orlando, Miami, Atlanta, Chicago, New York, Kansas City, Pittsburgh, Cincinnati, Dayton, Denver, Nashville, Philadelphia, St. Louis, Charlotte (N.C.), Phoenix, Memphis, Dallas, and Minneapolis. If your destination is a hub city, you can often book on a flight whose final destination is farther than your destination, but stops there nonetheless.

Consider a flight from Detroit to Pittsburgh. As I write this, it is less expensive to book a flight from Detroit to Canton, Ohio, on USAir—which requires a stop or plane change in Pittsburgh—than to buy a ticket directly to Pittsburgh.

Another example is a flight from Los Angeles to Atlanta that is almost twice as expensive as a flight (via Delta) from Los Angeles to Detroit, with a change of planes in Atlanta.

Finding phantom destinations is not easy, although it can be rewarding in terms of savings. When you attempt to book phantom destinations, you need to identify a city that is near (or in the same travel direction as) your destination city. It helps to collect current airline timetables, which are usually available at check-in counters and gates. These timetables provide you with detailed information regarding destinations and layovers.

Here are some other tips on finding phantom destinations:

☐ *Make a note of each airport you can depart from.* Because I live in Fort Lauderdale, I prefer Lauderdale as my point of departure. However, I frequently fly out of Miami and sometimes drive to West Palm Beach if the service I need or the price I like warrants it. Neither of these alternative airports is more than 45 minutes from my home or business. Different airlines service these three airports, with different flight and fare schedules. This is the key to finding and booking for phantom destinations: The greater your selection of airlines, the better your chances of finding an airline that provides a phantom destination for a bargain price.

☐ *List the airports you can fly into.* In many cases, only one airport will do. However, sometimes your eventual destination is not serviced by an airport, forcing you to fly to a nearby airport, then rent a car and drive to your destination. In these cases, you can improve your flexibility. The reason is that more than one airport might be in the vicinity of your ultimate destination, increasing the number of airlines and airports that you can use.

☐ *Find a travel agent who knows how to look for phantom destinations.* This can be quite difficult, though, because most agents aren't trained to look for these kinds of bookings. Part of the problem is that airlines change their fares and routes so frequently that it is difficult for an agent to keep track of current schedules. It is even more difficult to juggle schedules and fares based on phantom destinations.

Also, most computerized reservation systems have "search" programs, which look through different airlines' files in search of available flights and fares to your destination. Some agents have come to rely on these computer programs and don't want the added work of having to search for layovers and multiple destination cities. In any event, most agents will not book you to phantom destinations unless you request it and provide specific flight information.

The bottom line is this: If you have an agent that willingly finds and makes phantom bookings for you, think long and hard before you switch to another agent.

WARNING: If you book a flight to a phantom destination, make sure you carry all your luggage on board. Otherwise, your bags will be checked through to the destination city.

TIP

The principle of phantom destinations can also work for phantom originations. For instance, if you are flying from Atlanta to Chicago, check the airline's timetable to see where the flight originates. In this case, if the flight originates in Miami and there is a flight change in Atlanta, a ticket from Miami to Chicago might be cheaper than a ticket from Atlanta to Chicago. If so, consider buying a ticket from Miami to Chicago, then board the flight when it stops at Atlanta. Be sure your travel agent checks into these possibilities.

Work in Teams to Get a Free Round-Trip Ticket

Say your company has an office in Kansas City, with employees flying fairly frequently from Kansas City to New York and back. You are based in Miami, and occasionally need to visit the Kansas City office. If you buy a discounted round-trip ticket from Miami to New York and back, with a stop in Kansas City, you can actually create *two* round-trip tickets.

Figure 5–8 shows how this would work. Someone at the Kansas City office can use the flight coupons from Kansas City to New York and back to Kansas City. You use the other coupons to fly from Miami to Kansas City, then back to Miami. You save on your ticket and provide an associate with a free ticket.

The only hitch to this scheme is that the name on the ticket will not match one of the traveler's names. In all my years of traveling, though, I've never seen a ticket agent question any passenger on his or her identity—unless the flight was international. If you choose not to pass along the "free" round-trip segment, you could throw away those two extra coupons and still be ahead of the game financially.

Except. . . .

Unfortunately, most airline computers will cancel continuing portions of a flight when the passenger does not show up. In my example, if the flight coupon from Kansas City to New York does not get used (that is, no one checked in with that coupon), the computer is likely to cancel the balance of the flight.

Ticket	Miami to New York via Kansas City
	Coupon 1 Miami to Kansas City
	Coupon 2 Kansas City to New York
	Coupon 3 New York to Kansas City
	Coupon 4 Kansas City to Miami

Figure 5–8 *Team Flying. You use Coupons 1 and 4 for a round-trip flight from Miami to Kansas City. Someone else uses coupons 2 and 3 for a round-trip flight from Kansas City to New York.*

If this happens, you have several options. A day after your arrival in Kansas City, check your return reservation (from New York, remember). If the reservation is still intact, continue to check each day or so until the day of the flight. If and when you discover the reservation has been canceled, call the airline and make another reservation, but this time only from Kansas City to Miami. Make the reservation for the lowest available fare. When you arrive at the airport, remove all flight coupons that are not essential to the Kansas City to Miami segment. Check your bags at the curb, go directly to the gate, and check in.

The worst possible scenario is that you will have to buy a one-way ticket, the one you made a reservation for. Even by doing this, you will have beat the airline at its game.

Why Airline Computers Don't Provide a True Picture

The following scenario illustrates why the electronic age isn't always a benefit for travelers. Imagine you need to attend to business in Frankfurt and London. You can book a flight to one of these cities, then fly to the other and return to the United States. No problem—if you don't care about the cost of the flights.

You can ask your travel agent to find the lowest prices for these flights. But, as technologically proficient as your agent might be, you will probably be told that, due to your last-minute booking, the best that you can do is to purchase a one-way ticket to Frankfurt (the farthest destination point), take care of business there, then return to the United States through London, paying for a stopover. The fare quoted to me recently for such a flight was $2198—for a coach seat.

No computer will show you this explicitly, but even so, remember this rule: Most foreign airlines quote fares to European cities at the same rate as point-to-point service from the United States. Many travel agents seem to be "computer brainwashed" and don't believe this fact; they believe only what their computer screen tells them. International airline fares are based on published tariffs assessed to flights to cities in the United States. Most international airlines stick to this set price, which is often set by the local government. For instance, Miami to Paris can be $600 cheaper than a Miami to Frankfurt flight on most airlines. However, if you need to fly to Frankfurt, it might be more economical to book on a flight from Miami to Paris on an airline that first stops in Frankfurt.

The point: Check the fare structures provided by different international airlines. You might be able to fly to an international city not on your itinerary, which is a hub city for that airline, and simply walk off the flight and pay at a fraction of the price that you would pay to fly directly from the United States to your destination city.

Stretch the Rules to Their Limit

Pay close attention to this next scenario, because it can get complex. It can also save you hundreds of dollars when you are flying overseas to two or more cities. First, ask your travel agent to identify which is your destination city that will cost the most to fly to. Then, have your agent check the schedules for that country's airlines to look for inexpensive flights that terminate in your other destination city, but that have a plane change in the most expensive city. Then juggle your flight schedule so that you *purposely* miss your connection.

Let me explain. Say you have business in both Paris and Frankfurt. The cheapest price recently quoted to me for a nonrestricted ticket from Miami to Frankfurt was $1098 each way, coach. However, if you book on a Lufthansa flight from Miami to Paris, with a stop in Frankfurt, the price would be $793 each way. If possible, you should plan to fly to Paris, take care of business and spend the night, then select a late morning or early afternoon Lufthansa flight for your return (via Frankfurt) to Miami.

In this instance, the Lufthansa flight would arrive in Frankfurt too late to allow you to catch the connecting flight to Miami. When this happens, the airline will usually pick up your tab for your hotel stay in Frankfurt for that night. You then arrive in Frankfurt in time for an afternoon meeting, and later stay free at a local hotel, courtesy of the airline. The next morning you can have a leisurely breakfast meeting and catch your flight from Frankfurt back to Miami. Not only did you save a bundle, but you got a free overnight stay in Frankfurt—although you've only paid for the flight and stayover in Paris. This bargain is courtesy of Lufthansa and is quite legal.

TIP

If you are planning to travel to England, Ireland, Scotland, Amsterdam, or Paris, take note of these discount airlines and ticket agencies:

London/Paris
Nouvelles Frontieres
  1-2 Hanover Street
  London, W1
  (44-1) 629-7772

or

  87 Boulevard Grenelle
  Paris, France
  (33-1) 427-30568

London/Dublin
RyanAir
  Phone in London (44-1) 435-7101
  Phone in Dublin (353-1) 774-422

London/Amsterdam/Edinburgh/Glasgow
British Midland Airline
    Phone in London (44-1) 589-5599

Getting the Most from Frequent Flyer Programs

When the airlines first started their frequent flyer programs, they did so with these three goals in mind:

☐ Build client loyalty.
☐ Build repeat business.
☐ Fill empty seats.

Today, frequent flyer programs have become so complex, even for the airlines, that these goals often don't get met. In fact, airlines often complain that frequent flyer programs are difficult to manage and interfere with other flight programs. However, because frequent flyer programs have come to be expected by business travelers, most airlines can't afford to be without one. Actually, many airlines do not have their own frequent flyer programs, but are members or associates with other airlines, hotels, and rental car agencies. This cooperative effort helps defray costs for the airlines but can cause confusion for business travelers.

Airlines have compounded the confusion by adding special incentive programs to fill seats on less-traveled flights. These programs, often called "bonus miles," offer you double or triple the normal points earned if you fly the least direct flights, with the most stops, to your eventual destination. (By the way, you can actually earn "bonus miles" when you ticket to out-of-the-way destinations in order to use phantom destinations and other flight-juggling tricks that save you money.)

Although business travelers often grumble about the way in which airlines enforce the "rules subject to change without notice" part of a frequent flyer program, these programs make economic sense. I've put together the following list of major airline frequent flyer programs so that you can review and compare the different awards offered. Again, keep in mind that these programs can, and do, change.

Air Canada—Aeroplan

Participating Airlines: Air BC, Air France, Air New Zealand, Air Nova, Austrian, Cathay Pacific, Lufthansa, Royal Jordanian, Singapore Air, Northwest Territorial

Participating Hotels: The Charlottetown, Coast Hotels, Courtyard Inns, Hilton (U.S.), Holiday Inn (Canada and Europe), Keddy's Hotels, Ming Court Hotels, Prince George Hotel in Halifax, Radisson, Sheraton (selected locations), Vista International, Westcoast Hotels (U.S.), Westin

Affiliated Rental Car Agencies: Avis, Hertz

Other Bonus Offerings: Announced to members

How to Contact: Customer Service, 1411 Fort Street, Montreal, Quebec H3H 2RB, Canada, 800-361-8253 or 800-361-5373

Alaska Airlines—Gold Coast Travel Program

Participating Airlines: Hawaiian Airlines, Horizon, L.A.B. Flying Services, MarkAir, Northwest, SAS, Thai Airways, TWA

Participating Hotels: Red Lion Inns, Westmark Hotels

Affiliated Rental Car Agencies: Budget

Other Bonus Offerings: Visa card, one mile per each dollar spent

How to Contact: Gold Coast Travel, P.O. Box 24949, Seattle, WA 98124, 800-654-5669 (in WA), 800-942-9911

Aloha Airlines—AlohaPass

Participating Airlines: Aloha Airlines

Participating Hotels: Some hotel packages offered

Affiliated Rental Car Agencies: Some awards on car rentals offered

Other Bonus Offerings: From time to time, directly to members

How to Contact: AlohaPass, P.O. Box 30028, Honolulu, HI 96820, 800-367-5250

America West Airlines—FlightFUND

Participating Airlines: America West Airlines

Participating Hotels: Compri Hotels, Doubletree, Marriott

Affiliated Rental Car Agencies: Dollar

Other Bonus Offerings: FlightFUND Visa, one mile per each dollar spent; MCI Telephone, five miles per each dollar spent

How to Contact: FlightFUND, 51 West 3rd Street, Tempe, AZ 85281, 800-247-5691

American Airlines—AAdvantage

Participating Airlines: American Eagle, British Airways, Cathay Pacific, Qantas, Singapore Air

Participating Hotels: Fairmont (selected locations), Forum, Hilton, Inter-Continental, Sheraton, Wyndham Hotels and Resorts

Affiliated Rental Car Agencies: Avis, Hertz

Other Bonus Offerings: MasterCard or Visa, one mile per dollar spent; MCI Telephone, five miles per dollar spent

How to Contact: AAdvantage Department, MD 5400, P.O. Box 619623, DFW Airport, TX 75261-9623, 800-433-7300

Braniff—Get-it-All

Participating Airlines: Braniff Express

Participating Hotels: Compri Hotels, Doubletree, Hyatt

Affiliated Rental Car Agencies: Budget, National

Other Bonus Offerings: Offered to members from time to time

How to Contact: Braniff Get-it-All, P.O. Box 7999, Dallas, TX 75209, 800-346-8108

Canadian Airlines International—Canadian Plus

Participating Airlines: Air Atlantic, Aloha, British Airways, Calm Air, KLM, Midway, PEM-Air, Time Air

Participating Hotels: Canadian Pacific Hotels and Resorts, Capri Hotels, Corner Brook, Delta Hotels, Glynmill Inn, Kelowna, Marriott, Ramada

Affiliated Rental Car Agencies: Budget (Canada), Thrifty, Tilden (Canada)

Other Bonus Offerings: MasterCard, one mile per dollar spent

How to Contact: Canadian Plus, P.O. Box 13107, Vancouver, BC V6B 9Z9, Canada (Call Canadian Airlines)

Continental Airlines—OnePass

Participating Airlines: Aer Lingus, Air France, Alitalia, Bar Harbor, Continental, Continental Express, Iberia, Lufthansa, Royale, Sabena, SAS

Participating Hotels: Compri Hotels, Consort Hotels, Doubletree, Marriott, Radisson, Wyndham

Affiliated Rental Car Agencies: Eurocar (Europe), General, Hertz, National, Nippon, Thrifty, Tilden (Canada)

Other Bonus Offerings: Gold MasterCard, one mile per dollar spent

How to Contact: OnePass Service Center, P.O. Box 4365, Houston, TX 77210-4365, 713-952-1630

Delta Airlines—Frequent Flyer

Participating Airlines: Air Canada, Air New Zealand, ASA, Business Express, Comair, Delta Connection, Japan Air Lines, Lufthansa, Sky West, Swissair

Participating Hotels: Hyatt, Marriott, Preferred, Trusthouse Forte

Affiliated Rental Car Agencies: Alamo, Eurocar (Europe), Hertz, National, Nippon, Tilden (Canada)

Other Bonus Offerings: None at this time

How to Contact: Frequent Flyer, P.O. Box 20532, Hartsfield International Airport, Atlanta, GA 30320, 800-323-2323

Hawaiian Airlines—Gold Plus

Participating Airlines: Hawaiian Air Lines

Participating Hotels: None

Affiliated Rental Car Agencies: Avis, Dollar, and Tropical only in Hawaii

Other Bonus Offerings: None at this time

How to Contact: Gold Plus, P.O. Box 30008, Honolulu, HI 96820, 800-367-7637

Midway Airlines—FlyersFirst

Participating Airlines: Midway Connection

Participating Hotels: Omni, Stouffer

Affiliated Rental Car Agencies: Avis, Budget

Other Bonus Offerings: None at this time

How to Contact: FlyersFirst Department, P.O. Box 388009, Chicago, IL 60638, 800-621-5700

Midwest Express—Frequent Flyer

Participating Airlines: Midwest Express

Participating Hotels: None

Affiliated Rental Car Agencies: National

Other Bonus Offerings: None at this time

How to Contact: Frequent Flyer Program, P.O. Box 37136, Milwaukee, WI 53237-0136

Northwest Airlines—WorldPerks

Participating Airlines: Alaska, Big Sky, Express Airlines, Inc., Mesaba Aviation, Northwest Airlink, Piedmont (selected locations), USAir (selected locations)

Participating Hotels: Hyatt, Marriott, Radisson

Affiliated Rental Car Agencies: Avis, Budget, Eurocar (Europe), National, Nippon, Tilden (Canada)

Other Bonus Offerings: Visa, one mile per dollar spent; MCI Telephone, one mile per dollar spent

How to Contact: WorldPerks, P.O. Box 1713, Minneapolis, MN 55440, 800-435-9696

Pan American Airlines—WorldPass

Participating Airlines: Pan Am Express

Participating Hotels: Forum, Inter-Continental, Sheraton

Affiliated Rental Car Agencies: Alamo, Avis, Dollar

Other Bonus Offerings: WorldCard MasterCard, one mile per dollar spent

How to Contact: WorldPass, P.O. Box 11902, Alexandria, VA 22311-0962, 800-348-8000

Southwest Airlines—Company Club

Participating Airlines: Southwest Airlines

Participating Hotels: None

Affiliated Rental Car Agencies: None

Other Bonus Offerings: None

How to Contact: 800-445-9267

Trans World Airways (TWA)—Frequent Flight Bonus

Participating Airlines: Air New Zealand, Alaska, Horizon Air, NY Helicopter, TransWorld Express, Virgin Islands Seaplane Shuttle

Participating Hotels: Adam's Mark, Hilton (U.S.), Marriott

Affiliated Rental Car Agencies: Dollar, Thrifty

Other Bonus Offerings: None

How to Contact: Frequent Flyer Bonus, P.O. Box 767, Murray Hill Station, New York, NY 10156, 800-325-4815

United Airlines—Mileage Plus

Participating Airlines: Air France, Air Wisconsin, Alitalia, Aloha Airlines, British Airways, Iberia, KLM, Lufthansa, Presidential, SAS, Swissair, United Express, West Air

Participating Hotels: Hilton (U.S.), Hyatt, Kempinski Hotels, Westin

Affiliated Rental Car Agencies: Alamo, Hertz

Other Bonus Offerings: Mileage Plus First Card, one mile per each dollar spent

How to Contact: Mileage Plus, P.O. Box 17003, Inglewood, CA 90306, 800-421-4655

USAir (Piedmont)—Frequent Traveler

Participating Airlines: Allegheny Commuter, British Airways, Finnair, Hawaiian Air Lines, Lufthansa, Northwest (selected locations), Philippine, Piedmont, Swissair

Participating Hotels: Marriott, Omni, Radisson, Stouffer, Westin

Affiliated Rental Car Agencies: Eurocar (Europe), Hertz, National, Nippon, Tilden (Canada)

Other Bonus Offerings: Visa Card, one mile per dollar spent

How to Contact: Frequent Traveler Program, P.O. Box 65, Winston-Salem, NC 27102-0065, 800-872-4738, 800-874-4738 (Canada)

It makes sense to belong to as many frequent flyer programs as you plan to use—as long as you don't have to pay to join. For programs that require a

fee to join, make sure you will use the participating airlines frequently.

**WARNING: Most frequent flyer programs in-
clude a credit card program (typically a Visa or
MasterCard in which one frequent flyer mile is
credited for each dollar purchased with the card).
However, different programs have different rules
for corporate cards. A corporate card issued for
each traveling salesperson might earn mileage
only for one frequent flyer number—one that's not
yours. In this situation, the credit card program
will pay off only if you apply for and use your
own, personal card.**

Many airlines have additional bonus programs that don't really fit under the "frequent
flyer" heading. For example, Virgin Atlantic has
an instant bonus of one free economy ticket for
each business-class ticket you purchase. If you
expect to fly on an airline that is not listed in the
frequent flyer programs provided in the preceding list, ask your travel agent to find out if any
bonus programs are offered.

Some airlines offer incentives over and above
their existing frequent flyer programs. These incentives include allowing a companion to fly with
you at half fare, or giveaways for purchasing certain seats on certain flights. For instance, Pan
American recently offered to issue a free ticket
to the Caribbean if you purchased a regular coach
seat to Europe during a certain period.

Other usual incentives that are often connected to frequent flyer programs are bonus mileage for flying during certain times of the week,
or to specific destinations. It is not unusual for
these bonus programs to offer up to triple mileage
over certain times of the year.

When new cities are added to an airline's
route, special promotion rates as well as added
mileage can work to give you the best of all benefits if you can also include that city as a hidden

destination instead of your actual desired city of departure.

As with nearly everything the airlines offer there are strings that limit or restrict the use of the advertised bonus. These strings generally come in the form of blackout dates for travel or specific time limitations on when you can start and end the travel at the rate promoted. It is important for you to know exactly what the restrictions are before you are persuaded to take the promoted flight or schedule as the later inconvenience or inability to use the benefit offered may not be worth the effort to partake in the advertised promotion.

How to Get the Seat Selection You Want

Most airlines allow travel agents to make advance seat selections when customers purchase tickets. The seat assignment is based on your responses to questions that your agent asks, typically whether you prefer smoking or nonsmoking (for international flights) and whether you prefer a window or aisle seat.

If you will be traveling with an associate and you want to sit together, it is best to select one window and one aisle seat. The reservation computer system fills up window and aisle seats first, then assigns center seats on an as-needed basis. So, if you request two adjoining seats (aisle and center or window and center), there is a good chance that the third seat in the row will be assigned by flight time. By booking an aisle and window seat in the same row, you reduce the chance that someone will fill the third seat in your row. This can increase your comfort during the flight, because you will have more arm room. Also, many jets have a fold-down accessory in the backrest of each center seat in coach that forms an extra-wide arm rest and snack tray.

If you are flying alone in coach, you can use the following tips to ensure that you are assigned the best possible seat:

☐ Ask your travel agent to examine the most recent configuration of the aircraft you are booked on to find the available seat that best suits your need. Do not rely on seating charts published in travel books and magazines, because those charts are often outdated. Also, airlines will be refitting their aircraft throughout the first four or five years of the 1990s. First-class and business-class seating will change the most, with coach seating remaining fairly stable.

☐ Exit seats have extra leg room.

☐ Seats in front of exits usually do not recline as far back as others, and sometimes they don't recline at all.

☐ Last-row seats usually do not recline.

☐ On international flights, the first or last row in nonsmoking can be only one row from smokers.

☐ If there is an in-flight movie that you want to see, the location of screens might dictate where you should sit in order to view the screen comfortably.

☐ If there is a second exit behind the first, the first exit row might have more leg room than other seats, but the seat might not recline.

☐ The first two rows in coach often are assigned to children or parents with small children.

☐ Window seats have very little shoulder and arm room on the window side.

☐ Reconfirm your seat selection when you check in. Even though you are holding the boarding pass issued to you by your travel agent, the airline can cancel your seat assignment as much as 30 minutes in advance if seats are needed.

☐ Board the aircraft as soon as your section of the aircraft is permitted to board. It can be a mistake to board at the last possible minute, thinking you are saving yourself the trouble of waiting in line at the gate. Two passengers are often erroneously assigned the same seat. When this happens, the person who is already seated usually has priority. Also, overhead storage and folding bag compartment space is at a premium on many flights. If you board too late and find all available cabin storage space gone, you will have to check your bags.

Summing Up the Airline Game

Although this chapter tells you how to deal with airlines and their ever-changing and often-confusing fare structures, you should keep in mind that other modes of travel are often viable. Depending on your time, comfort, and money requirements, automobile or train travel can often do the trick. In Europe, especially, where cities and countries are connected by excellent road and rail systems, air travel might actually be more costly and less efficient than other means. The key to using these and other alternatives to your best advantage is a knowledgeable and hard-working travel agent. When the airline game seems to be getting the best of you, a good travel agent can be the perfect trump card.

6

Dealing with Overbooked Flights and Nightmares

The more you travel by air, the more often you will feel that the airlines view you as little more than a number or just another warm body. An airline may bump you to another flight, lose your luggage, or leave you stranded—without even offering an apology. Unless you take precautions, you can expect to spend a good part of your travel time trying to resolve these and other problems.

Although your rights as a passenger are not universal, you are protected by numerous rules and regulations, which provide you with some form of central control and uniform regulation. Knowing these regulations will help you when your rights have been violated and when you need to seek compensation.

This chapter will show you that the rules and regulations are slanted toward the airlines and other carriers (bus, train, or boat), but that you do have rights and a voice that can be heard.

Fortunately, the airlines are also businesses and frequently bend the rules to be more helpful and offer more compensation to inconvenienced travelers than the rules require. Keeping passengers happy and continuing to fly their airline is a very important part of business.

Check In Early—Or Else

Having a reservation does not guarantee you will get to your desired destination. Here's a case in point. Newlyweds Ted and Marie had planned their London honeymoon carefully. They had booked their flight early, secured the lowest possible apex fare, made their hotel reservations, and had already purchased some difficult-to-get theater tickets. They were confident that, because everything was so well planned, nothing would spoil this wonderful trip.

Ted and Marie arrived at the airport 45 minutes prior to the departure time and stood near the end of a lengthy line, awaiting their turn at the check-in counter. It was in this line where their well-woven plans began to unravel.

This couple had unknowingly broken an important rule of international travel: Check-in for international flights is 30 minutes in advance of the departure time. Unfortunately, Ted and Marie were still in line when that 30-minute deadline came due.

Ted and Marie were early, but not early enough. Only a few moments before they reached the counter, the grossly overbooked flight reached capacity. When Ted and Marie placed their tickets on the counter, a quick glance at his watch told the airline agent that it was now 15 minutes before the scheduled departure time—15 minutes too late for Ted and Marie to be given compensation.

TIP

Check in early enough to get your boarding assignment. When you are traveling internationally, this requirement is even more important due to longer lines, security and customs checks, and other potential delays. Try to arrive *two hours* in advance of a scheduled departure. Then relax until the flight.

Ted and Marie's problems were only just beginning: All flights to London and the vicinity, for the next three days, were sold out. Their apex tickets were good only on the booked aircraft, and they were nonrefundable. The airline station manager agreed to "let" them come back the following day and sign up as standby passengers. He told them to be sure to arrive early this time.

Ted and Marie did arrive early, but, once again, not early enough. Two hours before the departure time, there were already more standby passengers on the list than there would be seats to accommodate them. Another fully paid day in a charming London honeymoon suite had been wasted.

Ted and Marie never made it to London; instead, they went on a "never thought we would be *here*" Mexican Riviera cruise. And as nice as it was, it was not what they wanted, planned, or had dreamed of.

Passengers Who Don't Get Bumped

The following categories of passengers are least likely to get bumped from a flight. Their order of priority treatment depends on the airline reservation agent who is calling the shots.

☐ First-class passengers, although they may be downgraded to whatever empty seat is still available

☐ Business-class passengers, although they, too might find their ticket downgraded

☐ Children traveling alone

☐ Adults traveling with children or pregnant women

☐ Handicapped travelers

☐ Passengers who are ill

☐ Law officers with prisoners

☐ Very senior citizens

☐ Government officials and other VIPs

☐ Friends of the airline's employees

☐ Certain airline employees

If you are a regular traveler with a specific airline, make it a point to get to know the station manager or the airline representatives who handle check-in. These acquaintances may help you out when you most need help. But don't try to act like a VIP when you are not. You'll only appear to be a nuisance to the airline representatives.

TIP

Air Travelers' Fly Rights, a booklet published by the U.S. government, is available to the public. Send $3 to the Superintendent of Documents, U.S. Government Printing Office, Washington, DC 20402, and request stock number 003-006-00106-5.

Why Airlines Overbook Flights

To understand why airlines overbook flights, you must first remember that, on any given flight, there may be a dozen or more differently priced seats: First class, business class, excursion seats, second- or third-stop passengers, and so on. As described in Chapter 5, airlines constantly try to cover themselves against no-shows by overbooking their flights. Each airline has a "secret" formula to determine how many seats can be overbooked without denying boarding to any passengers.

Of course, this formula doesn't always work. However, if you are feeling especially kind-hearted, you might try for a moment to understand the airline's dilemma. If every passenger holding a reservation showed up for the majority of domestic flights, the airlines would leave thousands of passengers at the gate each day. In reality, very few travelers actually get bumped. You won't be one of the few if you follow the tips I provide in this chapter.

When a Flight Is Overbooked

Assume that you arrive at the airport within the required check-in deadline, as stated on your ticket or boarding pass. If the flight has been over-booked, your on-time status doesn't matter much—as we've seen with Ted and Marie. You might feel that it's unfair for the airline to blame you for its long lines, but the airline doesn't see the situation your way. You have to be early enough to receive a boarding assignment.

A *boarding assignment* might not be the same as a boarding pass. Your boarding pass should be checked in at the counter or boarding gate prior to your boarding. This is when your actual boarding assignment is given. Often this process is nothing more than stamping your boarding pass and returning it to you. However, there is no way for you to know in advance whether your boarding pass is a guarantee that you can board, so you should assume that it provides no guarantee. If, by chance, all seats on your flight have been assigned before you reach the check-in counter, you may not get on that flight at all—despite the fact that your ticket and boarding pass have been in your possession for days or weeks.

Current airline regulations require each airline to offer some type of compensation to passengers who have valid reservations on an oversold flight. First, the airline is obliged to call for volunteers who will give up their seat for payment and/or other compensation. If there are insufficient volunteers to equal the number of unboarded passengers, the airline can either increase the compensation offered or deny boarding to the remaining passengers and reimburse them accordingly. If the airline can get some volunteers to give up their seats for the compensation offered, there are no real losers.

Here are some additional facts about overbooking that should help you deal with the situation if it arises:

☐ If the airline is able to seat you on another flight that arrives at the desired destination within one hour of the original flight's scheduled arrival time, the airline owes no compensation to you.

☐ If the alternate flight is scheduled to arrive later than one hour from the arrival time of your original flight, but less than two hours later, you have a right to be paid denied-boarding compensation equivalent to the airline's one-way fare to your destination. Keep in mind this is based on the regular coach one-way fare, not a first-class ticket. In any event, the amount of compensation shall not exceed $200.

☐ If the delay is greater than two hours domestically and four hours internationally, the airline must double the compensation, using the same coach-seat formula, but not to exceed $400.

If you are denied boarding on your reserved flight, and are not offered any compensation, first check whether one of the following "exceptions" applies:

☐ Your reservation or ticket is invalid if you show up late (according to the conditions on the back of your ticket).

☐ If your ticket is a super saver for the following day, and you hoped to get on in the rush of a late check-in, or you simply made a mistake and showed up for the wrong flight, you're out of luck.

Volunteering as a Way to Cut Your Travel Costs

If a flight is overbooked and you have time to spare, you might consider volunteering to give up your seat to a bumped passenger. Depending on the circumstances of the flight and your ability to negotiate with the airline, you just might find volunteering to be the best way to go.

Read the following suggestions carefully to ensure that you get the most out of volunteering your seat and your time.

☐ As you check in, tell the ticket agent that you're willing to give up your seat if the flight is overbooked. As more passengers arrive, remind the agent of your intent.

☐ When you hear the official call for volunteers, make sure you respond promptly. If it looks like there are enough volunteers, the agent will not come looking for you.

☐ Deal with one agent (you'll get a better response that way), and find out exactly what the airline is offering. Find the answers to these questions:

1. When does the next flight to your destination depart? How many stops or plane changes will there be? Will you be guaranteed a boarding pass for that flight? Will you be given an upgrade to business or first class?
2. Will you be given a pass to the first-class lounge, or club lounge, while you wait?
3. If you will miss a meal you are entitled to on your reserved flight, will you receive a first-class meal voucher while you wait?

4. Will you get free overnight accommodations if necessary?
5. Will you receive monetary compensation or "free tickets"?
6. Are there any restrictions on the tickets?
7. Will the airline pay for phone calls needed to alert anyone who may be waiting for you?

WARNING: It is a rare occurrence when an airline will out-and-out refuse to respond to your demands for fair compensation. Chartered flights, on the other hand, are not regulated by the same rules that govern most other commercial flights. The low price of chartered flights suggests this basic consumer rule: You get what you pay for.

TIP

To protect your investment in any transportation service, you can purchase trip insurance. This insurance will guarantee you a refund should your charter (or other carrier) fail to deliver you the passage you thought you were getting. Ask your travel agent for more details.

When You Arrive and Your Luggage Doesn't

From the time you check your luggage until it arrives at your destination, it will be handled by numerous people. Sometimes it's a wonder that your luggage ever arrives at all; often it doesn't. Chapter 2 covers ways to protect yourself against luggage theft and lost luggage. This section provides additional information about an airline's responsibilities and liabilities for bags gone astray.

The Airlines' Responsibilities

In 1929, the Warsaw Convention set standards for airlines' obligation and responsibility for lost luggage during international flights. The standards remain unchanged. Unfortunately, these standards are quite inadequate. The normal liability is set at a maximum of $9.07 per pound of checked luggage. Also, these standards apply only to luggage that did not exceed the maximum flight weight. In addition to the checked luggage responsibility, the airlines have an additional liability of $400 per passenger for unchecked items. However, if you are flying on a non-IATA airline or on a chartered airline, the obligation may be considerably less. The liability information is included on the back of your ticket.

Purchasing Insurance for Your Luggage

Domestic carriers have a greater liability to their passengers, but it is still easy to pack more into a case than the airline will pay you to replace. The maximum liability is $1250. However, you can insure your luggage through the airline. When you check in, ask the ticket agent about "increasing your valuation." The airline will generally charge about $1 for every $100 over the $1250.

You can also take out a temporary travelers insurance policy with your own insurance company. Even if you have homeowners insurance, it may not cover all the items in your luggage.

Last-Minute Charges

Occasionally when you check in, the agent might tell you that you have the wrong ticket code for your seat and that the price you paid on your ticket is incorrect. Either your travel agent made a mistake, or you made a flight change with the airline over the phone and unknowingly requested a more expensive seat or flight (and the reservation agent failed to warn you about the price difference over the phone).

Don't waste your time and energy by complaining in these situations. Airlines have the right to charge you the correct fare, no matter what your ticket says or how much you've already paid. However, one possible way to avoid the extra charge is to ask how full the flight is. If it is wide open, and there are no standbys on the list, see if you can speak with the station manager about treating your ticket as a standby.

You may also find yourself paying for additional fuel or security charges when you check in. Although these charges should have been included in the price of your ticket, there are times when one or the other was added after you purchased your ticket. Here again, you have no choice but to pay up.

Defensive Travel Tips

Many of the following tips have been mentioned in earlier chapters, but they bear repeating here—because they are important and they *work*.

☐ Provide clear instructions to your travel agent.

☐ Obtain a travel itinerary showing dates, airport, flight numbers, departure, arrival, and connection information. The itinerary should also list the class of service provided, seat information, and meal service offered, including special meals you requested. Review this information and make sure it is what you expect. If not, find out why the itinerary differs from your wishes.

☐ The two days before your flight, make sure your name and all your details are confirmed directly with the airline.

☐ On the day of the flight, recheck the departure time. Even though a new departure time may have been scheduled, arrive early enough to ensure you get your seat. Other passengers may show up at the airport for the original departure time.

☐ If there have been any changes on your ticket, and by this I mean stickers attached to change the flight, do not rely on the information shown on the ticket. Confirm any differing data with the airline.

☐ Have alternative flight information. If you discover your flight is going to be unusually late or is delayed due to mechanical or weather-related problems, you may still be able to switch to a more reasonable flight. Another advantage of knowing about alternative flights is the ability to negotiate if you are bumped and are denied compensation for other airlines.

☐ If you check your baggage before you learn that a flight will be considerably late, you may be forced to wait out the delay. However, if a flight has arrived and is delayed due to mechanical problems, most airline reservation agents will not put luggage on board until they are sure the aircraft will be used for that flight. In this case, you can often demand that your luggage be returned. Sometimes it works.

☐ Keep your cool. However, if you feel you've been wronged, write to the airline and complain, complain, complain. A letter, written without a lot of name calling, can often result in some benefits to you: upgrades, free drinks, and the like. Send your complaints to any or all of the following:

—The airline
—Your travel agent
—ASTA (American Society of Travel Agents)
  4400 MacArthur Blvd. N.W.

Washington, DC 20007
(202) 965-7520
—The U.S. Dept. of Transportation
Office of Consumer Affairs
400 Seventh Street, S.W.
Washington, DC 20590
(202) 366-2220

Avoiding Airline-Caused Mishaps

This chapter has provided some basic strategies for combating problems that arise from overcrowded flights and airline employee mistakes. Most of these problems happen infrequently, but you must always be on your guard. Follow the advice I've provided, and you may never encounter any of the situations described here.

One parting comment: A friend, who travels with more nonchalance than any business traveler I've known, once told me: "Don't ever let anything get to you when you travel. There's always another flight." Simple advice, but true enough when you are trying to keep your blood pressure down and your travel spirits up.

7

The Ills of Travel and How to Avoid Them

Travel can make you sick—literally. The human body is just not designed to sit rigidly for hours in the cramped seat of a small pressurized tube hurtling through turbulent air at 30,000 feet at more than 500 miles per hour. And nothing can ruin an important business meeting faster than a travel-related illness that impairs your ability to think and act.

Air sickness and jet lag are two of the more commonplace maladies of travel. Other travel-related ailments are not uncommon. Some of them, such as diarrhea and intestinal gas, are as unpleasant to discuss as they are to experience. However, your ability to deal with the physical problems caused by traveling will depend on your knowledge of their causes and your ability to take steps to remain healthy.

Following are eight ailments that can plague the frequent business traveler:

☐ Jet lag

☐ Motion sickness

☐ In-flight earaches

☐ In-flight toothaches

☐ Traveler's diarrhea

☐ Intestinal gas

☐ Depression

☐ Viruses and other diseases

This chapter focuses on the preventive steps you can take to avoid the discomfort and serious illness that these maladies can bring to your trips.

The most important preventive step is one of common sense: Know your health and your physical limitations and plan accordingly. Travel is mentally and physically exhausting, even for the health-minded. You can be in good physical health yet still be prone to air sickness, jet lag, or travel-related stress. Try to adjust your travel schedule to take advantage of the limits of your internal "body clock" and other physical difficulties that accompany travel.

TIP

Make sure your annual physical check-up is just that—annual. The symptoms of a seemingly mild physical problem might not become apparent during your normal daily activities. However, when the plane you are in suddenly drops 100 feet or more in a pocket of turbulence, that "mild" problem could quickly develop into a life-threatening one.

Understand the Effects of Your Medication

If you are taking any medication, ask your doctor *and* your pharmacist to explain all possible travel-related reactions that you might experience from the medicine or from the problem for which the medication was prescribed. Make it clear that you will be traveling in the near future.

A medication that normally has few, if any, serious side effects might have a disastrous effect at 10,000 feet. For instance, altitude causes some drugs to be absorbed into the bloodstream more quickly than usual. Your doctor might tell you it is safe to take one drink while you are taking medication. However, the combined increase in the absorption rate of both the alcohol and medication at a high altitude could be dangerous or potentially lethal. At the very least, you do not want to meet your business contact at the destination gate in a state that suggests you cannot comprehend who you are or why you are there.

Also, ask about the effects of combining your prescription with any over-the-counter drugs that you might take when you travel—such as pain or motion sickness medication, or a remedy for diarrhea or upset stomach. For instance, some medications for diarrhea have a high sodium content, which can elevate blood pressure, which could be elevated further to dangerous levels by a prescription medication you are taking.

Understanding Jet Lag

The human body operates according to regular cycles—the heart pumps so much blood per minute, the pituitary gland expects you to be exposed to a certain number of hours of daylight, and so on. In short, your body has its own natural, internal clock that regulates your physical activity.

If you need further proof of this, ask yourself these questions: Do you wake up many mornings a few minutes before your alarm goes off? Does your stomach growl if your meals are late? Do you feel a mild sense of fatigue at the same approximate time during work days? Do you feel sleepy at the same time each night? Positive answers to these questions are signals of your internal clock.

Jet lag is the physical and mental disorientation that results when you travel into a different time zone. In general, your body initially becomes confused by the different external signals it gets when you cross one or more time zones. It even tries to compensate by "resetting" its internal clock. Numerous studies have been conducted on jet lag, with differing conclusions. However, most researchers agree that the key to overcoming the symptoms of jet lag is to help your body reset its internal clock as quickly as possible.

WARNING: A typical transatlantic flight to Europe will arrive in the morning or early afternoon. Considering the fatigue that a transatlantic flight causes, it would be crazy to attempt to conduct any important business on the day you arrive. Instead, rest and relax.

TIP

Here's a brief plan that you can use when you arrive at your destination after a transatlantic flight. If you can get to your hotel before 11:00 A.M., take a brisk walk for about 30 minutes. I have found that a short nap following a light lunch works well for me, as long as I do not sleep for more than three hours. Following the nap, it is important to get up and out of the hotel while there is still some daylight.

To get as much sunlight as possible, sit at an outdoor cafe (weather permitting), read the paper on a park bench, or just take a walk and enjoy the sights. These kinds of activities help your body see and feel daylight fade into night—a trick that can work wonders in getting your body to adjust quickly to the new time zone. After sundown, take a light dinner and retire at a reasonable hour. Allow a few extra hours of sleep time, because you might sleep more fitfully than normal.

How to Beat Jet Lag

In their book *Overcoming Jet Lag,* authors Charles F. Ehret and Lynne Waller Scanlon describe an elaborate method for tricking the body into a speedy adjustment following a time-zone change. Their system seems to work for many people I have spoken with, so I'll describe the highlights here. Ehret and Scanlon advise you to establish alternating feast and fast days prior to your departure, with your travel day being a fast day. (Feasting, according to the authors, means large meal portions, whereas fasting refers to small meal portions.) For both feasting and fasting days, breakfast and lunch must be high-protein meals, with dinner being a high-carbohydrate meal.

According to Ehret and Scanlon, caffeine also plays a major role in helping your body clock to reset itself. Their plan takes more than 160 pages of their book (which I highly recommend). To provide you with an overview, I've put together Figure 7–1, which provides a synopsis of the role of caffeine and caloric intake for flights that pass through five to six time zones.

There will be times when you cannot follow this program, simply because you receive notice of your trip with too little time to plan your diet, caffeine intake, and sleep schedule. However, you will benefit in these situations if you adapt the program as much as possible.

WARNING: Alcohol disrupts your normal cycles. It is advisable to avoid alcohol on the day of departure and for at least a day after your arrival. Also, you should attempt to follow the local schedule (in your destination city) for meals, active hours, and sleep.

Direction	Day	Suggested Regimen
Each Direction	Two days prior to flight	Avoid caffeine except between 3:00 and 4.00 P.M.
Westbound and Eastbound	Three days prior to flight	Eat a generous high-protein breakfast and lunch, and a high-carbohydrate supper (feast day).
Westbound and Eastbound	Two days prior to flight	Two days before the flight, eat as described above, but in much smaller portions. A total of 800 calories is ideal. Do not snack after supper (fast day).
Westbound	One day prior to flight	Load up as you did for three days before the flight. You may snack after supper (feast day).
Eastbound		Do the same as for Westbound travel, but do not snack after supper.
Westbound	The day of the flight	Sleep as late as possible. As soon as you wake up, drink three cups of coffee or strong tea. Do not have any more caffeine today. Also, eat late and in the quantities prescribed for three days before the flight.
Eastbound		Wake up earlier than usual and eat as you did for two days prior to the flight, except have no caffeine until 6:00 P.M. At that time, regardless of where you are, load up on caffeine—two or three cups of coffee or strong tea. Reset your watch to correspond with the time zone for your destination, and go to sleep as soon as possible (fast day).
Westbound and Eastbound	The day of arrival	Thirty minutes before your normal breakfast time, but using the time zone for your destination, activate your body and brain with mental and physical exercise. Eat as you did for three days prior to the flight, except take no caffeine (feast day). Do not nap on this day, and try to fall asleep at a reasonable hour, using the destination time zone.

Figure 7-1 *Suggested Regimen for Combating Jet Lag*—**Overcoming Jet Lag**

When to Use Your Internal Clock to Your Advantage

For short trips (four days or less), I have found that it can be better to make use of your internal clock rather than to attempt to adjust it. I've provided some tips below for dealing with time changes in westbound and eastbound travel.

Westbound Travel

☐ When you travel to the west, use your clock at home to determine when to get up. For example, I live in Fort Lauderdale. So, if I travel to Denver, I've gained two morning hours, meaning I'll be more alert in the morning. If I normally wake up at 7:00 A.M. Eastern Standard Time, I'll wake up in Denver between 5:00 A.M. and 7:00 A.M. Mountain Standard Time.

☐ Use the extra morning hours to relax and awaken. Go for a walk, swim, or jog if you choose. The point is to prepare your body and mind for the business day ahead.

☐ Schedule business meetings for the morning, if possible. Remember, you are taking advantage of your body clock by moving ahead in time. At 8:00 A.M. or 9:00 A.M., the local businesspeople you meet might not be as alert as you. You can use this potential advantage to give yourself an edge in your business meetings.

☐ Try to finish all important meetings by early to mid-afternoon. Later afternoon in the West might be early to mid-evening at home, a time when you probably are not at your sharpest.

☐ Make it an early evening. Schedule social events for early in the evening so you can retire early. The idea is to get to bed when your internal clock says it's time to sleep.

Eastbound Travel

☐ Rest on your arrival day. Try to arrive at an early evening or late afternoon hour. Do not plan a business meeting and, after a light dinner, make it an early evening.

☐ Sleep late the first morning and have a high-protein breakfast. Even one or two time-zone changes can disturb your sleep habits, so do not plan any early morning meetings.

☐ Avoid scheduling any meetings until lunch-time the day after the arrival. You will probably be alert and at your peak in the early afternoon.

☐ If you must travel overnight to reach your destination or if you have traveled eastbound through four or more time zones, do not plan any important meetings until the day after your arrival.

Other Factors That Contribute to Jet Lag

Traveling through time zones is part of the cause of jet lag but not all of it. These additional five elements combine in different ways to contribute to jet lag.

☐ Oxygen starvation—a subtle but potentially devastating problem

☐ Dehydration

☐ Lack of sleep and/or rest

☐ Overeating or excessive drinking

☐ Anxiety

To combat jet lag effectively, do your best to reduce the influence of all five of these elements. Here are some tips that will help.

Oxygen Starvation: How to Overcome Altitude Sickness

You probably know that airplane cabins are pressurized. Without some artificial pressurization, the atmospheric pressure at cruising altitudes would not allow oxygen to be absorbed into the bloodstream. But did you know that the pressure simulates an altitude of 4000 to 8000 feet?

Aircraft are not pressurized at sea-level pressure for several reasons: There would be a high risk of excessive damage in the event of a break in the pressurization hull. Also, the expense and extra weight that would be required for the aircraft to retain sea-level pressure at 40,000 feet would not be practical.

Oxygen constitutes about 21 percent of the total elements in the air around us. At sea level and up to certain altitudes, the pressure is sufficient to force oxygen into the bloodstream as we breathe. However, some people are unable to function normally above certain altitude levels, or more correctly, at altitudes where the atmospheric pressure becomes critical for their absorption of oxygen. People who have respiratory problems may find that flying in a cabin pressurized at 7000 feet is uncomfortable or even dangerous. Smoking, illness, or medicine can have an additional negative effect on oxygen absorption.

WARNING: Oxygen deprivation, even in small amounts, can result in temporary tunnel vision. This situation can produce some anxious moments, because your peripheral vision begins to fail, causing your outer paths of vision to become progressively darker. Eventually, you will be able to see only the area directly in front of your eyes. The problem might not be noticeable during the early stages if you are watching a film in a darkened cabin or reading a book. If you do fall victim to tunnel vision, avoid driving a car, especially at night, until your peripheral vision returns.

Lack of oxygen also can cause nausea, headaches, and a sense of fatigue that can last a day or more. Airlines carry portable oxygen bottles to aid people who may experience discomfort from this "altitude sickness." However, many people are affected by the reduced levels of oxygen to such a minor degree that they don't associate the "bad feeling" they have with a lack of oxygen. If you do experience discomfort, it might be wise to ask a flight attendant for assistance.

I learned an interesting trick in the Air Force that you can use to combat altitude sickness. It's called *pressure breathing,* a technique designed to increase the atmospheric pressure in your lungs, which in turn increases the amount of oxygen that is absorbed by the bloodstream.

To do pressure breathing, take a deep breath, hold it for two seconds, then exhale about 20 percent of the air, very slowly and through your mouth, gradually restricting the outward airflow through your lips. When you have exhaled about 20 percent of the air (still retaining 80 percent in your lungs), your lips should be pursed tightly so that no air is coming out. Continue to try to push the air outward, as though you are trying to push the air across the barrier of your sealed lips. Don't press too hard. Hold the pressure for about two seconds, then exhale normally. Inhale and exhale normally, then start the procedure again.

Do no more than 10 pressure breaths with alternating regular breaths. You might feel light-headed due to the additional oxygen entering your system. At the same time, you may feel less nauseous or notice your headache is gone or that your peripheral vision is improved.

You also might feel a little silly while you are practicing this technique in a cabin filled with strangers, because it looks a bit like you are trying to play an imaginary trumpet. But if you have developed a splitting headache, nausea, and/or tunnel vision, the beneficial results of pressure breathing can more than make up for the potential embarrassment.

How to Overcome Dehydration

When you are traveling in the pressurized cabin of a jet, the air you breathe is actually coming from outside the plane. The very cold outside air is heated to a comfortable level for passengers, but during the process it dries out. The result is extremely low humidity in the aircraft, causing you to lose moisture through your skin and through respiration. Some aircraft are equipped with humidifiers to return some of the moisture to the air but rarely return the moisture to a healthful level.

TIP

Complain about dry, intemperate air immediately. If an aircraft is equipped with humidifiers, the flight crew can increase the moisture level in the air. Adjusting the temperature of an aircraft can be more difficult, because temperature control is usually divided into zones, so that one section of a plane is frequently warmer or cooler than another. Your complaint will usually lead to positive results. If not, complain again.

TIP

A moisturizing cream can help increase your comfort level and keep your skin smooth during and after a lengthy flight. However, no moisturizing cream will stop the dehydration process.

The key to overcoming dehydration is to maintain your level of body fluids. Drink plenty of water or juice during the flight. However, it can be difficult to get all the water or juice you need if flight attendants are busy serving other passengers. The best approach is to build up your body's fluid level *before* your flight. Start as soon as you wake up on the day of the flight, forcing yourself to drink double the amount of fluids you normally drink. Above all else, *avoid alcohol and caffeine.*

Lack of Sleep or Rest

Don't burn yourself out before your trip. Some businesspeople are tempted to work late hours for a week or so before a trip. Their goal is to "get ahead" of their workload so that the office will run efficiently while they're away. This is a bad way to start a business trip, because your reason for traveling is probably as important as— if not more important than—the odds and ends that you try to take care of before you leave. You should be as rested as possible when you leave for a business trip.

If you feel that you must spend some extra time in the office before your trip, at least begin to ease into waking hours that are closer to those of your destination.

TIP

For domestic travel, you can prepare your body if you are flying from one coast to another. If you are traveling from anywhere along the East coast to a West Coast state, begin waking at least two hours earlier than normal for three days prior to the trip. From the West Coast to the East Coast, begin sleeping a few extra hours and going to bed later than normal for three days prior to the trip.

Avoiding Overeating and Excessive Drinking

Both excessive eating and excessive intake of alcohol tax your body's restorative capabilities and can disrupt the operation of your internal clock.

Also, alcohol speeds up water loss, just as a diuretic does. If you drink alcohol before or during a long flight, you will have to compensate by drinking even more water or other nonalcoholic beverage to avoid dehydration.

Reducing Anxiety

Your ability to relax before and during a business trip will help to reduce the effects of jet lag. Many of the planning techniques covered in earlier chapters will help to reduce your level of pretravel stress. I'll have more on relaxation techniques later in the book.

Overcoming Motion Sickness

If you are susceptible to motion sickness, and at this moment are traveling in a boat, car, bus, train, or aircraft, I recommend that you skip this section of the book until your feet are sturdily on *terra firma* and you are seated in a comfortable chair. Why? Some people become motion sick just by hearing about motion sickness.

Most researchers of motion sickness seem to agree that the problem is not caused by any single malfunction of the body. Instead, it seems to be a progressive process caused by the body's being deceived so that it does not accept or understand what the eyes are observing. Smells, sounds, and even your previous meal can each play an important part in triggering motion sickness.

If you have ever suffered from motion sickness, you know that it doesn't help to hear that it's all in your mind and that eventually you will become accustomed to the odd movement of the boat or car or that sooner or later you will get used to those odd, unnerving smells and the impossible movements taking place around you. No, as you grow increasingly nauseous, nothing matters except your desire to hug a tree. At that point, your salvation might depend on finding a person who knows how to return you to the world of the living.

If you have never been motion sick, don't think that you are immune to this ailment. Anybody can become motion sick if the right combination of sensations exists. An unusual motion coupled with some incomprehensible smell—like kippered herring, a cold cigar, buttermilk, or sour orange juice—can trigger motion sickness in a person who normally is not susceptible to it.

How to Beat Motion Sickness

Of course, the best way to beat motion sickness is to avoid traveling. That's not very realistic for most people, so the next best approach is to take preventive steps. You can begin arming yourself with a little knowledge of what to look for. Here are the 10 most common sickness symptoms. Keep in mind that you might not experience them in this order and that you might not experience all 10:

1. Inability to get comfortable
2. A sudden fixation on the possibility of becoming sick
3. Cold sweat
4. Sudden irritability
5. Overproduction of saliva
6. Dizziness
7. Nausea
8. More sweating and perhaps a chill
9. An oncoming attack of diarrhea
10. A sour taste in the mouth

Taking Preventive Medication

Preventive medication works well for many people. Ask your doctor to recommend one that is well suited for you. If you are currently taking medication for some other purpose, you should be extra careful, even when you select an over-the-counter motion sickness preventive.

Some of the more common over-the-counter preventives are antihistamines, including Bonine (meclizine), Dramamine (dimenhydrinate), Marezine (cyclizine hydrochloride), and Transderm Scopy (scopolamine). All of these drugs can produce side effects or may be detrimental to your health. If you are asthmatic, or suffer from glaucoma, enlargement of the prostate, high blood pressure, or heart problems, consult your doctor before you take any of these medications. Some antihistamines take effect faster than others, but none of these will work if you wait until you are already feeling the symptoms of motion sickness.

However, there are some natural preventatives that can work even after you are feeling ill.

Ginger Root

Ginger root can be purchased in most health food stores and some drug and grocery stores. Ginger has a settling effect on the stomach and is available in a hard-candy type of tablet, in fresh and dried root form, as a powdered spice, in ginger ale, and as sugar candied.

Green Olives

If not too salty, green olives seem to slow the flow of saliva and also have a stomach-settling effect when eaten very slowly (and without the martini, of course).

Coca-Cola

Drink the original Coca-Cola only, please. Coke over ice, sipped slowly, can add fluids and settle upset stomachs. This is not as effective in aircraft as it is in other forms of transportation, perhaps due to the effect of carbonated gas expanding in the stomach at high altitudes. However, you can remove most of the gas by briskly stirring the drink.

Cold Beer or Campari and Soda on Ice

Either very cold beer or Campari and soda sipped slowly works well in rough seas when taken on an empty stomach. I know what I've said about using alcohol during travel, but often one of these remedies will stay down after everything else has already left.

Green Apples

Nibbled slowly, green apples have the same effect as green olives but might taste better. Apples eaten with dry crackers are excellent, both as a preventative before you become sick and after you become sick. The combination has a settling effect on the stomach.

Dry Crackers

Crackers absorb saliva and help soothe the stomach.

Try to Relax

Relaxing is usually the most difficult part of any prevention plan for motion sickness. If you are susceptible to motion sickness, you will probably be anxious simply from the fear that you will become sick no matter what you do. But getting comfortable and staying comfortable while you travel is possible with a little planning.

If you will be flying, try to time your flights so that there will be no meal service. This will reduce the number of odors that might trigger sickness. On long flights, you might try a noon flight, then skip lunch or bring something that you know you will like as a snack (but nothing with a pungent odor).

For many people travel by car is less traumatic than most other modes of travel, simply because you can pull off the road, put your feet on firm ground, and try to relax before you continue. If you are a passenger in a car, try to sit in front. Your risk of becoming sick is reduced because you will be able to focus better on distant points than you can from a rear seat. The movement and sound of travel also tend to be less bothersome in the front seat.

TIP
The more comfortable you are, the easier it will be to relax. Try wearing a jogging outfit on the plane. If necessary, change into and out of the outfit during the flight. You can slip into the rest room as soon as the plane reaches cruising altitude, change into your jogging outfit, and hang up your business apparel. Then change back before the plane lands.

Try Exercising
Even in the confining space of a coach airline seat, there are many exercises you can do. Stretches, isometrics, slow turns, and bends can all help to keep the blood flowing and can help take your mind off less pleasant things.

Two excellent exercises are putting your arms inside the arm rests and pushing out, then putting your arms on the outside of the arm rests and pushing in. The same kinds of exercises can be done with the feet and legs. Just arching the back and holding the position can relieve a lot of tension.

Get up and walk around the cabin from time to time. While you're up, get a tall drink of water.

Do Something to Divert Your Thoughts
Reading won't divert your thoughts from motion sickness if you begin to feel ill whenever you read while traveling. Instead, bring something along that does not require reading. Try knitting or bringing a list of things to think about—such as problems at the office you need to resolve, a proj-

ect that you'd like to start, or memories of an especially pleasant event.

Watching an in-flight movie or listening to tapes can work, too. There are many excellent "books on tape" available that can make even a transcontinental journey pass more quickly.

Being sociable with someone seated next to you can be diverting as well as entertaining and a great way to meet someone interesting. Remember, the most interesting conversationalist is a person who asks questions about the other person and genuinely listens to the answers. I have mentally awarded booby prizes to traveling sideshow biographers who start talking about themselves the moment the flight leaves the ground and don't stop until the flight lands. But even listening to one of these world-class bores can help ward off motion sickness.

Sleep, if You Can

Some people find that the best way to prevent motion sickness is to go to sleep. Of course, it is easier to become drowsy if you have taken an antihistamine or have mastered the art of relaxation. Taking a sleeping potion of some kind is the only way a lot of travelers are able to fall asleep on board a moving aircraft, bus, train, or ship. However, this should only be used as a last resort. Drugs that induce sleep almost always have side effects, the least of which is a drowsy feeling that will hang on for a half-day or longer when you wake up. Of course, great care should be taken when you mix a sleep-inducing drug with any other medication.

Get Fresh Air

You can't very well roll down the window on a jet to suck in some fresh air, but when traveling by ship or car, it can help to breathe fresh air in and out, slowly. Don't stick your head out the window of a moving car, though. A small bug or piece of debris striking you in the eye at 60 MPH can cause physical damage.

Avoid Visual Reminders of Movement

The constant recognition that you are moving is a problem with slower forms of travel, such as a car, bus, or ship. The actual movement you see is a continual reinforcement of the conflicting movement the inner ear feels. When you are in a car or bus that's negotiating mountain turns, or on a ship watching the horizon rise and fall, each sensation of movement can nudge you closer to illness. Some people can become motion sick just by watching a film of this kind of movement.

Whenever possible, fix your vision on the most distant item you can find, such as a cloud, the moon, or a star. If that doesn't work, look at something that's stationary within the vessel to avoid viewing actual movement. Always avoid looking directly down, because this can aggravate the sensations within the inner ear.

Clearing the Air

Sorry to bring this up, but there might be a time when you've tried everything available to avoid motion sickness and you (or even someone near you) don't make it to the rest room or miss the opening of that "little white bag." The resulting smell can be enough to bring battle-hardened Marines to their knees. If this situation occurs in flight or on a train, quick action by an attendant will help you recover and can prevent others from falling ill as a result.

When nausea strikes, tossing wet, used coffee grounds on "tossed cookies" works quite well, assuming that the grounds don't have to be spread on a lightly colored sport coat or an attractive silk dress. The coffee grounds will absorb the offensive odor and actually leave a fresh smell.

For residual stains on clothing, the traveler's portable stain remover is soda water, sponged liberally onto the stain as soon as possible. (By the way, Perrier does not act as a substitute, although it is better than nothing in a pinch.)

Here are some detailed steps to take if nausea has already forced your stomach and its contents into reverse:

1. Wash your face and hands. Then use soda water to sponge off your soiled clothing.
2. Have your seat and surrounding area checked, cleaned, and deodorized with coffee grounds, then soda water.
3. Brush your teeth if possible, then rinse your mouth with something fresh and cold, like a 7-Up on ice.
4. Get comfortable as quickly as possible. You might feel better at the moment, but there's no guarantee that there won't be a second round of nausea. If possible, have plenty of cool, fresh air blowing on you, but keep your body from becoming chilled.
5. Sip a Coca-Cola over ice, very slowly, with a minute or two between sips. (You could also try one of the other natural preventives that I've mentioned earlier.)
6. Try to concentrate on something—anything— besides your discomfort.

WARNING: Different people get motion sickness from different modes of travel. For instance, if you never become motion sick when you fly, you might still be susceptible to motion sickness on a ship. In fact, the rocking movement of a ship causes motion sickness in more people than do other types of travel. On the other hand, a ship's movement can actually be relaxing for some peo-

ple. The point is to expect the best but plan for the worst, just in case.

Dealing with In-flight Earaches

This painful ailment seems to be a chronic problem for some travelers. Travelers' earaches result from the pressurization or depressurization of an aircraft as it first ascends until it descends completely. The inability of the pressure on both sides of the eardrum to equalize can cause sudden and constant pain, which won't subside until the pressure is equalized in some way. In severe cases, the only way to establish equal pressure is to have a doctor lance the eardrum. But in most cases, there is a less severe solution.

Another pressure-related problem is a plugged ear that does not return to its normal hearing capacity when you are on the ground. The inability to hear clearly with one ear can be disruptive in a business meeting that requires your full attention and listening skills.

WARNING: Chronic sinus problems and allergies, or even colds, can create additional problems in clearing or equalizing pressure in the ear. If you have any of these problems, ask your doctor to recommend a medication that will help keep the nasal passages and sinuses clear.

WARNING: Pharmaceutical companies manufacture similar or even identical drugs to deal with different problems. For instance, an antihistamine might be marketed under one trade name to combat motion sickness and under another name to fight cold symptoms. Also, travel at high altitudes increases the effectiveness of many medications. Make sure you are not doubling or even tripling a dosage by taking an identical or similar compound to combat different symptoms. As al-

ways, consult your doctor before you combine any
medications.

How to Equalize the Pressure in Your Ears

The following are five techniques that work well
to equalize ear pressure. The best technique is
the one that you are equipped to do and/or are
most comfortable in carrying out.

☐ *Chew gum or suck on hard candy.* Some airlines pass out hard candy or gum prior to departure or landing. The chewing motion of gum
and the sucking of candy can help keep your ears
clear, as will the continued swallowing of saliva.
As a preventive measure, take the gum or candy
both during the ascent and descent portions of a
flight. It's also a good idea to bring your own
gum or candy, because you can't count on the
airline to supply you with some.

☐ *Yawn.* Again, the motion of the jaw plays a
role here, as well as the opening action of the
throat during the yawn. The tube that runs from
the inner ear into the throat area can usually be
cleared or opened by repeated yawning. Once
might not be enough. Keep yawning until you
feel the pressure being relieved.

☐ *Do pressure breathing.* This technique, which
I described earlier in this chapter for motion sickness, also helps to relieve ear pressure. Another
technique is to hold your nose closed, then try
to blow out of your nose. Do this gently, though,
because you can actually increase the pressure in
your ears by overblowing. Follow any pressure
technique with yawning and swallowing, in that
order.

☐ *Cup your hands tightly over your ears.* Create
a slight plunging effect on the outside of the ears
while you are yawning and moving your lower
jaw in a circular manner. Don't make sudden or

exaggerated movements; just move your jaw gently.

☐ *Gargle.* This approach works best if you gargle with something warm, like lightly salted, warm water. Mouthwash is acceptable if nothing else is available.

If you try one of these steps and find that it is not working, chances are that you haven't tried long enough. If the technique you are using does not cause you pain, continue it for a few minutes. Repeated attempts are often necessary for seriously plugged ears or earaches.

Easing In-Flight Toothaches

In-flight toothaches usually indicate a more serious dental problem. A budding abscess can suddenly and painfully announce itself when the cabin of a jet is depressurized. A small amount of gas in decay beneath a filling or inlay can expand suddenly at a high altitude, resulting in great pain. A filling can even pop out when the pressure within the decayed portion of the tooth pushes against nerves and an already loose filling.

Try one or more of these four techniques to temporarily relieve the pain of an in-flight toothache:

☐ *Apply oil of clove.* If your toothache is unexpected, you probably won't have any of this handy, but the flight attendants might be able to retrieve some from the first-aid kit. When pressed against a broken tooth or the gum around an aching tooth, oil of clove has a soothing effect.

☐ *Apply an ice pack to the outside of your cheek to numb the area.* You can create a makeshift ice pack quickly by wrapping a napkin around ice from a beverage cart. Don't apply the ice pack directly to the tooth, of course, because this will probably just increase the pain.

☐ *Take a pain killer.* If you have a bottle of pain-killing medicine available, take it according to the directions on the bottle or according to your doctor's instructions.

☐ *Hold a little brandy in your mouth in the area of pain.* The brandy should be at room temperature.

All four methods for relieving tooth pain are temporary. The pain itself indicates that you need to see your dentist. If you are away from home, won't return home soon, and are in great distress, find a dentist in the area of your stay. Hotel clerks can often direct you to a dentist near your hotel. If you are visiting a foreign country where communication might be difficult, contact the nearest American consul or embassy (or any English-speaking consul or embassy) and ask for help.

Dealing with Diarrhea

This isn't a pleasant topic, but the debilitating effects of diarrhea can be even more unpleasant, and might even spur you on a run for the nearest rest room when you are in the middle of an important business presentation.

This problem usually is the result of ingesting some bacteria or virus that your system is not accustomed to. Diarrhea is not restricted to any particular country or part of the globe. You can fall ill with it in any country or even in a region of the United States where you are not used to eating the foods native to that area.

Except for situations where diarrhea is a symptom of a more serious illness, the problem usually disappears on its own within a few days. However, few business travelers have the time to wait before the bacteria or virus has been eliminated.

Remedies for Diarrhea

Although there are medications that you can take to relieve diarrhea, many have side effects, so check with a doctor before you take something that might create problems worse than diarrhea. Kaopectate, Pepto-Bismol, and other over-the-counter remedies can provide a measure of relief but probably will not solve the problem entirely. More effective drugs, such as Loperamide, offer a faster end to the discomfort of diarrhea but are usually available only with a prescription. Some studies have indicated that, if no other remedy is available, aspirin may help to "firm up" the problem.

Some medications taken for other travel ailments can actually cause diarrhea. For instance, antibiotics tend to destroy the natural and beneficial flora of bacteria that reside in your intestines. When these bacteria die, the result is often diarrhea, which will end soon after you stop the antibiotic and allow your natural flora to return to normal strength. One way to aid this process is to eat a generous helping of active yogurt, most of which contains acidophilus, or the "good" bacteria that aid your digestive system.

WARNING: Two drugs that are available outside the United States to relieve diarrhea are considered unsafe and should not be taken. These drugs are Enterovioform and Mexaform. Both contain iodochlorhydroxyquin, which medical evidence suggests is very dangerous.

Diarrhea and Dehydration

The continued loss of body fluids caused by diarrhea can often lead to dehydration. If you find that you are suffering from diarrhea, increase your hydration considerably. Gatorade or a similar athletic beverage is ideal. These beverages work well because you need to replace not only water but also electrolytes like sodium and potassium. If nothing else is available, drink several glasses of water with a spoonful of honey and a pinch of salt added. In any event, frequent and clear urination is a sign that your attempt to hydrate your body is working.

Dealing with Constipation

Here's another unpleasant topic, but one that isn't as debilitating as diarrhea. Constipation can lead to headaches and a general irritability, which certainly won't help in business dealings.

Fortunately, constipation is a fairly easy problem to solve, with more than a dozen over-the-counter remedies—including laxatives and enemas—available for ending cases of constipation overnight. Most of these remedies are fairly taxing to the body, though.

A better way to deal with constipation is to recognize your susceptibility to it, then take preventive steps that deal with the causes of constipation. Most people have regular movements because their body functions within a daily routine of meals, rest, and regularly scheduled activities. When you travel, you disrupt this routine, with the result quite often being constipation.

Eating apples can often relieve constipation, but if you are in a country where apples might not be available or very edible, you'll want to try something else. Other high-fiber fruits that can end constipation, like figs, dates, prunes, and mangoes, often cause diarrhea to those people unaccustomed to eating them.

But you can add a healthful amount of fiber to your diet in the form of oat bran. The key to using oat bran successfully is to make it a part of your daily diet, not just when you are traveling. In fact, when you begin using oat bran, the result can often be a mild case of gas. This problem usually disappears as your system adjusts to the bran. Bran coupled with plenty of liquid represents a natural approach that's easy on your system.

Coping with Intestinal Gas

"Rocky mountain barking spiders," as mountain climbers often call intestinal gas, can be potentially embarrassing if the involuntary "barking" occurs during a business meeting. Altitude again might be the culprit here, at least in part. Ascending in an aircraft or traveling in cities at a high elevation can cause the gas within your intestines to expand—and expanding gas tries very hard to escape.

Avoiding Gas-Producing Foods

Altitude isn't the only cause of gas. Many foods are gas producers for the body. Some people seem to be better methane producers than others, but even if that isn't the case for you, altitude coupled with a gas-producing diet can lead to noisy results.

If you want to avoid intestinal gas during business travel, your best bet is to avoid gas-producing foods 24 hours prior to your trip. The following are all culprits that should be checked off your diet during travel (with the exception of bran, which should not be a problem if you have been ingesting it regularly, prior to your trip).

☐ Brussel sprouts

☐ Bran

☐ Cabbage and cabbage products

☐ Eggplant

☐ Carbonated beverages (except as a remedy for motion sickness)

☐ Beer

☐ Beans and other legumes

☐ Radishes

☐ Pickles

☐ Spicy food

☐ Mangoes

☐ Most raw vegetables

All bodies are not created equal. If you know of other foods or beverages that usually produce gas in your system, add those foods to this list.

When Preventive Measures Have Not Worked

If intestinal gas should strike, some natural techniques can help overcome the problem. Many joggers will tell you that running seems to relieve excess gas. Two other approaches require that you be in a place where you can move your body freely.

The first approach is a Hatha yoga technique. Lying flat on your back, on the floor, stretch your arms above your head (along the floor). Relax for a few seconds. Then slowly bring one knee up toward your chest as far as you comfortably can. Hold your knee with both hands, fingers interlaced just below the top of the knee, with your elbows against your body. Your chin should be down, and you should make a relaxed effort to put all of your spine against the floor.

As you are performing this exercise, breathe in slowly, telling yourself to relax every joint, muscle, and nerve in your body as you inhale. As you exhale, increase the pressure on the knee, bringing it a bit tighter to your chest. Hold this position for 15 seconds as you exhale, then slowly extend your leg back to the floor. With your arms at your sides, lie flat and relaxed. Repeat this procedure with your other leg. Do the exercise three times for each leg, alternating between the right and left legs.

Finally, perform the same exercise, but this time pull both legs to your chest, making sure you now press your shoulders down, against the floor, while you put both arms around the knees and pull them to your chest. Breathe as indicated earlier, and hold for 15 seconds. Do this part of the exercise three times—or more, if necessary.

The next approach is what I call the "gravity gas removal method." Lie on your stomach, and with your feet and knees flat on the floor, slowly move your head toward your knees. Without lifting your head more than a few inches off the floor, slide your hands under your head for support. This will raise your buttocks into the air. When your rear is as high up as you can push it, slowly arch your back, back and forth (pushing your spine in the air, then pulling it tightly to the floor while maintaining your head as close to your knees as possible and your rear end as high as you can push it). Do this five times. Then, with your rear end still in the air, rest in this position for a minute.

One or both of these techniques, plus a short, two- to three-minute walk or jogging in place, should remove any excess gas from your intestinal system. Keep in mind that gas is continually produced, so you might have to repeat these procedures every hour or so until the problem disappears.

Traveler's Depression

Most seasoned travelers have experienced what I am about to discuss. In fact, I can't think of anyone I know who has traveled frequently and hasn't had at least one attack of traveler's depression. This is an overwhelming feeling that hits when the rigors of travel begin to take their toll on your emotions as well as your body. Fatigue clouds your thinking, you can't seem to shake off jet lag, you might have partied too much, and you might have a touch of a cold or flu. When these and other combined effects lead to depression, the business at hand no longer takes priority, if you have any interest in business at all.

Some telltale signals of the onset of traveler's depression is a shortened temper or a feeling that you are going to die at any moment. When depression strikes, the first step you should take is to recognize that this mood is temporary. Repeat to yourself that the depression is temporary—until your mind believes it.

Next, try to relieve yourself of the source of frustration or fatigue. If you can reschedule appointments, do so. Then get plenty of rest. Sometimes a hot bath followed by a sound night's sleep can work wonders. If you are crunched for time, a long nap followed by some light exercise can also produce excellent results.

Avoiding Viruses, Food Poisoning, and Other Diseases

Many travel conditions are ideal for the transmission of bacteria and disease. Being in close quarters within crowded airports, bus and train stations, and on aircraft is a recipe for catching something contagious. This situation is compounded when you are traveling to a country that is medically hazardous.

If you plan to travel to an underdeveloped country, or Central or South America, you should have your travel agent check the medical alerts for these areas. Often, you can take preventive steps by getting inoculated (see Chapter 8). Malaria also is on the upswing in many countries, and can be avoided easily with the appropriate medical preventive steps.

One of the Centers for Disease Control's annual publications, *Health Information for International Travel,* can help you to keep abreast of health dangers in foreign countries. The booklet is published each June and can be obtained by contacting the U.S. Government Printing Office in Washington, D.C. The phone number for this office is (202) 783-3238.

TIP

This is common sense but worth stating anyway. When you travel, let moderation be your motto. Overindulgence and temptation are perhaps the two biggest risks to your health and business when you travel. Whenever you're tempted to visit a prostitute, engage in a night of excessive eating and/or binge drinking, or some other mischief, think of the consequences. Do I need to tell you about the dangers of venereal disease, AIDS, or food poisoning? And is whatever you have in mind worth risking your business dealings, your career, or even your life?

8

Importance of Immunization & Vaccination

The previous chapter touched on many of the illnesses that can befall the traveler. Overcoming jet lag and motion sickness can be managed fairly easily with the right techniques and remedies. But if you are traveling in an area where malaria or cholera is at epidemic proportions, no amount of over-the-counter antibiotic is going to help. Disease and pestilence are everywhere, and as a traveler, you can be highly susceptible to a serious, even deadly, disease, simply because your body is not prepared to fight against foreign substances that invade suddenly.

Prior to departure on any trip, *anywhere,* it is a good idea to update your immunization status. A sad fact: It has been estimated that over 80 percent of the adults living in the United States have not maintained up-to-date immunization for contagious diseases. Many adults don't even know when they last had a vaccination, or what it was for.

Prevention Is the Only Way to Avoid Malaria

Many countries do not request vaccinations or warn of health problems, even though a real health risk might exist in that country. Malaria, for example, continues to be a serious problem for many parts of the world. You run the risk of catching this disease in South America, Central America (including Puerto Vallarta and other coastal areas in Mexico), Africa, Turkey, India, Indonesia, Asia, and elsewhere. To make matters worse, each country can have different strains of malaria or viruses. Malaria can be fatal, and if it does not kill you, it can remain part of you for the rest of your life.

Prevention begins well in advance of your travel to a malaria zone, so don't think this is something you can deal with when it happens. You can receive up-to-date information on malaria risk and other immunization needs through the International Association for Medical Assistance to Travelers (IAMAT). This nonprofit organization will send you a highly informative and useful package of material when you become a member (for a nominal donation).

Contact IAMAT at 417 Center Street, Lewiston, NY, 14092; or in Canada at 188 Nicklin Road, Guelph, Ontario N1H 7L5; or in Switzerland at 57 Voirets, 1212 Grand-Lancy-Geneva. Send $30 U.S. (or equivalent currency) and request your package and membership. Also be sure to ask for the full set of 24 world climate maps. One of the booklets you will receive is a worldwide list of physicians and clinics that can treat your problems and communicate with you in English. There are maximum charges established previously (in 1988), which are as follows:

☐ Office visits cost $20.

☐ House or hotel calls are $30.

☐ Night, Sunday, local holiday visits run $40.

☐ Medication, tests, and so on, are extra.

A frequently updated chart entitled World Immunization Chart lists all the countries of the world and indicates specific vaccinations or immunizations that are recommended to prevent disease (even though most of these vaccinations will not be required by either the country in question or the United States for your return).

Emergency Contacts

The State Department Overseas Citizens' Emergency Center, Washington, D.C., provides information on current health conditions around the world. Call Monday through Friday (except holidays) from 8:30 A.M. to 10:00 P.M. Eastern time, at 202-634-3600. In an emergency, this 24-hour number is available: 202-647-1512.

Medical Resources

To get help in a life-threatening situation, time and the ability to communicate will be extremely important. To aid in dealing with a life-threatening event, you should keep a copy of the following list wherever and whenever you travel:

Air-Evac International: 800-845-2569
    (CA 619-292-5557)
Arranges for emergency evacuation

Centers for Disease Control: 404-329-2572
Gives assistance with poisons or drug problems

Data Vue Products: 915-698-7312
Provides microfilm cards of your medical
    history

Europe Assistance Worldwide Services:
    202-347-2025
Gives help for travel to Europe or Asia,
    medical assistance, and evacuation

Health Care Abroad: 800-237-6615
  (VA 703-255-9800)
Provides free information on health conditions,
  insurance policy, evacuation (24-hour
  service)

International SOS Assistance Inc.:
  800-523-8930 (PA 215-244-1500)
Worldwide medical assistance for corporations
  or individuals

Local Emergency number: 911
For any emergency at all

Medical Alert Foundation: 800-344-3226
  (CA 209-668-3333)
Provides Medical Alert tags

N.E.A.R.: NATIONWIDE/WORLDWIDE
  EMERGENCY AMBULANCE RETURN:
  800-654-6700
Provides worldwide ambulance assistance

Passport Agency Emergency number:
  202-632-5225 or 202-632-1512 or 202-655-
  4000
Deals with emergencies that relate to passport
  problems

Poison Control Center: 800-282-3171
Gives emergency information about possible
  drugs or poisons

State Department Overseas Citizens'
  Emergency Center:
Emergency numbers: 202-647-1512 or
  202-634-3600
Helps with many emergency problems,
  including evacuation home; your at-home
  friends can call this number if they suspect
  you have been arrested or are missing, or
  they need to get money to you; it's an
  essential number to call if there is a death
  abroad

United States Foreign Service Offices (Embassies or Consulates)

NOTE: In the following list, the numbers indicated are local. No long-distance area codes have been indicated. If you are calling one of these numbers from another city in the same country, be sure to tell the local (or hotel) operator the name of the city to which the number corresponds.

The telex codes are essential if you plan to send any telex messages to a person or company within that country. Businesspeople often give you their telex address without including the country code. Having this list can prove to be valuable when you need to save time in getting a telex sent quickly to the correct place. A few of the countries indicated have several telex codes. Rather than give you all of them, without your knowing which would be correct for you, I have left them out. If you deal with such countries, be sure to have the country code for the telex addresses you may need.

COUNTRY, CITY	TELEPHONE NUMBER	TELEX CODE
AFGHANISTAN, KABUL:	62230/35 or 62436	930
ALGERIA, ALGIERS:	601-425/255/186	936
ANTIGUA, ST. JOHNS:	462-3505/6	306
ARGENTINA, BUENOS AIRES:	774-7611/8811/9911	390
AUSTRALIA, SYDNEY:	264-7044	790
AUSTRIA, VIENNA:	315-511	847
BAHAMAS, NASSAU:	322-4753/56	382
BAHRAIN, MANAMA:	714151	955
BARBADOS, BRIDGETOWN:	436-4950/7	386
BELGIUM, BRUSSELS:	531-3830	846
BELIZE, BELIZE CITY:	7161 or 7162	310
BERMUDA, HAMILTON:	295-1342	380
BOLIVIA, LA PAZ:	350251 or 350120	multiple
BOTSWANA, GABORONE:	53982/3/4	991
BRAZIL, BRASILIA:	223-0120	391
CAMEROON, YAOUNDE:	23-40-14	978
CANADA, OTTAWA:	238-5335	389
CHAD, N'DJAMENA:	3269 or 3513	984
CHILE, SANTIAGO:	71-0133/90	multiple
CHINA, BEIJING:	522-033	716
COLOMBIA, BOGOTA:	285-1300/1688	396
COSTA RICA, SAN JOSE:	331155	303
COTE D'IVOIRE, ABIDJAN:	320979	969

COUNTRY, CITY	TELEPHONE NUMBER	TELEX CODE
CUBA, HAVANA (SWISS):	320551, 320541	307
CURACAO, WILLEMSTAD:	613066	384
CZECHOSLOVAKIA, PRAGUE:	536-641	849
DENMARK, COPENHAGEN	423-144	855
DOMINICAN REPUBLIC:	541-2171	multiple
ECUADOR, QUITO:	562-890	393
EGYPT, CAIRO:	355-7371	927
EL SALVADOR, SAN SALVADOR:	26-7100	301
FINLAND, HELSINKI:	171-931	857
FRANCE, PARIS:	296-1202	842
GERMANY E., BERLIN E.:	2-202-714	840
GERMANY W., BONN:	339-3390	841
GREAT BRITAIN, LONDON:	499-9000	851
GREECE, ATHENS:	712-951	863
GRENADA, ST. GEORGE'S:	440-1731/4	320
GUATEMALA, GUATEMALA CITY:	312235	305
GUYANA, GEORGETOWN:	2-54900	312
HAITI, PORT-AU-PRINCE:	20354 or 20368	349
HONDURAS, TEGUCIGALPA:	32-3120	311
HONG KONG, HONG KONG:	5-239011	780
HUNGARY, BUDAPEST:	329-375	861
INDIA, BOMBAY:	823-611	953
IRAQ, BAGHDAD:	718-1840 or 719-3791	943
IRELAND (REP.), DUBLIN:	688-777	852
ISRAEL, TEL AVIV:	03-654338	922
ITALY, ROME:	652-841	843
JAPAN, TOKYO:	583-7141	781
JAMAICA, KINGSTON:	929-4850	381
JORDAN, AMMAN:	644371	925
KENYA, NAIROBI:	334141	963
KOREA, SEOUL:	722-2601	787
KUWAIT, KUWAIT:	242-4151/9	959
LEBANON, BEIRUT:	417774 or 415802/3	923
MEXICO, MEXICO D.F.:	211-0042	383
MOROCCO, CASABLANCA:	224-149	933
NETHERLANDS, ROTTERDAM:	117-560	844
NEW ZEALAND, AUCKLAND:	32-724	791
NICARAGUA, MANAGUA:	66010 or 66015/18	388
OMAN, MUSCAT:	738-006	926
PAKISTAN, KARACHI:	515-081	952
PANAMA, PANAMA CITY:	27-1777	328
PARAGUAY, ASUNCION:	201-041	399
PERU, LIMA:	338-000	334
PHILIPPINES, MANILA:	521-7116	multiple
POLAND, WARSAW:	283-041	867
PORTUGAL, LISBON:	725-600	832
QATAR, DOHA:	870-701	957
SAUDI ARABIA, RIYADH:	488-3800	928
SINGAPORE, SINGAPORE:	338-0251	786
SOUTH AFRICA, PRETORIA:	28-4266	960
SPAIN, MADRID:	2763-400	831
SWEDEN, STOCKHOLM:	783-5300	854
SWITZERLAND, GENEVA:	990-211	845
SYRIA, DAMASCUS:	333-052 or 332-557	924

COUNTRY, CITY	TELEPHONE NUMBER	TELEX CODE
TAIWAN, TAIPEI:	708-4151	785
THAILAND, BANGKOK:	252-5040	788
TUNISIA, TUNIS:	782-566	934
TURKEY, ANKARA:	265-470	821
TRINIDAD, PORT-OF-SPAIN:	622-6371	387
U.A.E., ABU DHABI:	336-691	multiple
URUGUAY, MONTEVIDEO:	409-051 or 409-125	398
VENEZUELA, CARACAS:	264-7111/6111	395
YUGOSLAVIA, BELGRADE:	645-655	862
ZAMBIA, LUSAKA:	214-911	965

For Medical Emergency Where Treatment Is Required

COUNTRY, CITY	MEDICAL ASSISTANCE	LOCAL NUMBER
Argentina, Buenos Aires	IAMAT Center	791-9956
Australia, Sydney	Traveler's Medical Serv.	221-7133
Austria, Vienna	IAMAT Center	439-706
Bahamas, Freeport	Lucayan Medical Center	352-7288
Bangladesh, Dacca	Red Cross Society	400-011
Belgium, Brussels	IAMAT Center	513-4975
Belize, Belize City	IAMAT Center	45-261
Bolivia, La Paz	IAMAT Center	371-826
Botswana, Gaborone	IAMAT Center	52-221
Brazil, Rio de Janeiro	IAMAT Center	246-4180
Cameroon, Yaounde	IAMAT Center	224-523
Canada, Ottawa	IAMAT Center	738-1210
Chile, Santiago	Clinicas las Condes	211-1002
China, Beijing	Capital Hospital	(ext 372) 553-731
Colombia, Medellin	IAMAT Center	251-5639
Cote D'Ivoire, Abidjan	Center Medical	321-526
Cyprus, Nicosia	Nicosia Clinic	77-022/3
Denmark, Copenhagen	IAMAT Center	387-828
Dominican Rep., Santiago	Clinica Corominas	582-1171
Equador, Guayaquil	IAMAT Center	301-785
Egypt, Cairo	IAMAT Center	350-3105
El Salvador, San Salvador	Clinica Medicas	(ext 178) 25-0277
England, London	IAMAT Center	235-5995
Ethiopia, Addis Ababa	Tikur Anbessa Hospital	151-211
Fiji, Labasa	Labasa Hospital	81-444
France, Paris	American Hospital	637-7200
Germany, Dusseldorf	IAMAT Center	663-444
Greece, Athens	HYGEIA	682-7940
Hong Kong, Kowloon	TST Medical Clinic	(3)723-1199
Hungary, Budapest	IAMAT Center	138-688
Iceland, Reykjavik	St. Joseph's Hosp.	19-600
India, New Delhi	IAMAT Center	692-544
Indonesia, Jakarta	IAMAT Center	714-591

COUNTRY, CITY	MEDICAL ASSISTANCE	LOCAL NUMBER
Iran, Teheran	IAMAT Center	655-128
Iraq, Baghdad	IAMAT Center	542-1505
Ireland, Belfast (North)	IAMAT Center	776-600
Ireland, Dublin (Republic)	IAMAT Center	882-683
Israel, Jerusalem	IAMAT Center	633-712
Italy, Rome	IAMAT Center	777-695
Jamaica, Kingston	F.I.S.H. Clinic	927-1106
Japan, Tokyo	Tokyo Hospital	392-6151
Jordan, Amman	IAMAT Center	624-096
Korea, Seoul	St. Mary's Hosp.	(ext 1463) 593-9121
Mexico, Mexico City	IAMAT Center	520-3132
Netherlands, Rotterdam	IAMAT Center	360-339
Pakistan, Karachi	Dawood Clinic	724-701
Panama, Panama City	Clinica San Fernando	616-666
Peru, Lima	British American Hosp.	403-570
Philippines, Manila	IAMAT Center	885-725
Portugal, Lisbon	IAMAT Center	531-315
Spain, Madrid	Anglo-American Clinic	431-2229
Sudan, Khartoum	Khartoum Clinic	44-479
Sweden, Goteborg	IAMAT Center	220-011
Switzerland, Geneva	IAMAT Center	314-756
Thailand, Bangkok	Adventist Hospital	281-1422
Turkey, Istanbul	Admiral Bristol Hosp.	131-4050
U.A.E., Abu Dhabi	Al-Damluji Clinic	338-428
Venezuela, Caracas	Centro Medico, Anexo B	515-362
Yugoslavia, Belgrade	Interna Klinika A	620-537
Zaire, Bukavu	IAMAT Center	25-18

9

How to Survive In-Flight Calamities

The Best Defense: Realize What Can Go Wrong—Then Beat It!

Are you sitting down? (Seated or standing, if you are in an aircraft as you read this, I strongly suggest that you skip this chapter until you are safely in your hotel.) Although I hate to be a doomsayer, you should be aware of the potential disasters that can befall you when you travel by air. You might never have to deal with any of these situations, and I hope you don't. But if you are in one of these rare situations, it is best to be prepared.

Not all of the following airline calamities are life threatening, but each can, at the very least, disrupt your travel plans, and most can scare you out of your skin if you are not prepared:

☐ Malfunction prior to departure

☐ Aborted flight due to weather

☐ Crew mutinies

☐ Malfunction during flight

☐ Sudden interruption of flight prior to arrival at the destination (crash)

☐ Hijacking

Malfunctions Prior to Departure

The symptom is usually something like this: The flight leaves the gate on time, taxies for takeoff, then after what seems like an eternity, turns around. A voice announces that the flight has returned to the gate but is expected to depart within a few minutes. Much later, after the flight is finally underway, a passenger asks one of the flight service staff if the problem was with one of the engines. If the discussion is honest (which it probably wouldn't be), something like the following exchange might take place:

"No," the flight attendant admits. "The pilot just refused to fly an aircraft that was in disrepair."

"Oh," the passenger says. "So the mechanics were able to repair the aircraft in such a short time?"

"No," the flight attendant replies. "That's how long it took to replace the pilot."

Don't laugh. I have heard of cases where pilots have been pressured to fly less-than-safe aircraft. If you read or hear about an airline that has been cited for excessive maintenance violations, find another carrier. Also, send a letter to the president of the carrier to let the company know why you plan to find other means of travel.

In reality, flight crew members are the watchdogs of the airline industry. These professionals often are the first to catch the minor—and I do stress minor—maintenance problems that some members of airline management would rather ignore for the sake of "the bottom line."

Because it is not uncommon for a redundant part or instrument to need repair, there is no need for you to panic or become unglued when you see workers pulling up the carpet to get at a wire or swarming around one of the engines to perform some basic repair. FAA rules require modern jets to undergo major overhauls of the engines and other parts periodically. Back-up systems also are in place to support critical functions. All repairs, even minor ones, must be filed with the FAA.

So when a flight is delayed due to maintenance problems, don't become alarmed. Chances are that the fix is very minor. Otherwise, the paperwork involved in informing the FAA would take longer to complete than the repair itself, and the flight would be canceled.

Weather Problems

If you have ever flown through a heavy thunderstorm, you probably have gained a new respect for the power of natural forces. At the same time, you probably have increased your level of confidence in the strength of modern aircraft and their ability to take punishment. But storms are still dangerous. The FAA and pilots are very aware of this, which explains many of the thousands of delayed or canceled flights each year in the United States alone due to bad weather.

Weather Conditions That Cause Delays

Three types of weather disturbances cause the majority of delays or diverted destinations:

☐ Storms

☐ Wind shear

☐ Fog and other visibility problems

Snow and ice storms have been the cause of many aircraft crashes, generally on takeoff. The extra weight of the snow or ice that has not been cleaned off the aircraft, or the jamming of an important and needed movable part due to ice, can cause major structural failure. The result in some tragic instances has been the crash of the flight.

The irony of these incidents is that most aircraft should never have this kind of problem. If weather conditions are that severe, the flight should never take off from or land at that location. But in rare situations, unpredicted weather situations will arise suddenly and endanger aircraft.

Snow and ice encountered in-flight are not much of a problem with high-performance aircraft, except when they limit visibility for landings. Smaller aircraft that cannot ascend to altitudes to escape the snow and ice may encounter flight difficulties and be forced to turn back or seek an airport to wait out the storm.

Thunderstorms are dangerous but, for radar-equipped aircraft, almost entirely avoidable. There have been instances, however, when local flight patterns or local flight control has forced an aircraft through or too close to a thunderstorm. Prior to this situation, the pilot will alert the passengers that they should remain seated with their seat belts securely fastened. A sudden drop of one thousand feet or more has been experienced by aircraft in severe storms, and in such events, injuries can easily result. But, again, thunderstorms are a visible and relatively predictable event.

Fog is more insidious and is caused by the temperature differences between the land or water and the air above it. Fog is much more of a problem for an aircraft that is landing than for one taking off. Even when an airport is "closed" due to fog, some aircraft are still able to leave, until conditions get so bad that even aircraft departures are not allowed.

Accidents in fog do occur. The worst case occurred in the Canary Islands when a departing 747, loaded with passengers, crashed into another 747 that was taxiing across the runway at the time.

Local commuter aircraft are far more susceptible to weather problems than are larger aircraft. Not all commuter aircraft are able to get above weather disturbances, and many are not as well equipped to deal with complicated instrument flights in inclement weather.

Wind shear, another serious weather danger to aircraft, is the result of a sudden shift in the direction of the wind. Because an aircraft's movement is first through the air, then over the ground, the direction in which the air is traveling is critical. All aircraft must make adjustments for the direction of the wind in order to fly from Point A to Point B.

If the wind is moving from east to west, and if an aircraft takes off from Miami and flies in a straight line headed for New York, the actual track across the ground would take the aircraft well west of New York. To counter this, on departure from Miami the aircraft must point at a destination somewhere out in the ocean to the east of New York and allow the wind to push the aircraft to the west.

I point this out because that adjustment is very subtle and hardly noticed in jet aircraft. However, when the aircraft is making an approach to land, wind direction becomes more critical and adjustments harder to make. The pilot must bring the plane to a point where it no longer wants to stay in the air, right over the place where the runway is.

A sudden and violent change in the direction of the wind can cause the aircraft to veer to one side or, if the wind shear is a down-draft, to land very hard, or crash. This is a very rare event.

How to Avoid or Limit the Effects of Weather on Your Travel Plans

I've included these scenarios not to frighten you but to point out that air travel has its risks. As safe as air travel is, you can reduce risk by taking steps to avoid or sidestep weather-related problems. Often these steps will do more than ensure your safety in flight; they will help you to get to your destination with a minimum of delay.

A good place to begin is to review several factors related to your trip:

☐ Are you traveling to or from an area that may be prone to a weather problem during the time of your trip?

☐ What weather patterns are typical for your departure and arrival locations at the current time of year?

☐ Even if you are traveling to and from problem-free areas, is your aircraft coming in from a problem area? That is, will it be delayed at some point before it reaches your point of departure?

☐ How flexible are your plans?

☐ Is the trip necessary at this time, or will next week do?

Local weather conditions for your departure area and arrival point are easy to ascertain. The weather problems may occur daily, such as the usual thunderstorm around the Orlando area in August, or the snow flurries in Buffalo in January. When you need to fly into these areas during months of typically severe weather, make an effort to discover the best time of day to fly into or out of those cities.

Fog is usually heaviest in the morning and late evening, whereas thunderstorms occur heaviest in the late afternoons. Snowstorms and ice storms can occur at any time of the day or night, but are usually part of a large weather pattern and therefore are somewhat predictable.

If you are making a trip to any tropical area during the hottest time of the year, make the arrival time as early in the day as possible.

Night flights in modern aircraft can often be the smoothest, because the night air is the most stable. Also, thunderstorms are clearly visible at night due to their flashes of lightning.

Finding Out About Weather Problems

Your travel agent has several ready sources of weather information. It is always a good idea to ask your travel agent to check out the weather conditions before booking you on a flight.

However, the information available to your agent is usually generic, and will probably prove to be less timely or specific than information that you can gather yourself. If you want specific and highly current weather information, try the following sources:

Cities 1-800-247-3282	Gives you an update on the weather conditions in more than 250 cities in the USA, by local area code
Flight Service (check your phone book for a local number)	This is the federal weather phone service for all pilots. You can ask for weather en route to and at your destination, for the time of your flight.

Why You Should Choose Commuter Airlines Carefully

Because smaller aircraft are more affected by weather disturbances than larger jets, the company's maintenance of the aircraft and the training of pilots should be examined carefully. Many commuter airlines are associated with major airlines, because this situation benefits both airlines in scheduling and selling tickets. This association can create the illusion that the major airlines are larger than they actually are and that they serve more cities than they really do. The small airline is taken under the wing of the major carrier but in reality remains just a small airline trying to draw as much business as possible and is frequently owned separately.

Even when a commuter service is "owned" by a major airline, the passengers who fly in these commuter aircraft often do not discover the small size of the plane until they are ready to board the flight. Some travel agents do not tell their clients about the type of craft they will fly simply because they do not bother to check, or if they do check, they don't know the difference.

I don't mean to imply that small, commuter aircraft are not well cared for or that aircraft for major airlines are better maintained. It's just that you are at a greater risk in bad weather when you travel on a small craft. The bottom line is that, if you are traveling to a remote destination, make sure your travel agent tells you what kind of craft you will be traveling in. At least you will be in a position to decide whether you want to find another carrier or travel at a different time.

How to Pick the Best Places to Stop Over

If all flights to your desired destination are one or two stoppers, then select the stops with the least likely delay potential. Weather isn't the only criterion for determining the potential for delay. As a general rule, I try to find flights that have stopovers at small airports. The reason is simply that the reduced traffic also reduces the chance for delay. However, when possible, look for relatively uncongested airports such as Charlotte, North Carolina, or Pittsburgh, Pennsylvania, that also serve as hub cities. This way, you will have several flights to choose from in case a delay occurs while you are on the ground.

TIP

Every time an aircraft must stop at an intermittent airport, the chances for delays increase. Whenever and wherever you are on the ground, inclement weather can move into that area and close the airport, or the aircraft can simply be forced to wait for passengers who have been delayed on incoming flights. If your schedule is critical and you can afford to do so, select flights that are nonstop or that at least make as few stops as possible.

Avoiding Changes of Aircraft

Even if your flight must stop, try to find one that does not require you to change aircraft. This is a good idea for many reasons. Chiefly, if you must make a stopover, you have a better chance of avoiding delays or missed connections if one leg of your flight is not dependent on the arrival or departure of another aircraft. Before you decide on a flight selection, always ask the airline or your travel agent whether you must change planes.

What Happens When the Crew Mutinies

Sounds unlikely, doesn't it? True, the flight attendants or copilot won't throw the captain out of the plane in midflight, but there are situations in which the crew simply has worked the maximum number of hours they are required to (often by union rules). The result can be an on-the-ground "mutiny" that leaves you and your fellow passengers stranded.

Crew members work long hours and put up with a lot of abuse from passengers who do not understand or care about the problems that a flight crew has to contend with. First, most members of a flight crew log their hours based on the actual time the aircraft is between "depart the gate" and "arrive at the gate." This period does not include the time required to check in, make the aircraft ready, board the passengers, or deal with the same delays the passengers have to put up with. Nor does it include the time required to solve hassles at the other end of the line, including problems with customs, getting their luggage, finding transportation from their airport to their home or hotel, finding transportation back to the airport, and so on.

But regardless of one's sympathies for the hard work performed by the flight crew, it is terribly irritating to be left in the lurch en route to a business meeting.

Your rights to recover costs for a delayed flight are much less if the flight is canceled due to a "mutiny" than if the cancellation is due to weather or mechanical problems. The critical question in these situations is: Did you board the aircraft? Your case is best if you have boarded the aircraft, are forced to deplane, and are certain that the delay will prevent you from making a reasonable arrival time at your destination. The station manager in charge of the airport station is also the senior employee at the airport for that specific airline. He or she is the best person for you to deal with.

When an entire crew has to be replaced or if the aircraft returns to the gate for any reason, there is apt to be a long delay. So take action as soon as you step back in the airport terminal.

The station manager will probably be more will-ing to deal with your problem if there is still time to find alternative travel plans on another flight.

Act quickly, or you might miss your only opportunity. Until the full extent of a delay is known and a contingency plan is selected, airline employees are not going to announce the details of a delay. That single first-class seat on a one-stop flight leaving in 10 minutes might be yours if you act immediately.

Dealing with In-Flight Malfunctions

In-flight mechanical problems occur more often than you might realize. Normally, the problem is not a cause for alarm, simply because modern aircraft contain back-up systems that can func-tion temporarily in the event of a failure in the main system.

However, many malfunctions can render an aircraft less stable, which by nature endangers passengers, if only to a slight degree. Even though you are relatively safe in the event of such a mal-function, you might experience fear or discom-fort. Also, the policy of most airlines is that the safety of an aircraft and its passengers comes first, even if that means turning a 747 around in the middle of the Atlantic and heading back to Lon-don, rather than landing on the airstrip of that small island right below the aircraft.

Here are five facts and tips to remember in the event of an in-flight emergency:

☐ If a crew member announces an in-flight prob-lem, even one that sounds like an emergency, it is probably not as serious as you think. The truly serious problems occur so suddenly that there is no time for the crew or passengers to do much of anything. Thus, the very fact that there is time to react to a problem is a good sign and means the odds for a safe landing weigh heavily in your favor.

☐ No matter how disturbing and roller-coaster-like the flight might become, realize that the aircraft is designed to take much greater punishment than any flight can reasonably expect to encounter. The bumpiness of the flight might seem frightening, but as long as you are securely buckled into your seat, the situation is probably not that dangerous.

☐ The flight crew has been well trained to deal with every possible emergency, and you must listen to them. Don't ignore the safety precautions that flight attendants point out prior to departure. You might be a seasoned passenger, but you aren't a seasoned crash victim.

☐ Remain calm. This is not as difficult as you might think, and will increase your chances of surviving a life-threatening situation. It is okay to be frightened without panicking. Some fear can help you remain attentive and prepare your body for a developing emergency. Adrenalin is a wonderful high.

☐ Be ready to act. If the aircraft makes a crash landing, be prepared to evacuate according to the flight crew's prior instructions. Even if you remain calm, other passengers might become paralyzed with fear. You may need to become a catalyst to force others to act.

In-Flight Safety Precautions

You can take several steps to reduce your risk from an in-flight problem. The most obvious step is one that I see hundreds of passengers ignore each year: Keep your seat belt buckled and securely fastened whenever you are seated. Perhaps travelers feel that, just because flight attendants are moving about the cabin, passengers should feel completely safe.

Wrong.

First, flight attendants are at risk when they move about the cabin. However, they are also trained to handle turbulence and other problems. You haven't received any such training. Any sudden change in altitude or balance of the aircraft can send you flying into the overhead compartments, then onto the floor, then back to the overhead compartments, and so on.

WARNING: At the first sign of a potential in-flight emergency, remove sharp objects from your shirt pockets. The pens and pencils that you might carry in your shirt pocket as a normal part of business can be fatal daggers in a crash. Pens, pencils, and other long, pointed items do not belong anywhere on your person if the flight is headed for an emergency landing. The same holds true for contact lenses.

Why You Should Sit Next to an Exit

This is not just a safety measure, but one of comfort as well. Seats that are next to emergency exits generally have more space between them and the seat in front than other seats within the same seating category.

However, on some flights, two exits are located next to each other. In other words, one row and the next row back can each contain a window exit. With this configuration, you will want to sit in the second of the two rows because the seats in the first row, even though they have extra leg room, may not recline fully (or at all).

Which Part of the Aircraft Is Safest?

The airline industry has never publicly acknowledged which seats are safest on any given aircraft. I don't really blame the companies; if they did announce which seats were "safe," these would certainly be the only requested seats on every flight.

Booking a "safe seat" can still be difficult, because there just aren't enough to go around. As soon as I or any other writer points out that the rearmost seats in the aircraft are probably the safest, someone will point out that, at least on international flights, this is generally a smoking section.

My preference, though, is to sit several rows in front of the wing. Here's my reasoning: The section of the aircraft where the wing and the cabin come together is generally the strongest part of the plane. Also, this section is also usually far enough forward to be in a quiet part of the craft, and usually is close to one or more exits that lead directly to the wing for a quick and safer exit from a downed craft. In the event of a "nose down" encounter with the ground, the area just ahead of the wing will still be far enough back from the nose to remain intact following the initial crash.

Again, I mention these facts not to invoke fear but to help you to prepare *just in case*. For the vast majority of in-flight problems and emergencies, the plane will land safely. However, it may not land at your intended arrival location.

What to Do if You Don't Arrive at Your Destination

Here you are, back at your point of embarkation, or worse, in some strange place, all due to a malfunction that caused an unscheduled stop. In these cases, the airline will usually go to great lengths to help you in your hour of inconvenience. But at the same time, the airline will be as practical and as economical as possible.

If you find that you are not getting the assistance you expect under the circumstances, demand satisfaction. But don't let your voice get too loud and don't make reckless threats to sue everyone in sight. The patient, determined, and calmly assertive individual is more likely to get results in this situation.

One good approach is to suggest a solution that will satisfy you. For instance, if there is another flight headed to your destination that you could reasonably catch, confide to the airline representative that an acceptable solution would be to book you on the available flight. Usually, these types of arrangements can be made. Again, behave reasonably and you will be more likely to be treated reasonably.

Dealing with Terrorism

Airline hijackings reached almost epidemic proportions in the 1970s. But in a majority of those cases, the hijackers were expatriate Cubans who were homesick and wanted to return to their homeland in the only way that seemed possible—by hijacking an aircraft. Usually, these planes landed safely, although the passengers experienced the fright of their lives.

Today, air hijackings have expanded to include terrorist activities. Terrorists are far more dangerous than many of the hijackers of past years. They are angry, desperate, and often eager to make martyrs of themselves and innocent passengers to make a political statement. The airlines and airport security officials know this and in many cases have unfortunately only added to the confusion.

Consider evidence uncovered following the bombing of Pan Am Flight 103, which exploded December 21, 1988, over Lockerbie, Scotland. All indications are that international security agencies knew of a bomb threat and failed to take action. In the case of a recent flight I was on, security forces believed a bomb threat existed, but didn't know what action to take. If you want to survive or guard against hijackings, terrorist actions, and other potential airline calamities, you may have to rely on your own knowledge and abilities.

The Psychology of Flight Security

To some degree, the very attempt to keep a would-be terrorist off an aircraft by relying on the myriad existing security measures is like keeping a dedicated burglar out of your home by putting a single lock on the door. The fact is that modern security will keep the novice or that desperate Cuban national from hijacking an aircraft. For the most part, though, the so-called airport security checkpoints have holes you could drive a tank through. True, some airports have perfected the art of security to a level where only the truly insane and fanatical would attempt to supersede it. But how many terrorists are sane or unfanatical?

So, although existing airport security measures might weed out many garden-variety or amateur terrorists, they don't stand a chance against the trained pros or crazies who are determined to advance their cause. Also, because each skyjacking has unpredictable circumstances, it is difficult to train flight crew members in how to react in these circumstances.

What You Can Do to Survive a Hijacking

Recognize Which International Flights Are at Risk

Any international flight can be a target for terrorists, but some are more likely to be than others. Often, the time of year that you travel can be at least as important a consideration as the countries you are traveling between. Certain events attract terrorists. If you travel frequently on international flights, this very frequency can put you at a greater risk than the occasional holiday traveler. The five basic events listed here all attract terrorist activity. If possible, avoid traveling to countries when they are affected by these events.

☐ A major political or national holiday, or other festive event, adds importance to a terrorist act and provides automatic visibility.

☐ The anniversary of some event that is of importance to terrorist groups can be used by terrorists to commemorate the event.

☐ A recent political act can touch off a wave of terrorist activity, usually as a retaliatory act.

☐ The capture of one or more terrorists could cause other members of that terrorist organization to lash out at any airline affiliated with the country responsible for the capture.

☐ Public statements made by a terrorist organization against a country or other group of people add risk. The threat *might* be idle, but it can be used by other terrorist organizations to capitalize on the publicity potential.

To help in identifying events that could be meaningful to terrorists, contact the Citizens Emergency Center, Room 4800 N.S., U.S. State Department, Washington, DC 20520. The telephone number is (202) 647-5225. Ask it to describe any specific safety problems you may encounter in the area to which you are flying. Also ask if there is any reason you should avoid flying on certain airlines.

You should also be alert to current events while you are traveling. If you travel during a time of international crisis, keep abreast of any terrorist movement that might impact your travel plans. If you are abroad and do not speak the language native to the country you are in, try to find a copy of an international newspaper published in English. If this is not possible, try to find a radio and listen to a shortwave BBC or

Radio America broadcast to find out whether you are in any danger.

WARNING: Never transport a package for anyone, unless you are absolutely certain of its contents. Even then, it is best not to carry anything that you do not own. Remember, it was a bomb built into a small radio that caused the crash of Pan Am Flight 103 in Lockerbie.

If the practicality of business makes it rude or impossible to reject a present given to you at the last moment, tell airport security that you do not know what is inside the package or present and ask the official to put it through a detector.

General common sense will help keep you out of a lot of trouble, and although some of the following may seem too simple they should be your absolute habits when you travel anywhere internationally.

Fourteen Tips That Can Save Your Life

Here are some tips that can prevent you from becoming a target for terrorists when you travel internationally:

☐ *Maintain a low profile.* At all costs, avoid looking like a wealthy American. Also avoid dress that pegs you as an American student or professor (sweatshirt with the name of a university emblazoned on it or a tweed jacket with arm patches). Try to dress out of style. You don't have to dress like a slob, but just in a moderate, middle-of-the-road style that does not draw attention to yourself. Dress as would the least likely person in the world to have an enemy.

☐ *Avoid first-class seating if you are flying on high-risk routes.* This is the closest part of the aircraft to the pilot's compartment and is apt to become the hijacker's headquarters.

☐ *Sit in the middle of any specific compartment, near to but not next to a window exit if possible.*

Any serious hijacking is apt to be well organized, with enough terrorists on board the flight to take control over each compartment. However, each terrorist is likely to take up a post at the front of a compartment. Blend into a group of passengers to avoid being singled out as a hostage.

☐ *Do nothing to draw attention to yourself.* Do not challenge a hijacker; do not ask what a hijacker's plans are; do not even look in the direction of a hijacker. Eye contact may be dangerous.

☐ *Do not play the role of hero.* Play it absolutely safe unless you see some incredibly good opportunity to take control of a situation and if you know you are in the physical condition necessary to do so. Chances are that such a true opportunity will not occur, so be cautious first and heroic only as a last resort. It may be your last act.

☐ *Identify and make mental notes on how to use all available escape routes.* If the opportunity for escape exists, it might be in total darkness, and your survival might depend on being able to locate and use a mechanical exit with little or no light.

☐ *Recognize that an external attempt to overtake the hijackers could occur at any time the plane is on the ground.* Be alert to signals from outside the aircraft. If a SWAT team or other form of antiterrorist force storms the aircraft, the first thing you might see or hear is one or more sudden blasts from a device called a "stun grenade." Much like a superpowerful firecracker, the stun grenade throws off little shrapnel amid a loud bang and a severely shocking blast wave. It also has the ability to rupture eardrums, knock people down, and cause some physical harm. If a sudden blast occurs, put your head and the rest of your body down as far you can get but remain off the floor. If the blast is followed by the sharp cracking of automatic gunfire and more stun grenades, you can be sure an attempt to storm the aircraft is underway. You should be thinking about how to use the emergency exits.

The attack on the aircraft should be over within seconds. There is no chance of a prolonged fire fight in this kind of event. The hijackers will either give up, get killed, or try to blow up the aircraft. Once the sharp, hard cracking sound of automatic gunfire is over, it is time to move. Help others out of the plane in a hurried, but not panicked, manner.

☐ *Avoid military dress or even a military appearance.* Don't even check in bags that have a military appearance (like a duffel bag) or a military I.D. If your flight is the target of hijackers, the hijackers will be checking in, too, and will likely make a mental note of anyone who needs to be subdued quickly or will make a high-profile hostage.

☐ *Carry only "soft identification," or identification that will not target you as a hostage or a danger to hijackers.* If your job is in any way political or diplomatic, invest in some form of identification that suggests you are a passive and benign person.

One solution is to have a "pseudonation passport." These are not falsified passports, because they do not purport to be real. I know several business travelers who carry them in case a terrorist demands to see their passport. They can then hand over a quite authentic-looking document that describes them in a nonexistent language as being a citizen from Natarovia, or Saint Kits, or Quadaloop. People advertise the sale of this kind of passport in almost every issue of all English-language international newspapers.

A simpler approach is to have a few business cards made up in the name of Cummings Plumbing Supply, or something equally disarming. Any small print shop can do this for you, at a cost of less than $20. Use an address that is unlikely to offend, like this: Villa Santa Rosa, 555 Avinguda Princep Benlloch, Andorra La Vella, Andorra. This small country high in the Pyrenees between Spain and France is not likely to be on anyone's hit list.

If you are a diplomat or are traveling on military orders when a hijacking starts, hide your passport or orders somewhere far from your body. As a preventive measure, ask the State Department to issue you a regular passport in addition to the diplomatic one. You do not want to be the person singled out.

☐ *Relax.* I know, this is much easier said than done. But you simply will not be able to take action, when necessary, unless you are calm and in a ready state of mind. Do not take a tranquilizer unless you are going to pieces. If your seatmates offer you something to "calm your nerves," decline unless being put to sleep is better for your present state of mind than being hysterical.

☐ *Maintain a positive image of survival.* A positive outlook can supply you with the right mental skills you will need to escape your situation in good mental and physical health.

☐ *If the hijackers single you out, attempt to make the confrontation as personal and as human as possible.* There is no need to prove anything to anyone or to be embarrassed about crying or talking about your family. I know one businessman who has a photograph of his "wife and seven children." The photograph is a fake, but he wants to have it available in case he needs some sympathetic treatment by terrorists.

☐ *After the ordeal has ended, seek professional help, even if you think you survived unscarred.* Counseling can mean the difference between getting on with your life and having disruptive nightmares for years.

☐ *Never sign a release document.* Airlines may send out a team of insurance adjusters to reduce their potential claims from injured passengers. Just because you are not bloodied does not mean you have not been injured, so do not sign anything. Do and say nothing that can reduce your future rights to a claim if the airline is proven to have been negligent in any way.

Where and How to Complain

Because airline safety is a big job, it is not always managed as well as it should be. Report any situation that seems to be a safety violation of any kind, as soon as you can. Write a brief description of what happened and where (in flight, in the airport, and so on). Send a copy to each of the following:

1. The airline, to the attention of Security
2. Airline Transport Association (for domestic flights)
   1709 New York Avenue N.W.
   Washington, DC 20006
3. IATA (for International Flights)
   1730 K Street N.W.
   Suite 900
   Washington, DC 20006

≡ 10
How to Survive Political Unrest

The increasing climate of political unrest is a growing concern for travelers who frequently must cross international boundaries or do business in a country torn by civil unrest. War is something many people just read about in the morning newspaper. But for many business travelers, war zones are a travel reality.

One problem for U.S. citizens traveling abroad is that the United States is seen as a bully by many smaller countries. You might not make foreign policy or even know much about foreign policy, but aggressors in other countries might target you anyway if it is apparent that you are American. If terrorists or political factions need a scapegoat or hostage to make a point or to negotiate, U.S. citizens are ideal.

Political unrest tends to take many by surprise, including political leaders and policy makers. For instance, it was reported that Soviet intelligence never notified President Gorbachev about the impending attack by the Iraqis on Kuwait. The Soviets just didn't think Saddam Hussein was a serious threat. Unfortunately, political groups make threats constantly, and it is difficult to determine which ones are serious.

Unrest and war certainly aren't confined to the Middle East. Major U.S. urban areas during the 1960s were the scenes of violent racial strife. And American campuses in the late 1960s and early 1970s also were targets of violent protests and political mayhem.

Some of the paradises of this world have had their problems, and still do. Bermuda is an example. The first moment that I set foot there I thought I had gone directly past GO and to heaven. I was sure it would be one of my favorite business and vacation spots for years to come. Then, with great suddenness, a native uprising took place, causing several horrible days and nights for the whites who were on the island at the time. Paradise lost, again.

On the other hand, I suppose a law-abiding family from Bermuda would have had a couple of sleepless nights had they been vacationing in New York City during the night of the Great Power Outage. Political unrest is a relative concept; unless you know your way around any large city like a native and what to expect and where to go, gang activity or racial tension can be a major problem for you.

Safety Tips During Political Unrest

If you are caught in the midst of political turmoil, keep these six tips in mind:

□ *Find out which faction is against which faction.* Then determine which would be the most likely to protect you or the least likely to harm you. (You might discover that each side poses a threat to your safety.) This knowledge can save you when you have to decide who to confide in and whether to admit you are a U.S. citizen. If neither side is pro-American or pro-Western, then you must relate to neither side. Remember to maintain a low profile. Even if your passport says you are American, you can be of Picaran descent. Can you speak Picaran (or any convincing gibberish, in a pinch)? Your ability to bluff your way through a confrontation can save your life.

☐ *Realize that even the "friendly" side can be dangerous.* You are in a situation in which there may be no real friend, only varying degrees of enemies. If there is a deterioration of law and order, civil war might be the next threshold. If that is the case, you cannot trust anyone from either side—unless you know individuals personally and have confidence in what they tell you. Nonetheless, you must try to decide which side is the fire and which is the frying pan, because between the two, the frying pan is the safest bet.

☐ *Get to a safe place.* This should be your first goal when chaos rules the streets. What place is safe? If you are in the middle of a minor skirmish, like a labor strike that deteriorates into a mob, it might simply be enough to distance yourself from the mob scene. If the scene is more violent, find a nearby hotel. Make a reservation if things are getting nasty in the street. If things go poorly for the pro-Western faction, a hotel room is a far better place to be than on the street, or even in the lobby of the hotel. If you can, get to your own hotel. If you know the city and you know you do not have to traverse the mob or other scene of violence, take a cab, bus, or anything that will take you away from "them," and closer to your hotel.

The American Embassy is not my idea of a safe place. This is an instant target for an angry mob, especially if U.S. action bears the brunt of the mob's anger. The Swiss or Canadian Embassy would be a better choice, but any place not threatened will do.

☐ *Reduce your profile.* If you are on foreign soil, try not to look like an American. In fact, try to blend in with the natives. This might mean abandoning that $500 briefcase, which will target you as an important person—not a desirable identity during a period of unrest.

☐ *Have cash on hand.* It is a mistake to travel in any unstable part of the world without carrying hard currency. The U.S. dollar is still good and essential in most Central and South American areas. In European areas, the German mark or the Swiss franc will do nicely, as well as the dollar. Although the dollar is no longer king, in the rest of the world it is most certainly the prince of currencies. At any rate, if a violent situation deteriorates, all the travelers checks in the world may not be worth a dime. People will want easy-to-convert currency.

☐ *Do not go out at night.* Even when a nasty scene seems to have calmed down, do not trust the truce. Get your business done as early as possible, then leave for home or at least for a safe country.

There are many sad stories of travelers who have been caught in the middle of an angry mob. Mass hysteria replaces rational thought and, without reasonable actions, otherwise normal people can and do act in horrible ways. Never attempt to be a bystander when you see a crowd turning ugly, for any reason. Let the members of the press be the observers. You get the hell out.

The previous chapter covered some of the dangers that occur during aircraft hijackings—one of which is the chance that you will be taken hostage. You could become a hostage, though, on firm soil just as easily as on a plane.

If You Are Taken Hostage

According to experts I have spoken with, being taken hostage is not a death sentence. On the contrary, a hostage is a bargaining chip. If your hostage-takers kill you, their bargaining power is gone. It is in their best interest to keep you alive and healthy. If you believe you are a hostage risk, consider the following tips:

☐ Have a planned itinerary that is known only to those who need to know your whereabouts.

☐ Check in from time to time on a regular basis.

☐ Have several "code" names or phrases you can use when you check in, so that you can pass on and receive messages of importance. For example, "Oh, please tell Frank O'Hara that Beirut will love his new book" might be a coded message indicating that you are being held against your will.

☐ Travel with alternate identification. At least on the surface, you can be someone else. If you use this tactic, play it all the way. Do not show up at the airport in the company limousine, with half a dozen staff members escorting you all the way to the check-in counter, where you give up your mink-lined Burberry for a common London Fog prior to boarding the flight.

☐ Leave behind detailed instructions that will

- Explain the important factors of your assets, will, bank accounts, and critical details of your potential estate.
- Indicate who your family members should turn to if you or someone else gets word to them that you are being held hostage.
- Give sufficient facts that explain why someone might try to take you as a hostage.

— Remind those at home that any negotiating should be left to professionals but that the family should insist on being kept informed.

☐ Keep up-to-date on the political events in the areas in which you travel. The simple recognition of a face, or the knowledge of the "reasons" one faction is fighting another, can save your life.

☐ Do not be predictable. If you are staying in one town or hotel for several nights, vary your daily plans. Do not rise and follow the same routine every day. Avoid taking any steps that might announce where you will be and when during your travels.

No matter how many precautions you take, realize that someone has to be taken hostage. If it happens to you, what do you do?

☐ *Relax and remain hopeful.* Hostage situations might not make the newspapers every day, but they are remembered. Be assured that people are taking steps to get you released.

☐ *If you have a medical problem and require attention, weigh the risks of calling attention to yourself.* If your medical alert is life threatening, or you have reason to believe that those who have taken you as a hostage will be sympathetic, then ask for attention, or even for release.

☐ *Be alert to everything going on around you.* If you are on a flight, observe what is happening without appearing inquisitive. If you have been taken away in a car or are being transported, listen to everything said and to the sounds outside. You may be able to hear clues that tell you where you are being taken, which will provide you with a better chance for escape should the opportunity arise.

☐ *Do not trust those who are keeping you hostage.* They are apt to want to lull you into submission so that you do not become difficult. To minimize their control over you, let them believe that you trust them, but don't. This may be very difficult to pull off, but as a practical matter, it is better for the keeper to believe the prisoner has been dominated than to realize the prisoner will be fighting and trying to escape.

☐ *Do not set mental goals regarding when you expect to be released.* This can lead to disappointment and depression if the event drags on for days, weeks, or longer.

☐ *Have advance ideas about what you might do to occupy your mind.* People have maintained their sanity and positive frame of mind during years of captivity by having something to concentrate on.

☐ *Do not try to use your high-school karate skills.* No matter how many martial arts skills you might possess, the terrorist will be armed and might blow your kneecaps off just to keep you still.

☐ *Do not be too proud.* Humans are emotional animals and many people from European or Middle Eastern parts of the world relate to human emotions, such as fear and tears. Being cold and aloof might do more to separate you and make you a candidate for execution.

☐ *If the opportunity to escape exists, and you are physically capable, then act and act quickly.* Only attempt escape if you feel that you have a reasonable chance to deal with events taking place outside. If you speak the language of the country you are held in, you know the area, and you believe you can get help nearby, then escape might be worthwhile.

The list of hostages who have escaped is impressive, and many have found safe passage through some of the most harrowing circumstances.

11

When What Can Go Wrong, Does

When you are in comfortable territory, in your home city or state, small problems can be solved easily. If your car breaks down, you can call a tow truck or a friend for help. If your credit cards are over their limit, there's usually a cash machine nearby. Even many big problems can be handled in a fairly routine manner; if someone you are with becomes gravely ill, for example, you probably know where the nearest emergency room is. But when you are traveling, small problems can quickly turn into big problems, and big problems can mushroom into disasters—if you are not equipped to deal with the situation. When you are traveling, your usual support network of friends, family, and business associates might not be available to help you in a time of crisis. And if you are traveling in a foreign country, language and cultural barriers can make it difficult to communicate your problem.

This chapter provides some examples of problems that can and often do occur to the frequent traveler, and offers ways to prevent them from happening or, if a problem already exists, how to prevent it from getting out of hand.

Here are eight potential problems to plan for when you travel:

☐ A person you are traveling with becomes seriously ill or dies.

☐ You are arrested.

☐ You are in an accident.

☐ Your rental car breaks down.

☐ Your credit cards are refused.

☐ Your hotel has no record of your reservation.

☐ You are mugged, robbed, or your property is burglarized.

☐ You are in a fire.

When Your Travel Companion Becomes Ill or Dies

Of course, illness and death can strike you or your fellow associates at home as well as during travel. If a problem like this occurs at home, you will have others around who can provide assistance. If the problem happens when you and your associate are away from home, it might be up to you to know what steps to take. So it makes sense to learn how to handle medical emergencies that can arise during travel.

Sudden Choking

Travelers spend a good deal of their time dining out, often eating unusual foods and in unusual quantities. If you suspect someone seated near you is choking on food (usually because a piece of food is blocking the windpipe), request help from the restaurant staff immediately and with urgency. Often waiters are well trained in dealing with these kinds of emergencies. If you are unable to find help within seconds, take action yourself. Follow these steps immediately:

1. Have the person try to cough up the food.
2. Try to calm the person; reassure him or her. When a person chokes, panic can set in extremely quickly, compounding the problem.
3. Send someone for help. Do not leave the choking person unless absolutely necessary.
4. Quickly lay the person down on his or her side and, with the heel of your hand, strike hard in the middle of the back between the shoulder blades. Do this several times in quick succession. For children small enough to be lifted by their feet, do so and strike the child's back forcefully several times. A larger child or small adult can be placed over your lap with the person's head near the floor and hit as indicated in the back.
5. Clear the victim's mouth to see whether anything can be removed.
6. If the person becomes unconscious, you should begin artificial respiration.

Another approach that gets rapid, effective results is the Heimlich maneuver. However, this maneuver requires greater strength than the preceding procedure and should not be performed on a child less than one year of age.

1. If the choking person is standing, get behind him or her and wrap your arms around the person's waist. Make a fist and put it just above the navel and below the rib cage.
2. With the thumb side of your fist lightly against the person's abdomen, grasp your

fist with your other hand and press it into the victim's abdomen with a quick upward thrust. Repeat several times if necessary.

3. If the choking person is lying down, put the person on his or her back and kneel astride the hips (or next to the hips for young children). Face the victim.

4. Place the heel of one hand on the victim's abdomen slightly above the navel and below the rib cage, and your other hand on top of the first. Press into the abdomen with a quick, upward thrust, repeating several times if necessary.

If a Person Is Not Breathing

In a drowning or other accident where the victim is not breathing, you must start mouth-to-mouth resuscitation as soon as you have the person sturdily in your grasp, even if you are still in shallow water. Once you are out of the water, lay the person face down to see whether any water will drain out. Then follow these steps:

1. Turn the victim on his or her back and quickly make sure there is nothing loose in the mouth and that the person's tongue is not blocking the throat. Clear the tongue from the throat if necessary.

2. Place a coat or something soft (if immediately available) under the person's head. Then arch the head back, as though the person was trying to look as far backward as possible. Push or pull the jaw as far out as you can.

3. For an adult victim, pinch the nose and cover the open mouth with your own and blow strongly into the victim's lungs.

4. Turn your ear to the mouth and listen for any air escaping toward you. Take another breath and continue this vigorously, at a

pace of 12 to 15 times per minute. A child will require less air, but at a faster pace— up to 20 to 25 short breaths per minute. You must listen every few breaths for the air coming back out. If none is coming out, you are not getting any air into the lungs. Something might be stuck in the throat. Perform one of the methods just described for dislodging an object from the throat, then continue the resuscitation.

5. If the person vomits or spits up water or other matter, turn the person on his or her side and wipe out the mouth before continuing with the resuscitation.

6. Do not give up. People have been revived even after four hours of this treatment.

Make Sure the Paramedics Are Called

Even if you feel your attempts at resuscitating a victim are getting nowhere, make sure paramedics or an ambulance has been summoned immediately. No matter how dead a person might look, it might be that vital signs are so shallow that they are difficult to detect. You should never discontinue a life-saving procedure until someone qualified to assess the situation has arrived.

Guard the Victim's Personal Possessions

In the moments that surround the chaos of an accident or sudden death, there are people who will take advantage of the situation and attempt to steal the victim's possessions. The whereabouts of a briefcase, portable computer, and carry-on bags will take a low priority during the critical moments of an emergency. Thieves know this. At the first reasonably safe opportunity, make sure the personal effects of the ill or dead person, as well as your own, are visible and within easy reach. If possible, place the belongings in a safe place or entrust a responsible person to guard them.

Make Yourself Understood

There will be times when you find it difficult to make others aware of a serious problem. In the confines and general noise of an aircraft, it is not always easy to make yourself heard or to contact a crew member to explain what you know about a person in distress. Add to the confusion the difficulty in communicating to those around you if you are on a foreign carrier. In the case of a road accident, all of these communication problems might exist and even be compounded by the fact that you have been injured yourself and cannot move or speak well.

In any of these circumstances, it is important to assert yourself. Force yourself to be heard and understood as much as possible when you have information that can be helpful. Once you have alerted others nearby, someone will probably come forth who can communicate both with you and the others. If not, try repeating, slowly and loudly, one or more of these appropriate words: *Doc-tor, Hos-pi-tal, Po-lice, Me-di-co.*

If you are trying to communicate by phone, the problem can be more difficult. Your first step is to request someone who can understand you. Convey the urgency of the situation in the tone of your voice. If you are in a hotel room, a call to the reception area of the lobby is a good idea, because someone there is probably able to speak English.

If all else fails, dial 911. This emergency number works in many countries outside the U.S. Often the people who staff these emergency switchboards are multilingual and can help.

"Okay, Pal, You're Under Arrest"

Frightening words, these, especially if they are uttered to you in a strange city or country. So you're the pillar of the community, a respected businessperson in your hometown, and the father or mother of seven little angels? This has to be a big mistake. How *dare* the officer arrest *you*?

Now is not the time to become incensed. You will only make a bad situation worse. Instead, your ability to extricate yourself from this situation depends on how well you remain calm and coherent.

Consider some possibilities. You engage in some activity that seems to you to be perfectly harmless but is a serious breach of law in the country you are visiting. Perhaps a local has approached you and asked to buy your radio or your leather jacket—at a great price. Free-market enterprise at work, right? In some places, you could be accused of selling contraband or of some other black-market violation.

Another situation: Your dress, skin color, accent, or other features peg you as a foreigner. In some cities and towns, this automatically marks you as either a suspicious character or an easy hit for a con job—often done with the cooperation or even participation of the local police.

The best way to avoid these situations is to know the customs and laws of a country before you cross its borders. However, this isn't always possible unless you've lived in the country for a while or are traveling with someone who has. If you do find yourself in such a precarious situation, maintain your calm. It is possible that you can explain to officials that you did not mean to break the law, you were simply unaware that you were violating anything. But perhaps not. . . .

Your Legal Rights Change When You Leave the United States

Americans traveling abroad forget how much freedom there is in the United States. In some countries a prisoner—even a foreigner—has virtually no immediate rights at all. Countries at war can always make a military arrest, in which case you might not even get a trial before you are locked away behind bars or even shot.

Although much of Western Europe has a legal system that grants some rights to an arrested individual, it is not unusual for the following procedures to apply:

1. A person may be held for up to seven days, while an interrogation or investigation is made, without being allowed to see or talk to anyone outside the detention area. This rule obviously varies from country to country. England has one of the strictest detention laws; Holland is much more relaxed on this point.
2. Establishment of bail may be slow or nonexistent. If you are a foreigner, you are an automatic flight risk. A trial may take a long time to come to court (sound familiar?), and you may be held without bail for as long as it takes (months or even years).
3. Trial by jury may not exist or be allowed for the offense you are charged with.
4. There may be no such thing as plea-bargaining.
5. Police who cannot communicate with you may become frustrated or confused, and take whatever you do or say out of context. They may not like you very much, either, simply because you are an American. They may try to shut you up in a very painful way.

If you should be arrested abroad, remember these important tips:

☐ Do not engage in any name calling. Never show disrespect or anger for a police offer who might question you.

☐ Save your energy and argument until you are out of the arrest environment and can deal with someone who has greater authority.

☐ Never, but never, attempt to bribe anyone in any situation where you are unsure about the customs or how to handle the bribe. You might only strengthen the case against you.

☐ Ask the judge or other person of authority to explain your rights or to appoint someone who will. If you do not speak the local language, you may have a major problem unless you can encourage the authorities to find a translator for you. Remember, the more cooperative you are, the more cooperative the authorities are likely to be.

☐ If you are allowed to make a phone call, make sure you have planned in advance and know who to call and where to reach your party. If the hour of the morning or night makes it impossible to call an attorney, call your hotel and explain what has happened. Implore them to contact your office (or travel agent, if necessary) and to notify the American Embassy of your plight.

☐ Get legal help as quickly as you can. Do not try to deal with the justice system on your own, even the U.S. justice system. Possibly a local lawyer can resolve any misunderstandings quickly and either reduce or eliminate the need to spend time in jail.

☐ If you are allowed to post bail, do not skip town. The risk isn't worth the chance that you might be caught.

When You Are in an Accident

If you are in an accident abroad, your ability to deal with the situation might depend on the insurance coverage you have. Keep in mind that insurance purchased in the United States does not necessarily apply outside of U.S. borders, and even if your policy does apply to foreign travel, the coverage might be different and woefully incomplete.

Make sure you have looked into supplemental insurance to cover your foreign travel—before you leave. Also check with your business and credit card companies to determine what coverage you might be offered under their umbrella policies. If you are sued for an accident while you are traveling abroad on business, it may be that your company can be held liable, not you personally. Find out before you leave home and make sure you are covered for all possible accident situations.

The following is your list of procedures in case of accident. Make a copy and put one in each car you and members of your family drive, and stash another in your briefcase for those trips out of town in rental cars.

☐ Get the names, addresses, and phone numbers of several witnesses.

☐ What other vehicles were involved? Write the name, address, and phone number of other drivers, vehicle license numbers, driver's license information, and any insurance information the drivers can provide.

☐ If you are in a cab or bus, get the company name and insurance company; the driver's name, address, and phone; and the identification (license and number) of the cab or bus.

☐ If the accident takes place on a train, make sure you keep all information regarding the departure time and destination of the train.

☐ Write a description of the location of the accident, including nearest cross streets and relevant landmarks.

☐ Note the time of the accident.

☐ Write a description of what happened. Get it down while you are still on the scene (but in a calm, rational state of mind). Details tend to fade or blur into one another over time.

☐ Jot down the name and number of the police officer in charge (if one arrives).

☐ Get the police case number or accident report number from the officer in charge at the scene of the accident.

☐ Note who was injured and where treatment was given.

☐ If a camera is available, have someone take as many photos as possible to show the location, damage, witnesses, your condition, and any injured persons.

☐ Even though you may not feel injured, you should realize that excitement, confusion, and mild shock all can keep you from recognizing or feeling an injury, even a broken bone. Have yourself checked by any attending paramedic. If any possibility exists for injury, see your doctor immediately. If there is any possible injury, go to your doctor.

☐ Never admit fault, even if you feel sure you were at fault. Circumstances might be discovered later that place the blame on another party. You will then have to explain your admission of fault.

☐ Relax as best you can. The best way to deal with an emergency or a shocking situation is to remain as calm as possible.

When Your Rental Car Breaks Down

One rental car resale company advertises that used rental cars are a wise purchase because they are driven only by nerdy businesspeople who wear thick glasses, carry briefcases, and are overly cautious about everything. These aren't the types of people to drive a vehicle carelessly or reck-lessly.

Although this stereotype car renter might truly reflect the general condition of a rental car conditioned for resale, minor mechanical problems are actually *more* likely to exist with a rental car than with your own car. Part of the problem stems from the fact that mechanical problems often go unreported by previous users of a rental car, who don't want to be delayed, charged, or blamed for anything that is wrong with the vehicle. The mechanical problem is passed from driver to driver until you are behind the wheel, traveling down a mountain road, and notice that your brakes are failing.

When you rent from a major car agency—like Budget, Thrifty, Hertz, Avis, or Dollar—you can probably get a replacement vehicle easily and with only minor inconvenience.

However, suppose you decide to rent from a local agency to save a few dollars per day in fees. You need to make some sales calls a few hundred miles from the agency's office and while you are out of town, the car breaks down. You might find yourself stranded and even have to pay to have the problem repaired.

Prevention dictates that you ask questions when you rent a car. Use the following list to find out everything you need to know before you get behind the wheel of a rental car.

☐ What is the 24-hour emergency phone number for the areas in which you will be driving? If there is no 24-hour number, consider another agency.

☐ What is the rental agency's responsibility if the car fails to function, for any reason?

☐ Will the car agency pay your expenses if you have to rent a car from another agency due to a mechanical failure?

☐ What insurance coverage is provided with the rental car for collision, liability, malfunction, and theft? What is the maximum limit of those coverages, and is there a deductible?

☐ Does your credit card insurance cover 100 percent of collision costs? If so, do not pay the collision damage waiver (CDW) offered by the rental car agency.

☐ Are there any exclusions or exceptions to your own insurance coverage or to the agency's CDW?

☐ Will the agency bring another car to your location if this one fails to work?

Assuming you have received satisfactory answers to these questions and have signed a rental agreement, inspect the car before you drive it. Walk around the car. If there is a scratch, dent, or broken part, make a note of it. Get into the car and inspect the interior. Do any parts look broken? Is any fabric torn or vinyl cracked? If so, make a note of it. Turn on the ignition. Does the engine sound like it's idling correctly? Do you hear any unusual sounds? Again, make any notes necessary.

If you notice any problems inside or outside the car, you probably are not in a position to walk back inside the airport terminal or wherever the rental car counters are located. Chances are you are in the middle of a rental fleet parking lot, miles from the airport terminal and driven to this spot by the agency's shuttle bus. In this case, you should drive the car to the exit point or to the rental office if there is one on the lot. At the exit from most rental car lots, a guard will be waiting to check you out of the lot. The guard will usually ask to see your rental contract. Make this person aware of your notes, and have him or her look at all the problems you have encountered. Then have the guard write on the rental contract that the car has been inspected and that the problems found are verified to have occurred before you rented the car.

If the guard or lot attendant does not have the authority to make this verification, get directions to the closest point where you can have an authorized person check those items. Too often, business travelers plan their schedules so tightly that there is no time to return a car after problems have been discovered. Try to add some time between your airport arrival and the time required to be at a meeting place. In most cases, you might not need the extra time, but if you do, you can take corrective steps without feeling rushed.

Once all this has been done, you will have the proper document necessary to make demands on the car agency for a replacement auto. If you discover a problem with the car once you have left the lot and you do not feel the car is safe to operate, insist that the agency provide you with a replacement.

If you do not receive a replacement, you might be entitled to compensation for the following:

☐ Gas and mileage charges you incur in returning the car, and added mileage and gas on the alternate car. When I had to drive more than 100 miles to exchange a National rental car, I insisted that the round trip of 200 miles be deducted from my final bill. I also requested to be compensated or not charged for the fuel I had used to drive the 200 miles. The rental agent agreed to both demands.

☐ Inconvenience. This is a difficult topic for an agency to handle, because too many customers make unreasonable demands for compensation. However, if you calmly explain in detail the ways in which you have been inconvenienced, an agent might agree to compensate you in some way. Aid the negotiations by suggesting that your contract price be downgraded to that for a lower-class vehicle. Or ask that you be charged based on the weekly rate instead of the daily rate you had initially signed for.

When Your Hotel Reservation Has Disappeared

So, you've taken care of any rental car problems and have arrived at the hotel ready to relax, eat a pleasant dinner, and get a good night's sleep. The sign on the marquee near the hotel lobby says "Welcome Shriners." When you announce yourself to the hotel desk clerk, you are told that no reservation exists for you. And, of course, the visiting Shriners have taken every available room in this hotel and possibly at most other hotels in the city.

There are two techniques you can use to guarantee that a hotel reservation will not vanish on your arrival:

☐ Obtain a confirmation number or other locator number when your reservation is made. Bring this number with you at check-in. This code links your name and other information to your request. If an agent spelled your name incorrectly when the reservation was made, the confirmation number might be the only way to cross-reference your reservation.

☐ If you receive the reservation notice that many hotel companies send, review it to ensure that the date of arrival and length of stay are correct. Carry this confirmation notice with you when you travel, because it can prove that you have a confirmed reservation.

If you do not receive a confirmation notice in the mail, confirm your reservation by phone at least 24 hours before you arrive. If your name has been spelled improperly, if you or your travel agent wrote down your confirmation number incorrectly, or if the hotel reservation agent booked you for the wrong week, you need to know this before you arrive at your destination. This notice gives you time to clear up the problem or to find other accommodations.

For international travel or travel that must be managed extremely carefully, ask your travel agent to send a telex requesting that a confirmation telex or fax be sent in reply. Have a copy of that return telex with you when you arrive at your hotel.

If Nothing Else Has Worked

Even when you take care to confirm your reservation, there can be times when you still will be told that you have no reservation. Why? Because the hotel employee has canceled you out of the system erroneously. It isn't unusual for someone to call to cancel a reservation only to cancel *your* reservation accidentally. Alternatively, you may have fallen victim to a growing practice that the hotel industry seems to have learned from the airlines: overbooking.

Even worse, you might have neglected to guarantee your room with a credit card or advance payment, and you arrived later than the 6 P.M. hold time. To avoid this, simply phone the hotel prior to the end of the hold time if you think you will be late. Your reservation will generally be extended, even though you do not guarantee it with a credit card. Make sure you get the name of the person you speak with, in case you need to deal with that person later.

Assuming you have made a valid reservation, you are at the right hotel, and you are on time, what should you do when you are denied the right to check in?

1. Plant yourself like a potted fern in front of the hotel desk. Make it clear that you do not plan to move until your problem

is resolved. Do not let anyone divert you to "the manager's office" or to some other quiet place where they can deal with you on the hotel's terms. A complaint made at the check-in desk will be heard by other customers and will prevent the reservation clerk from doing his or her work. As long as you control the location of the disagreement, you will maintain bargaining leverage.

2. Present evidence of your reservation. If you are simply past the hold time for the reservation, remind the clerk that you called from the airport (or wherever) and mention the name of the person you spoke with. Stress that this person promised to hold the reservation for you. If you are on time and the hotel simply does not have a reservation for you, do not immediately assume that you cannot get a room. Some reservation agents like to play games with the power they have, and I'll let them have their fun as long as I get my room in the end, and I am not inconvenienced.

3. When you are told that you do not have a confirmed reservation, say, "Even still, you have a room for me, don't you?"

4. If step 3 does not produce a room, ask "Why not?" This usually gets some kind of reply. The response probably will be some kind of runaround. When the reservations clerk finishes the nonanswer, ask, "What is the management of this hotel going to do about my need for accommodations as reserved?" It may be that the problem is an overbooked hotel and they really do not have a room for you and the hotel may do everything to convince you that you, your travel agent, the tour operator, or someone else is to blame.

Possibly, the hotel is not full, but the kind of accommodation you have reserved is not available. If you had requested a single room, which is generally the least frequently available type of room in the hotel, ask for an upgrade to whatever accommodation is available. If the clerk tries to charge you for the extra cost, insist on the available accommodation at the same rate as the room reserved.

5. If you still receive no satisfaction, ask for the manager (or the owner if it is a small hotel), to whom you should calmly explain that you need your reservation serviced immediately. Any respectable hotel will, at this point, own up to the responsibility, if you have evidence that you are right. The management will either find a room for you or will make a reservation for you at another hotel. If the manager does find you a room at another hotel that is more expensive than your reservation, insist that the manager pay the added cost along with the cost of transportation to the alternate hotel.

6. If you still have not obtained a room, now is the time to create some heat. Show the management that you are fully willing and able to create a scene if that is what it takes.

If nothing does work for you, you may be able to take legal action against the hotel. Be sure you have documented the events carefully and have the names of the different people you had to deal with while at the hotel.

When Your Credit Cards Are Refused

You are visiting Chicago, invited to dinner by your top prospective client and his or her partner. You want to make a good impression, so you offer to buy dinner, and your guests accept. Next comes the humiliation. The waiter reappears with a smug grin on his face and your credit card on a silver tray. "This card has been *refused* by your bank," the waiter says, loudly enough to alert the parking valets outside.

There are several reasons your credit cards might be refused. If you travel frequently and you haven't tracked your spending as closely as you should, you might find that one or more of your cards has reached its limit. If your spouse, son, or daughter also has a card on your credit accounts, you might be unaware that someone has been spending beyond a card's limit. If you entrust payment on your cards to your secretary or your accountant while you travel, your bills may not have been paid. It is also possible that the waiter entered the wrong credit card number when he telephoned for approval.

If your credit card is refused, you'll want to solve the problem as gracefully as possible, especially if you are with guests. Few things are as embarrassing as being refused credit in public. Try following these seven steps if one of your credit cards is refused.

1. Say, "There must be some mistake. I would like to speak with the manager, please." Then get up and walk in the direction of the cash register. You don't want your guests to be party to any of your embarrassment or frustration. *Do not wait for the waiter to respond.* The key here is for you to maintain total control over the situation.

2. When you reach the cash register or maitre d', ask to speak with the manager. The waiter has probably trailed along behind you. Forget that he or she exists. After all, the problem might have been this person's mistake. You should not be rude

(the problem might lie with you), but there is no reason for your waiter to gloat or to behave condescendingly.

3. When the manager arrives, ask how it was that your credit card was valid earlier in the evening elsewhere, yet now is being refused. If you come out assertively, you may put the manager on the defensive. But do it quietly.

4. At this point, give the manager another card, if you have one, and ask the manager to run this one through. If your second card is turned down, go to step 5.

5. Insist that you be allowed to speak with the credit card approval office yourself. Most restaurants will agree to this, because they are not eager to be stiffed for the meal.

6. Ask the credit card company why your account is on hold. Explain that you are a long-term client and do not understand why there is a problem. Has your last payment not been processed? At this point, your ability to get a positive response from your credit card company depends on whether your credit is good. In emergency situations, many banks extend your card limit.

7. If this tactic fails, you will have to acknowledge to the manager that your account has just reached its maximum. Ask if there is some way to settle the matter quickly and quietly. Would the restaurant be so kind as to bill your office? Or perhaps the manager will take your watch or some other valuable on your person as good-faith collateral until you return with cash or a check. You will likely have some bargaining power, because the restaurant's main goal is to be paid for the meal, not to throw a customer in jail.

If you are sincere, you can probably arrive at an agreement. Even if you have excellent credit and you are sure that your card is not even close to its limit, a situation might occur where you mistakenly believe that the restaurant takes your type of card.

Of course, the best way to avoid any of these situations is to be able to pay a tab in at least two or three different ways. However, I have been in situations where none of my cards were accepted and my travelers checks were also refused. I have had to leave other members of my dinner party at the table while I ventured out to buy money on a credit card.

How to Prevent or React to Being Mugged or Robbed

Being mugged or robbed isn't nearly as embarrassing as being refused credit, but it certainly is more dangerous. Unfortunately, muggings and robberies are on the rise in many parts of the world.

An Ounce of Prevention

The worst part of being mugged or robbed is the aftermath, when you realize that if you had only planned for this situation, you could have actually prevented it. Take a look at these seven tips to avoid muggings and robberies:

☐ *Act and dress in a low-key manner.* Do not appear to be flamboyant or rich. You can dress in style without looking ostentatious. If you are going to be in a crowded public place or a place that has a history of crime, avoid wearing jewelry, fur coats, and any other items that advertise you as a prime target for muggers.

☐ *Avoid dark streets, both at night and during the day.* If you find yourself on a dark street unexpectedly, it might be safer to turn around rather than to continue. If you are in a dimly lit neighborhood that has a lot of traffic, stick close to the edge of the street and walk briskly.

☐ *Walk in well-lit areas that you know are relatively safe.* In a strange city, don't rely on maps to get you from point A to point B. I have never seen a street map that will offer honest advice like, "Do not walk in this neighborhood unless you are absolutely insane." You've heard about foreigners visiting United States cities who get off a bus in a bad neighborhood and have all their money and possibly their life savings stolen. Use your intuition. If an area looks like it might mean trouble, play it safe and find another route.

☐ *Hold onto your valuables.* Women should hold their purses under their arms or even on the inside of their coats. Men should always be on the alert for pickpockets.

☐ *Avoid friendly people who promise to "give you a bargain," if you'll follow them around the corner.* When you are approached by such people, it is best not to stop or even talk to them. You can simply nod your head and in some nondescript language say "Nami nup nup Englissse" and move briskly along.

☐ *Take a cab at night to and from each unfamiliar place you must visit.* Even if an area is familiar, do not trust it to be safe if you have not been there for several years. Neighborhoods change.

☐ *Do not assume that, because a street is crowded, you are safe.* Crowded streets are favorite hangouts for the snatch-and-run thief and for pickpockets. Be alert for anybody bumping against your body.

How to React During a Mugging

Crocodile Dundee notwithstanding, most business travelers do not carry a Bowie knife tucked under their belt. Even if you had such a weapon, it would probably just get you into greater trouble in the event of a mugging unless you are skilled in hand-to-hand combat. And, of course, a knife might as well be a peashooter when your attacker is carrying a loaded gun. Most experts in the area of self-defense agree that the following strategies make sense for most muggings:

☐ *Do not panic.* If you stay calm, the mugger, who might be more frightened than you, will be calmer if you do not launch into hysterics.

☐ *Do not argue with your attacker.* Speak in low but understandable terms (assuming you and the mugger speak the same language) but speak *only* if you must.

☐ *Do not delay the inevitable.* Assume the person wants your valuables and give them up without delay.

☐ *Make a mental note of your attacker's clothing and physical appearance.* Try also to identify distinguishing physical markings, mannerisms, or speech patterns for use later with the police.

When You Need to Consider Taking Flight

If you are stopped and someone attempts to lure you away from the mainstream of people around you and into a dark alley or doorway, make an immediate assessment of your surroundings. If there are other people in the area, your mugger does not show a gun or other weapon, and you can distance yourself from the mugger quickly while making a ruckus, perhaps you should do so. The very fact that the mugger wanted to get you away from the mainstream of the sidewalk indicates the mugger's discomfort with committing a public robbery.

However, this is the kind of decision you have to make on your own, in the span of a few seconds and based on everything you know about what is happening and your own ability to escape. Most muggings or street robberies end with a loss of valuables but no physical injury. But purse snatchers often knock women down and any sign of resistance from a victim might cause a mugger to panic and lash out or even shoot the victim. Treat each mugging as a serious threat to your life.

As soon as the mugging is over and you have gotten into a safe part of town, find a police station and report the event. Be thinking of the events that led up to the mugging, because each detail can help police pinpoint the person or gang who has a similar *modus operandi*. Be ready to describe your attacker from head to toe.

Do not expect to retrieve what has been stolen from you. Your attacker will probably attempt to hide or sell your valuables before you can even report the incident to police. In any event, the police will take the descriptions from you and give you a case number so you can attempt to recover from your own insurance company, if you have insurance to cover this kind of loss.

Keep these facts and tips in mind regarding your valuables:

☐ If you own irreplaceable items, don't bring them when you travel unless they are absolutely necessary. Perhaps you have a $1000 watch that was given to you by your company and you want to show it off. Resist the urge. Why not travel with a less expensive watch and wear the more expensive one at home?

☐ Keep important identification separate from your valuables. If you hand over your purse, travel bag, or wallet to a thief, but hide your passport, driver's license, and other identifying documents in a shirt pocket or other separate location on your body, you will save yourself a lot of inconvenience after the mugging.

☐ Karl Malden is right: Don't carry a lot of cash. If you must have cash on your person, put the least amount reasonable in your wallet and the rest in a pouch or other place on your person where it does not show. I do believe it is important to carry a reasonable amount of cash and, in areas of political unrest, the cash you do have on hand can save your life.

☐ Keep track of your travelers checks. If they are lost or stolen, you can eventually recover the loss, if you have kept the check numbers or other identifying information in a separate, secure location.

In High-Risk Areas, Carry Something Worthless That Looks Valuable

Over the past many years, several of my coats were stolen from airplane closets, camera cases have not made it from the hotel lobby to the hotel room, suitcases have been lost forever, and burglars have tried to make off with things from my hotel rooms.

One night, in Beirut, my traveling associates and I were mugged by a tank. The tank rolled up in front of the car I had hired for the evening. Fortunately, the driver of the car was a professor at the American University of Beirut and knew the dangers in and around Lebanon. Out from the tank jumped a PLO officer who commanded us to stop. From out of nowhere, two armed gunmen emerged. One went directly to Antoine, the driver, while the other pinned me to the seat by pushing the barrel of his machine gun into the middle of my chest. Yet, despite the pain and discomfort of the barrel making a hole in my sternum, none of us complained as Antoine negotiated our passage. He told them there were no Americans in the car—only Japanese and French.

After what seemed like hours, Antoine pulled out a wallet from somewhere and held it up for a moment so everyone could see it was filled with cash, then he tossed it onto the street.

We were waved on, and only later did Antoine tell us that the wallet contained about $20 worth of Italian lire and nothing more. I shall never forget this lesson and recommend that when you travel through dangerous areas, carry a throwaway wallet filled with several bills that look impressive but have little real value.

Hotel Robbery

No, I'm not talking about the rates many downtown hotels charge. I'm referring to the hotel room burglar, a rare breed who often works alone. Such a burglar might even check into the hotel and live there for a while, pretending to be a businessperson with some large company.

My wife and I were in Orlando, Florida, when we discovered a room burglar in the midst of doing his job. Because this was our last evening at the hotel, we returned to the room earlier than on previous evenings. He was in the bathroom when I entered the room, and he said quickly, "I'm in here. Is this the sink that has been leaking? They sent me up to check it out," as he slid down to the floor looking under the bathroom sink. I went to phone the desk when he bolted for the door and in an instant was gone.

Once, in Dallas, I was wakened by a sound at the door, and a man entered the room. I leaped up, making a horrible sound that frightened both of us. One morning, this time in New York, I came into my room after going down for a breakfast meeting that did not fit my usual pattern at this hotel for the previous three mornings. As I entered, I found someone removing one of my jackets from the closets. "Is this the one for the cleaners?" he said, coolly, as he carefully maneuvered himself toward the door.

Business acquaintances have told me stories of having everything they own taken from their room while they were in the shower. All of these stories should suggest to you that hotels are not the safest havens in the world. However, there are several steps you can take to reduce the risk of having your hotel room robbed:

☐ *When you check in, do not display your valuables.* Don't present a wad of cash, a display case of jewelry, or anything that would appear to an onlooker to be worth stealing. Remember, maintain a low profile when you travel.

☐ *Do not ask for a safety box while you are checking in.* Call down from your room and find out the details regarding a safety box. When you check in, it is likely other people will be able to discover your room number and your name. People who use safety boxes frequently store other valuables in their rooms.

☐ *If you can avoid it, do not leave valuables in your room when you are not there.* Documents such as airline tickets, travelers checks, excess cash, items of jewelry, cameras, and quick pickup items should go in the hotel safety box.

☐ *Do not believe that you can hide valuables in your room from a determined burglar.* Hotel burglars know where to look and have no qualms about cutting open your designer luggage or even taking it with them.

☐ *Do put things away, however, and do not leave even moderately valuable items out in clear view.* This warning applies even at night when you are in the room. Make it a habit to use a drawer instead of a dresser top as the place to pile your loose cash and pocket items. Some burglars get a thrill from slipping into rooms of business travelers who have returned late at night after having too much to drink.

☐ *Invest in a lock or door jam that will provide absolute security from the inside.* Make sure it is simple to use and can be removed quickly in the dark without any finesse required in the event of an emergency.

☐ *Do not establish a regular pattern if that's at all possible.* Make it a habit to do the unexpected, like returning to your room only a few minutes after you have left it.

☐ *Avoid leaving evidence that you have left the hotel.* This means take your key with you and do not park in any parking garage that holds your car key for you (when it is gone, so are you). Do not tell the reservation desk or the phone operator that you will be out for the day. If you need to reach anyone who might call while you are out, it is better to call them rather than have them call you while you are out.

☐ *Women traveling alone might want to develop the habit of booking the room as husband and wife.* "Mr. Cummings is expected later," will take care of the situation and keep any burglars or other undesirables guessing. If you want to avoid paying for the cost of a double, then confide to the manager (over the phone from your room), that your husband will not be coming after all, so can you be charged for a single instead.

☐ *Do not ask for your messages at the reception desk.* The clerk will either ask you for your room number or will know you and look in the room key slot to see if there are any messages waiting for you. Either of these events will tell anyone around the desk where your room is. Call for messages from your room or from a house phone.

☐ *Do not leave one of those "make up this room" tags on your doorknob when you leave in the morning.* It is better to leave a "do not disturb" sign. When you return later in the day, call to have the bed and bathroom towels changed. Or if you are going to be around in the morning and can work around a maid, get one from the hallway or call housekeeping and ask if your room could be cleaned right away because you are having a business meeting in your room.

These steps will reduce your chance of having your hotel room burglarized or robbed, but they won't eliminate the possibility. Here are six steps to remember if your room is robbed or burglarized:

1. Relax, the event is over. You lived through it and should now chalk it up to experience.
2. Take inventory to determine what is missing. Do this before you call the desk. Once you have called for help, you might not have time to check your belongings thoroughly before the police or hotel detective arrives.
3. When you make your calls, first notify the desk, then report the incident to the city police.
4. While you are waiting for someone to arrive, make two or three copies of your list of missing items, describing each item in as much detail as possible. Keep one list, then give another to the police.
5. Try to think of anything suspicious that you may have seen or heard during the past 24 to 48 hours at that hotel. Did anyone talk to you at the bar? Did you tell any strangers where you were staying? Did you give your key to that pretty little thing or that cute guy the other night? Be ready to provide any details of suspicious occurrences to the police. They might recognize a pattern that will lead to a current suspect. But don't count on it.

6. Get a case number from the officer in charge. As soon as you can, during normal business hours, call your insurance agent and tell him or her that you were robbed and report the details.

In Case of Fire

Fires can occur in planes, ships, hotels, restaurants, nightclubs, and office buildings. If you are in one of these structures during a fire, what you learn in this section can save your life.

The following tips can help you survive a serious fire:

☐ Know your escape routes.

☐ Understand the way fire and smoke kill, and how you can survive in a smoke-filled structure.

☐ Do not break windows unless you must to escape.

☐ Always assume a fire alarm is signaling the real thing.

Know Your Escape Routes

Here's a good habit to develop: Whenever you enter an unfamiliar structure, whether it's a plane, boat, office building, or another structure, make a mental note of exits and exit signs that are visible. Note regular exits as well as emergency exits. If this safety measure becomes an automatic mental process, you will be in a good position to escape quickly from any emergency situation, in just about any structure.

Also try to find out how exits work—doors, hatches, and other types of exits vary in their operation depending on the age and type of structure. Knowing where an emergency exit is located will not do you much good during a fire if you do not know how to open the exit.

You should understand emergency exit procedures well enough to carry them out in the dark, which you might have to do if you are in a fire-engulfed structure in which the electrical system has been burned or shut off. In a plane, this might involve nothing more than reading the procedures printed on the nearest exit, then counting the number of rows you will have to pass to reach the exit.

In some emergency—fire or otherwise—that requires your departure from the structure, do nothing on your own until you have determined there is no leader to follow. On airlines, ships, and in some restaurants and nightclubs, the staff and/or crew are trained and drilled in emergency procedures and can save lives if their instructions are followed. However, do not spend much time looking for a leader prior to taking action yourself. If someone in a leadership position is available to help, you can be sure this person will act immediately; failure to receive instructions from anyone is a good sign that you are on your own.

On the back of most hotel room doors in many countries, you will find an evacuation plan that includes a layout of the floor you are residing on and the location of fire escape stairs. Take a few minutes to review the map and corresponding evacuation instructions. These few minutes of effort could provide you with the information you need to save your life and possibly the lives of others.

In the United States and most countries around the world, the local fire departments or fire prevention authorities make an effort to ensure that public buildings have adequate fire escapes. Unfortunately, although many buildings meet or exceed fire codes in terms of their structure, emergency exits and escape routes might be poorly maintained. It is not uncommon to find fire escape routes blocked, stairways being used as storerooms, escape doors locked, and other problems that can make an escape either impossible or dangerous. The point is to keep one or more alternative escape routes in mind in case your initial route will not work.

WARNING: When people panic and there is no clear escape or leader, they will function as a mob, with each person trying to flow with the movements of other people nearby. During a mob scene, people become frantic and desperate. Many will kick, claw, scream, climb over others, or do just about anything to escape whatever danger has caused the mob scene to develop.

If you get caught in the flow of a mob, you must fight to stay on your feet. If you are knocked to the floor, it will be difficult to return to your feet. Your best bet is to stick close to a wall, which offers support. If you do get knocked down, try to get to a wall by rolling toward it. Once you reach a wall, you should be able to stand again.

Understand the Way Fire and Smoke Kill

Smoke inhalation is by far the greatest cause of death in a fire. Smoke can contain toxic gases that are released from burning synthetic materials, including carpets, drapes, upholstery covers and stuffing, insulation, and soundproofing materials.

Even a relatively small, contained fire can send poisonous smoke throughout a structure. Aircraft and ships are so self-contained that smoke spreads quickly, possibly reducing the already limited number of escape routes. In modern buildings, air conditioning ducts and service corridors become natural passageways for smoke.

If you are in a fire, take every possible step to avoid breathing the smoke created by a fire. Because smoke is heated to a higher temperature than surrounding air, it rises to the tops of ceilings, then travels outward along every available pathway, ultimately filling a room from the top down. However, until a structure becomes engulfed with smoke, you can often find breathable air along the floor, even in the middle of a burning building. Your life may depend on finding that air.

So, the closer your face is to the floor, the cleaner and more breathable the air may be; don't hesitate to get on your hands and knees to look for breathable air when necessary.

WARNING: If you smell something in your room that suggests smoke or fire, look as quickly as you can at the air-conditioning vents in the room to see whether smoke is emerging there. If so, turn off the air conditioning immediately, then use wet towels to plug the vents.

WARNING: Never open a hot door. Before you attempt to exit a room, feel the door with your hands. If the door is hot, do not open it. If it is not hot, open the door and look out. If the hall or passageway is filled with smoke, quickly close the door and try to call someone who can sound a fire alarm. If your phone does not work, you will need to decide whether to exit your room, seek another exit, or wait for help. Take another look in the hall. Can you see the fire exit? Do you remember where it is? If your room has light, identify all possible fire escape routes posted on the door of your room or in the bathroom. If you think you have a good change of escaping, do so immediately.

Do Not Break Windows—Unless Absolutely Necessary

Break a window only to escape the smoke or flames of a fire and only as a last resort. When you break a window, the sudden rush of cool air may suck smoky air from the air conditioning vents into the room. It is also possible that smoke from outside and below will rush into the room.

If you have to break a window, make as small a break as possible, as close to the floor as possible. If your window has several panes, pick the bottom one. If the window is a single pane, it is probably tempered glass, which is very difficult to break. When tempered glass does break, it will shatter in small pieces, removing any protection you might have between your room and outside smoke.

TIP

Most sinks have an air vent (the overflow drain) connected both to the drain and the air pipe so the air pressure can equalize in the drain. If there is no smoke entering the bathroom from the overflow drain, you can, in a pinch, breath in the air from this vent. The drainpipe from the sink extends to the roof of the building, so the air you breathe in will come from the roof.

Believing That Every Fire Alarm Is Serious

I always assume a fire alarm is the real thing. I was in a Sheraton hotel in Washington, D.C., recently when the fire alarm sounded. I tried calling the reception desk, but nobody answered. I then looked out into the hall. Other guests were also peering into the hall from their rooms. I did not see or smell smoke or fire.

I quickly got dressed, tried to reach the reception desk again, then looked out the window and noticed fire trucks arriving. The total time elapsed from the start of the alarm to the arrival of the fire trucks was less than two minutes. I was out the door five seconds later.

The hotel was eventually emptied of guests and employees, but I was amazed at how long it took. People were even using the elevators to exit, even though it should be common knowledge that elevators *never* should be used to evacuate a building. (If there is a power failure, the occupants of the elevator will be stuck in what may rapidly become an oven.)

The alarm proved to be false. The guests returned to their rooms and the fire trucks left. A few hours later, the alarm sounded again, and again the fire trucks arrived. This time, it took even longer to evacuate the guests from the hotel. Again it was a false alarm, but either alarm could have been the real thing.

There is a tendency for people to disbelieve an alarm when one or more false alarms have already been sounded. However, consider that you might be a participant in a game played by a very cruel and sick arsonist. I would much rather experience some inconvenience than risk ending my life. When in doubt, follow the Cummings Evacuation Rule: Better to be safe than barbecued.

12

How to Deal with Customs Officials

In most situations, dealing with customs and immigration officials will be little more than a slight annoyance. Depending on a number of factors, including which country you are entering, officials might inspect your luggage, charge you duty for imported goods, confiscate items from you that are not permitted in that country, or possibly even search you and your luggage for smuggled goods.

The vast majority of passengers find even the more thorough customs inspections to be little more than a minor aggravation. However, the thought of being interviewed or searched seems to terrify some people. I have seen apparently innocent people break into tears, because they believe that a customs official's tough questions are going to land them in jail for smuggling.

As a frequent traveler, you're likely to come up with common, pointed questions about customs policies, procedures, and duties rather frequently. The answers to just about all such questions can be found (and carried with you) in a free booklet offered by the U.S. Customs Service entitled, *Know Before You Go.* For this or any other customs publications, write U.S. Customs, P.O. Box 7407, Washington, DC 20044 or call (202) 566-8195.

Why Customs Procedures Have Become Increasingly Strict

Even in countries where illegal immigration is not much of a problem, the smuggling of drugs and contraband will likely be a serious concern for customs officials. The drug trade is a global problem and is on the increase. As a result, more people are being stopped by customs officers than at any time in the past.

To cope with the clever strategies that smugglers use to transport their goods across international borders, customs agents have resorted to a number of detection techniques, including high-tech devices, drug-sniffing dogs, and informers who mingle in line with others. Customs agents even have profiles that describe a typical smuggler's appearance, dress, and mannerisms. Even though you are innocent of any wrongdoing, you can be stopped by customs if you fit one of these profiles.

Coping with a Search

Here's what to do if customs agents do stop you:

☐ Relax. You might unknowingly fit the agents' profile for a smuggler or the customs office might have received a tip regarding a smuggler who bears a resemblance to you. These stops are usually routine and should not be a cause for alarm.

☐ Ask what the officer wants and do not appear to be in a hurry.

☐ Do not glance about.

☐ If you have just slipped on your overcoat in anticipation of going outside, remove it now. Otherwise, you are apt to start sweating, which might arouse the officer's suspicions.

☐ Do not hesitate to open any bag that the customs agent wants to see.

☐ Do not say, "Oh, I forgot about the five bottles of scotch, and the 10,000 Havana cigars," and so on. Do not volunteer any information. Simply respond to questions, calmly and with composure.

☐ If an agent wants to search your person, he or she believes there is a high probability of finding something. Protest a body search, but do so mildly. Explain who you are, where you are coming from, and ask to speak to a superior prior to the search. However, if customs agents are determined to perform the search, you don't want to aggravate the situation or give the agents cause to make the search unpleasant.

☐ If the agents find something wrong, be very careful what you say from this point on. Keep in mind that there is no solace in the fact that thousands of people slip through customs each day with minor violations undetected. You could have a serious problem headed your way, so be cooperative and very careful.

☐ Do not rant and rave about how you are going to "report all of you" or something similar. These people have a difficult job. They bear the brunt of a lot of angst from a lot of people on a daily basis and are subject to flare-ups in temper.

☐ Do insist on your rights when you know you are right. These rights, of course, vary greatly, depending on the country you are entering. You have far more rights in the United States than you will have in, say, Turkey.

The key factor to consider is that you need to know what your rights are. This might involve a request to talk to an attorney before the situation gets out of hand. Either call an attorney in the United States or ask for one to be appointed to you. If it is not possible to call a U.S. attorney and you do not feel you can trust a local attorney, ask to speak to the U.S. Embassy or Consul's office. Sometimes the very fact that you press your need to speak to someone else can be impressive if done in a calm, determined manner.

The person who rants and raves may be treated like a fanatic, and in many parts of the world you most certainly do not want to be treated like a fanatic. Of the several dozen times I or my traveling companions have been stopped by customs or security people, I can say with all candor that I have never met a customs officer who did not try to bend over backward to handle a problem in a courteous and professional manner.

I cannot overemphasize the need to remain calm. Once, while traveling with my daughter, a security person stopped her in customs. Despite the fact that she had 20 years of international travel experience, she was taken aback at the personal confrontation. "He thinks I am a criminal," she said, then burst into tears and started to walk away from the bags and the officer. Fortunately I was able to calm her down. Otherwise, she might have triggered a full-blown body search and dismantling of our luggage.

What Not to Do

In addition to the tips I've just offered, there are some specific things that you should *not* do when you enter customs.

□ Never carry someone else's bags or articles through customs. I have seen men cry when confronted with items they did not know existed (so they said), because they were being carried as a favor to a friend. Even if you trust the person who asks you to carry his or her articles, you might not be able to explain the presence of some item that your friend believed was harmless.

☐ Do not carry a lot of foreign-made items with you, unless you can prove you have owned them prior to this trip. A copy of your insurance rider showing that all these items are covered, with the rider dated prior to your original departure, generally will do.

☐ Never assume you can slip any drugs into any country. You might be the one person the customs people choose as the example of the week.

☐ Do not make any sudden moves if you are stopped. If you fit the profile of some armed and dangerous person, the simple act of reaching for your wallet can be misunderstood. Remember, the person who provided customs with the tip (of a person fitting your description) might have been a ploy by the real drug smugglers to create a diversion. You may not know it or see them, but there may be one or more security guards with guns aimed at you.

Avoid Buying Imitation Name Brands Abroad

A growing problem in both the United States and other countries, and one that customs officials have gotten involved in, is the manufacture of "fakes," or imitations of products made and sold at much higher prices in another country. These counterfeit items often violate the trademarks of the originals that they imitate.

It is against the law for you to bring in these copies, so if you have purchased any, and customs officers see them, they are likely to be confiscated. Keep this in mind before you buy several dozen of some cheap imitation to give to friends at home.

Duty Charges

I have included a chart in Table 12–1 that shows the duty (in percent of the total value) that you may be charged on items brought into the United States as of the date of this writing. Keep in mind that the duty charged changes frequently. It is likely that many of the items shown may actually

Table 12–1 *Samples of Duty Charged on Items Brought into the United States*

Item	General Duty	Duty if from a Communist Country
Antiques		
100 years or older	Free	Free
Books		
Foreign author or language	Free	Free
Cameras		
Motion over $50 each	5.1%	20%
Still over $10 each	4.7%	20%
Leather Cases	7.4%	35%
Lenses	8.8%	45%
Candy	7.0%	40%
Chess Sets	7.0%	40%
China Tableware		
Bone	11.6%	75%
Not bone not over $56	30.7%	75%
Not bone valued over $56	11.9%	75%
Drawings and Paintings		
Works of art done by hand	Free	Free
Fur		
Wearing apparel	7.4 to 11.6%	50%
Other products	3.4 to 7.4%	50%
Gem Stones (Cut but Not Set)		
Diamonds	Free	10%
Others	0 to 3.4%	10 to 20%
Glass Tableware	15 to 42.5%	60%
Leather		
Pocketbooks, bags	8.1 to 10%	35%
Other Products	1.5 to 10%	35%
Perfume	5.9%+	75%+
Shoes (Leather)	8.5 to 10%	20%
Television Sets	4.2%	35%
Toys	10 to 10.9%	70%

be assessed at a different rate—or not at all—by the time you read this.

You can get a more comprehensive, up-to-date list of duty rates from the nearest Customs Service Office. Check your phone directory or ask your travel agent to order a copy of current duty charges for you. Duty charged on items from Communist countries can change overnight if that country is granted a Special Trade Status (which is occurring with increasing frequency).

Traveling to a Trade Show with Your Company Display

Whenever you cross into another country and you are loaded down with samples or displays, you may be told you owe duty on the items. Many business travelers who plan to attend trade shows, conventions, or just a couple of days of business meetings discover that the duty on trade-show items and displays is greater than their actual cost. If you are unprepared for this and cannot pay the duty, the item(s) may be confiscated on the spot.

One way to ensure that you will not have to pay duty on valuable items that you carry is to obtain an ATA Carnet. This is a simple customs document that includes several vouchers for listing each item you are taking with you. When you enter a foreign country, you will leave one voucher with the customs office on arrival and another when you depart the country. On your return to the United States, you will have the original document for your entry with United States Customs.

The Carnet is operated through the International Bureau of Chambers of Commerce and serves as a bond to ensure that you are not taking items into the country and selling them. There is no limitation to the number and basic types of items that can be covered—except that perishable and consumable items are not permitted, for obvious reasons.

The Carnet is essential when you travel with expensive camera equipment—even if you are not a professional and the equipment is for your own use. A customs official may challenge you and require you to pay duty on what he or she determines to be "excessive equipment for personal use."

You can obtain a Carnet by contacting one of the local offices of the International Bureau of Chambers of Commerce. You will usually have to post a bond through your own insurance company to cover the value of the items on your list. You will pay a fee for the Carnet, which is good for one year. At the end of the year, assuming you have had no violations recorded against the Carnet, you will receive a portion of the fee back and the bond will be released.

For further information on obtaining an ATA Carnet, contact:

> United States Council for International
> Business
> 1212 Avenue of the Americas, New York, NY
> 10036
> 353 Sacramento Avenue, San Francisco, CA
> 94111
> 1900 East Golf Road, Schaumburg, IL 60195
> 3345 Wilshire Boulevard, Los Angeles, CA
> 90010

> International Chamber of Commerce
> 38, cours Albert 1. 75008 Paris, France

Information can also be obtained through Chamber of Commerce offices in most countries around the world.

What to Do When You Cannot Prove You Are a U.S. Citizen

It is rather common for travelers to lose or forget identification proving their U.S. citizenship. It can be frightening to arrive in some foreign country or back in the United States and have no passport to produce.

Before you start on your journey to a foreign country, most airlines verify that you have a passport or (depending on the country you are traveling to) some other proof of U.S. citizenship. However, in the heat of the evening rush to fill a 747 with nearly 400 passengers, there might not be time to check each passenger's identification.

Once, en route on a flight to Saint Kitts in the Caribbean Islands, I realized I had forgotten my passport. Cold beads of sweat began to run down my face. My imagination got the best of me and I envisioned myself being tossed into some hot, roach-infested cell to await the next flight back to the United States. Then I remembered that I was carrying my voter registration card, which is a form of proof of U.S. citizenship, and I relaxed—until I double-checked and discovered that I didn't have my voter registration card, either.

If you find yourself in such a situation, try what worked for me. I went through my wallet and belongings looking for the most official-looking card possible. I knew the card would have to bear my photograph and could not be an obviously improper form of identification. For example, a driver's license, because it can be obtained by noncitizens, is an improper form of identification.

I decided not to inform anyone of my problem; I wanted to avoid arousing any suspicion or drawing any unnecessary attention to myself.

When the planeload of passengers passed through the customs and immigration entry checkpoint into this Caribbean country, I casually showed my official-looking identification, along with my ticket, and was waved through. On my return to the United States, no one even asked me for my passport.

Keep in mind that this approach should be reserved for that rare instance when you have forgotten your passport. It is a rather drastic approach, simply because it may not work. If your identification is challenged, you will have to remain very calm and be able to give the impression that you assumed what you were doing was acceptable.

However, if you try this ploy and it fails, explain the actual details of your problem. Never say anything that can be proven false (either by a review of the documents you are carrying or by a search of records made while you are enjoying the local hospitality). The truth works best; at least after your initial attempt to get through customs has failed.

While I traveled in Spain with a companion, we decided to cross into France for lunch. My companion did not have his passport with him, but we decided to try to make the crossing anyway. At the border crossing, I asked to speak with one of the officials and explained that we were on business and were staying in Pamplona. We were headed for Jean de Luz for the afternoon and lunch and would gladly leave something as collateral to ensure our return. After looking at our documentation, the official let us pass—with the stipulation that we were to return through that same checkpoint.

To test the situation, we decided to try another border crossing on our return into Spain. We chose the border crossing in San Sebastian, one of the busiest crossings in Europe. As I suspected, the French didn't even look at any of our identification and waved us on toward the Spanish side. Crossing through the no-man's land between two countries can produce a funny feeling, and I had a brief vision of being held in limbo between these two countries for the remainder of my life.

Spain refused to allow my companion to enter, so we had to turn back. Now we had a more serious problem. The officials in France won-

dered why we couldn't get into Spain. We resorted to honesty. I suppose that and the sad
looks on our faces made us believable. We were
allowed to pass.

The One Document That Is Almost as Good as Your Passport

A copy of your passport identification page and
any specially needed visa pages can save you
when no other type of identification will.

Being detained at a customs station or border
crossing can be quite an inconvenience; if you
are traveling by train or bus, you can be left behind while customs officials question you or
search your belongings. If you are unprepared for
this kind of event, being detained can be a prel-
ude to something worse. So take precautions. Advance planning and the use of the lists provided
earlier in the book are the keys to returning home
unscathed.

13
How to Survive Travelers Check Dilemmas

You've seen the commercial: a distraught couple traveling in Europe wonders what to do now that a pickpocket has stolen the man's wallet, with all of their cash, credit cards, and the "wrong" travelers checks. Next, Karl Malden looks you straight in the eye and reminds you that if you, too, had chosen the wrong travelers checks, you might have lost out.

Well, I've got bad news. There is no universal travelers check that will be accepted everywhere you travel. Although major hotels, rental car companies, and airlines accept all major travelers checks (and credit cards), you will discover that many hotels, restaurants, gas stations, shops, and other services around the world will not accept your travelers check (or credit card for that matter) for payment. To complicate matters, many establishments will accept credit cards issued by a company but not a travelers check issued by that same company. The reverse situation is also true. I have been in restaurants that accept American Express credit cards, but not American Express Travelers Checks.

If your travel is confined mostly to the United States, your problems will be limited to the minor inconvenience of paying cash at a store or restaurant that will not accept your travelers check, or that has a minimum purchase amount when you pay with a credit card or travelers check. When these situations occur outside the United States, your problem magnifies simply because it can be more difficult to get cash.

Some establishments view a travelers check the same as a personal check. They may or may not accept your travelers check, depending on a variety of circumstances—how you look, what you are buying, and what kind of identification you can produce. The cautious establishments may only accept your check with the stipulation that you:

☐ show your driver's license, credit card numbers, and other identifying information.

☐ allow yourself to be photographed.

☐ provide a local address and phone number.

☐ pay a fee that may run anywhere from 10 cents to 15 percent of the amount of the check. Because you already may have paid a fee when you purchased your travelers checks, any additional fee makes travelers checks more expensive than you may want to pay.

What Are Travelers Checks, Anyway?

Travelers checks were conceived as a variation on the "letter of credit," which was a rather convenient way to transfer funds several decades ago. Letters of credit are still used for certain types of business transactions, but they are no longer a convenient method of funds transfer for a traveler. So banks and other private, quasibanking institutions (American Express, for instance) issue checks that, in essence, guarantee to the person who accepts the check that funds have been paid to the grantor of the check and that the company stands behind the value of that instrument.

How Businesses Benefit by Accepting Travelers Checks

Domestic businesses find that accepting travelers checks is less risky than accepting a personal check, which may bounce. Internationally, some businesses actually prefer U.S. travelers checks over U.S. dollars, because the handling fee for processing foreign currency may be slightly more than the fee charged for processing travelers checks.

How You Benefit by Carrying Travelers Checks

The advantage to the traveler of using travelers checks is security—the knowledge that the checks will be replaced, at no cost to you, in the event they are lost or stolen. The convenience of travelers checks is also a benefit. The ability to travel from country to country with checks that are "bound to be good" in each country is much more convenient than carrying hard currency, which may have to be converted into local currency when you cross into a new country.

How the Issuing Company Also Benefits

Several companies, banks, and other financial institutions sell travelers checks because they increase the company's interest-bearing assets. The idea is that you exchange cash for the travelers checks today, although you may not use the checks for weeks—or, in some cases, years. The institution that sold you the checks earns interest on the money you provided until the travelers checks are cashed in.

Add to this the fee that you may have paid, and the fee that might be charged to the person or company that ultimately collects on the checks. You don't have to be an international economist to realize that the travelers check business is a good one to be in.

Will Any Bank Cash Your Travelers Check?

In the United States, I have never had an experience where a bank would not cash a U.S. travelers check, although in some instances I have had to show reasonable identification or deposit the checks into my personal account.

But the moment you step off U.S. soil, you should stop expecting every bank you enter to accept your travelers checks. True, thousands of banks around the globe *will* cash your travelers check. However, it may also be true that, depending on the country or city you are in, only one out of the dozen or so local banks will accept your check. Your problem, then, is to find that one bank in town that will do it. So, Karl Malden hasn't lied, he just hasn't given you all the facts. In Europe, as well as in other parts of the world, finding some place that will accept your travelers check can be a nightmare. It is one thing to enter a bank and ask to cash a travelers check drawn against the native currency. It is quite another thing to present a travelers check that has a face value in a foreign currency.

WARNING: Even when you do find a bank that will cash your travelers check, you may discover that they charge you a hefty fee. I have had to pay as much as 10 percent of the check's worth in London. Each travelers check company will

have (in major areas at least) offices or banks where the check can be cashed at little or no processing fee. Look for the main local office for your type of check. You can usually call the travelers check company to find out where these "cash-free" locations are. Keep in mind, however, that when you convert your dollars into the local currency, there will be a "fee" for that as well. Shop around for the best bottom-line deal in cashing your dollars into local funds. In general, it is safe to assume that one of the worst places to get a good deal is at the airport exchange counter.

Major Problems You Might Encounter with Travelers Checks

Three major problems can befall you when you carry travelers checks:

☐ They may be refused.

☐ They may be stolen.

☐ You might lose them.

When Your Travelers Checks Are Refused

This is one of those moments when you can break into a cold sweat. Your client and two other associates are at your table when you present your travelers checks to the waiter. The surly waiter tosses the checks into your dish of unfinished coconut cream surprise and announces, "What makes you think we would take *these*?"

Although travelers checks can come in handy, you should never rely on the fact that they will be acceptable for all goods and services that you buy. As is the case with credit cards, it is a good idea to ask in advance if the establishment accepts your specific brand of travelers checks. If so, also ask whether there are limitations or qualifications, including a minimum purchase, a hefty surcharge added into the bill, or identification that you will not be able to produce.

TIP

Among all the oddities that I've encountered throughout the world, one stands out: Many establishments that will not accept (or would prefer not to accept) my credit cards or travelers checks *will* accept freely and without any surcharge my own personal check. The reasons for this vary and in some cases are because of the fee the establishment must pay to the credit card or travelers check company. In contrast, a personal check can carry a lower processing fee.

It is therefore a good idea to carry some personal checks with you for situations in which a business will not accept anything else (besides cash, that is). In fact, you can save money when you use a personal check over a travelers check, especially if you have an interest-bearing checking account. You earn interest on your money until the personal check is cashed, whereas the travelers check represents cash you have already spent.

When Your Travelers Checks Are Lost or Stolen

If your checks are stolen, the result is not, I am sorry to tell you, as easy as the television commercials indicate—even if you are carrying the "right" travelers checks. First, if you expect to get an immediate refund for your unspent checks, you will have to provide a record showing the sequence of checks that you started with, and the numbers of the checks you have already spent.

When you buy your travelers checks, you are given a copy of the purchase order showing the series of numbers for your checks and the denominations of their values. The teller or clerk selling you the checks should advise you to keep these records separate from your checks in case the checks are lost. These purchase records and your notations showing which checks have already been spent enable you to get a faster replacement of the checks.

Before you purchase your checks, ask this question: "If my checks are lost or stolen, and I am in a different city, what exactly do I do to recover my money?"

The answers will be anything from "I don't know" to a detailed account of the process you must follow. Unfortunately, the actual process will not be the same as what you are told. So what really happens?

First, you can and should call the number or place that is specified on instructions you get as you purchase the checks. When you report the loss or theft of your checks, you must provide the full series of numbers for the checks you have purchased. All the checks you take with you should be purchased as one lump sum, with an uninterrupted sequence of numbers for all checks. I try to follow this rule, but frequently have checks remaining from earlier trips, which means I have a set of checks acquired at different times and often different purchase points. This will greatly complicate your recordkeeping and reporting procedures unless you make a separate list at the start of any trip, showing all the check numbers and their values. I describe more about this bookkeeping a bit later.

Once you have reported your loss, what occurs next depends on your credit rating. If a person could simply buy checks, report them stolen and get new ones, then cash the old ones at an unsuspecting bank, you would see a sudden and dramatic rise in the crime rate throughout the world. In the real world, the return of your lost checks will be "provisional," depending on your ability to warrant that what you have reported is true. If you have a credit card, you will be in better shape, because your card will be accepted as collateral. The travelers check company will tell you this is done in case you have "mistakenly" already cashed one or more of the checks you have reported stolen.

I have tested this statement, though, and now believe that the company mainly wants added assurance that you are not trying to make a fraudulent claim. In one case, I later discovered that I had made a mistake in the number and amount of the checks stolen from me. One day recently a "charge" for the mistaken report appeared on my credit card bill—over a year after the reported theft. The point is, the company does not seem to be too concerned about this type of problem—as long as your credit is in good standing.

In most cases, with the proper documentation, you will be given a refund, although it may not be for the entire amount of your claim. You can also expect that the process required to recover your money will be time consuming and, in general, a hassle. If you are within the United States, the replacement moves along pretty quickly. But if you are on the road in Spain, somewhere near Ubeda, you might have to wait several days for your refund. If you are in the middle of a Brazilian rainforest or some other location without a phone, it can be next to impossible to get a refund within any useful period of time.

In any event, make sure you have recorded the following six items of information as soon as possible after you discover a loss:

☐ The numbers of all the checks you purchased

☐ Where you purchased them

☐ How you paid for them

☐ The date they were purchased

☐ How many you have spent

☐ Where they were spent

At the very least, you will always be able to report the entire loss to the place where you purchased the checks and allow that office to sort out which ones you actually cashed. This may take some time, but you will eventually be reimbursed for 100 percent of your loss. That's not much consolation when you have to sell your solid gold Omega watch for $50 to pay for your hotel room in Tangier. So make sure your recordkeeping is complete and up to date. Of course, make sure you keep these records separate from your travelers checks and in a safe place.

A System for Tracking Your Travelers Checks

Before I travel, I make sure all my travelers checks are together and in the proper sequence. I then note any checks that may be missing from the sequence. It is not difficult to pull a check from its pack out of order. Unless you note this in advance, you might not report your lost or stolen checks correctly.

Then I enter into my computer (or type out on a typewriter) the list of checks (fabricated ones, here), in the format indicated:

AMERICAN EXPRESS
    $20.00
783–543–670 _____

          671 _____

          672 _____

spent   673 xxxx

          674 _____

$50.00

211–776–341 _____

342 _____

spent   343 xxxx

344 _____

345 _____

$100.00

998–532–294 _____

295 _____

296 _____

297 _____

573–192–831 _____

832 _____

833 _____

I print two copies of this list. I put one copy in my wallet and another in my briefcase. If you have a copy machine that has a reduction feature, you can make your list even smaller, but make sure it's readable. When I spend or cash a travelers check, I simply make a note of the place and date on the appropriate line.

TIP

If you get free travelers checks, turn in all your "old" unspent ones to keep all the new ones in an uninterrupted sequence.

WARNING: If you commonly use a nickname in place of your legal name (such as Jack, rather than John, in my case), and you plan to travel to other countries, make sure that the name on your

travelers checks is the same as the name on your passport, which may be the only identification acceptable.

Contacts to Use if Your Checks Are Lost or Stolen

Following is a list of major travelers check issuers and ways to contact the companies from major travel sites.

AMERICAN EXPRESS: In the United States, 1-800-221-7282; in Alaska or Hawaii, 1-800-221-4950; in Canada, 1-800-221-7282. Outside the United States or Canada, contact the nearest American Express Service Company, its affiliates, or representatives; or look in the Yellow Pages of the local phone book, under "Travelers Checks" or "Banks." If you have the number of the place where you purchased the checks, you can call that number, if necessary. If the purchase location is your personal bank, the bank staff often will provide the fastest and best results.

BANK OF AMERICA: In the United States, except Alaska, 1-800-227-3460; from all other locations, call the United States collect at 415-624-5400.

BARCLAYS/VISA: In the United States, call 1-800-227-6811; in Europe, call the London office at 937-8091. For other locations, check the Yellow Pages, as indicated for American Express checks.

CITICORP: In the United States and Canada, call 1-800-645-6556; in Mexico, 813-626-4444; in Europe, call London at 438-1414.

THOMAS COOK/MASTERCARD: In the United States, except New York, Alaska, and Hawaii, 1-800-223-9920; from those excepted States and all other parts of the world, call the United States collect, 212-974-5696.

When you buy your travelers checks, ask for a more specific list of numbers that will be suitable for the specific areas of the world where you plan to travel.

Also, try to use the following nine tips for handling cash, checks, and credit cards when you travel:

☐ Know how much cash you have, and which checks and credit cards you have with you at any given time. Make frequent copies of all the documents and credit cards you carry when you travel. This will help you to replace a large number of important items if you lose your wallet or if it is stolen.

Avoid carrying more money and checks than you need for a given trip. You can do this by creating a simple expense plan. For instance, if you are to be gone for five days, and anticipate that, excluding your prepaid bills and expected credit card use, you should not need more than $200 in cash. Make note of the amount, then *stick to it*. Track your cash expenditures in your daily record of expenses, which you will want to keep for your income tax reporting. (I've devoted an entire later chapter to income tax recordkeeping.)

☐ When you travel, get into the habit of leaving your valuables in a safe place during the day. All better hotels have some type of safe or safe deposit box system that is available to you, even if it costs a nominal fee. Use these boxes to store your excess cash, taking with you only sufficient cash for the needs of the day, with a reasonable surplus for emergencies. In this way, you will limit your loss if you are mugged or lose your wallet.

☐ Keep a record of your travelers checks separate from where you carry your checks. This really sounds obvious, but too many people lose their checks along with the records of the checks. It is a good idea, before you leave, to keep at home a record of the amount of money you have in travelers checks, the series numbers, the denomination of each check, and the location and date you purchased the checks.

☐ Do not display your wealth. When you begin your trip, you may have a fat wallet or purse. Avoid creating the impression that you are a worthy robbery target. Remember too that wealth is relative, and although you may not think of yourself as "rich," if you have something worth stealing, you are rich in the eyes of a mugger or burglar. You should not only dress modestly, from head to toe, but carry luggage that provides the same general impression. I have seen travelers who were dressed like vagabonds but had some of the most expensive luggage, briefcases, and shoes I have ever seen.

☐ Hook or fasten the majority of your travel valuables to apparel that you will continue to wear throughout the journey. In other words, don't leave all your checks, cash, and other valuable documents in the jacket that you plan to store in the overhead compartment during your flight.

If possible, buy a small money belt or cotton sack bag that can hang around your neck, and keep the valuables there during your travel from one destination to another. After you have checked into your hotel and have left your reserve in a safe place, you can revert to more conventional methods for storing your valuables.

☐ Do not assume you can safely hide your valuables in your hotel room. A thief often checks the "unthinkable" places first, then checks the more conventional hiding places next.

☐ Learn the tricks that pickpockets use and be alert for them. (I include more on this next.)

☐ Never show how much money you have in public. If you carry all your cash in one place on your person, you reveal all your money whenever you make a purchase. It's far better to keep your stash of cash separate so that you can transfer cash, in privacy, onto your person in amounts that you'll need each day.

☐ Never leave your valuables in the open in your hotel room if the maid or cleaning people are in the room, even if you are there.

How to Avoid Pickpockets

So many pickpockets have nibbled at my wallets that it is almost a game for me. I sometimes take an old wallet, stuff it with cut paper, place it in my back pocket, and then wander into a crowd to see how quickly my pocket will be picked. Usually, because the wallet is so thick, and I generally know what to look for, I end up thwarting would-be pickpockets just as they are about to nab my funny-money wallet. Do not play this game, however; it can be risky.

If you want to witness a pickpocket, simply find a public place where people are leaning over a rail or wall to look at something below. It will only be a matter of time before a team of pick-pockets will arrive to take advantage of the situation.

Put yourself in the pickpocket's shoes and try to imagine what to look for. Knowing the situations that make pocket picking easy can be the difference between observing a crime and being the victim of one.

What Pickpockets Look for

The following five conditions provide a pick-pocket with (pardon the pun) excellent pickings:

1. *A ripe victim.* This is indicated either by a display of wealth or by an inexperienced, un-

prepared person who allows him- or herself to become a target. For instance, someone who has had one too many drinks has impaired awareness—a perfect victim for a pickpocket, especially if the person looks wealthy or has a fat wallet.

2. *A group of people or a crowd.* The more people who are around an intended victim, the better it is for the pickpocket. A move for the wallet or purse might be perceived as nothing more than another bump from somebody in the crowd.

3. *A natural distraction.* Whenever something occurs that will distract a person's attention, the pickpocket will have the advantage. Ideal locations for a pickpocket include lookout points and railings (where people are looking intently for something beneath them).

4. *A logical move.* This is the bump that seems logical and natural, but is generally created as a diversionary tactic by the pickpocket. Pickpockets often work in teams, with one person providing the distraction and the other providing the "extraction."

5. *A clear getaway.* This is essential. Pickpockets will avoid a situation where their ability to escape the scene is limited.

WARNING: To stop a pickpocket theft in progress, it is better to scream than to call attention to the criminal. You have no way of knowing how large the pickpocket team is and whether there are members willing to "shut you up" so that their compatriots can escape.

What to Do if You Are the Intended Victim of a Pickpocket

The following steps all help you to prevent or handle a robbery attempt on your wallet or purse:

1. If you feel a tug on your wallet or purse, make sure your valuables are still with you and se-

cure. Then turn and face the direction of the tug. If the movement was caused by a pick-pocket, the person is apt to drop his or her head and move away quickly.

2. Don't assume that you know how a diversion will take place. It could be that the first tug is designed to get you to turn so that someone else can take your purse or wallet, or your now-unattended camera bag.

3. Note the faces of those around you. If you move to a new location and recognize several of the same people at this new location, make sure your valuables are safe and that you re-main alert.

4. If you have to engage in a struggle to keep your purse or other valuables, you must make an immediate decision about hanging on or letting go. Begin shouting to attract attention. If the thief does not let go and does not try to escape—release your valuables. Better to be poor and healthy than dead and wealthy.

5. If the pickpockets manage to get your wallet, purse, or camera bag, report the crime im-mediately. Get a police case number that you can show to your insurance company. With-out this number, you may find it difficult to collect on an insurance claim.

6. Contact your credit card companies imme-diately to report your loss. Ask for emergency replacement cards if you need them. Always keep a list of your credit cards and their num-bers separate from your cards. Before your trip, empty your wallet's contents onto a copy machine and keep a photocopy of everything you need to report in case of robbery.

14

How to Survive the Rental Car Racket

Every seasoned business traveler I know has a unique horror story about car rentals—and most business people I've met have a deep, passionate loathing for at least one rental car company. Yet all of us, myself included, continue to rent cars and do so in growing numbers. We're so dependent on automotive travel, renting a car when we travel is a natural result.

However, we can do something about the ways in which rental car companies treat us—and that's the reason for this chapter.

To Rent or Not to Rent? That Should Be the Question

In some cities, renting a car is more of a liability than a benefit. When you add the total cost of renting the car and paying for parking, taking cabs can be a far more economical and less frustrating way to travel through many cities. In New

York City, for example, there is no reason to rent a car unless your business extends outside the city.

Before you travel, you should think about each city you will visit and try to determine whether having a rental car is essential and cost effective. Consider the alternative forms of travel for each city and then compare these modes of travel with the difficulties you will face in dealing with a rental car.

Determining the Real Cost of Renting a Car

One argument that people make in favor of rental cars in a city like New York goes something like this: "Sure, driving is a hassle, but try to get a cab at 10:00 in the evening during a heavy rain." True, but try to find a parking place at 6:00 in the evening within 10 city blocks of anywhere near where you need to be. Chances are you'll have to walk several blocks (in the rain, too).

A better way to approach this problem is to set aside convenience for a moment and consider the overall cost involved in renting a car. Here's a list of expenses that can be involved in a typical car rental situation:

☐ The actual rental for the car that the company quotes you

☐ The fuel the agency charges you for—both before and after you use the car

☐ The insurance you pay per day

☐ The parking cost you pay per day at your hotel

☐ The parking fees you will pay wherever you go

☐ The fuel you have to buy along the way

☐ Tips you pay when the valet porters bring your car

☐ Tips you pay when the valet porters take your car

☐ Sales tax charged

☐ Hidden charges you never find out about unless you watch your credit card bills like a hawk

☐ The fee to waive the collision damage liability

☐ Your frustration at not finding a parking place

☐ Your exasperation at having to deal with an accident, breakdown, flat tire, or other malfunction

WARNING: Sales tax can be a devastating surprise internationally, bringing the final price to as much as double the original price quoted. I have paid a 33 percent rental tax in some foreign locations, on top of the local city tax of 10 to 20 percent. If you start with a $200 per week rental base price, then add $40 for city or airport tax and insurance charges of $84 ($12 per day times seven days) your total bill is $324. Add to that $106 for the 33 percent rental tax, and your grand total is $430. This is more than double the $200 per week you initially thought you would have to pay.

TIP

Know what the total charges consist of before you rent. Make sure your travel agent checks for added city and country tax. These taxes vary from place to place. You might be able to save a bundle by renting your car in Germany instead of Austria, or Portugal instead of France. Not only will you save substantially on taxes, but the actual car rental rate might be cheaper.

The Insurance Rip-Off—The Gold Mine of the Rental Car Racket

Collision and damage waiver (CDW) is what you pay the rental car company to be relieved of the liability for any damage to the car. Although this sounds like an insurance policy, if it were, the rental car company would have to register with the state in which you rented the car as an insurance company. Rental agencies don't, of course. Also, if this were an insurance situation, it would be under the control of that state's insurance bureau. It isn't.

If you own a car, you most likely already have a collision policy that insures you for other cars that you drive, including rental cars. There is usually a deductible associated with this policy. This is true insurance and is regulated by the insurance commission in your state.

How Leasing Agents Mislead You

When you rent a car, the agent might ask, "Do you want full coverage?" What they really are saying is, "Pay us this exorbitant amount per day, and we will waive the right to come after you and take you for every penny you have if you put so much as a scratch on one of our beautiful cars."

The cost for this hospitality will vary and should be considered when you compare the overall costs of renting a car and using a cab or limo. On one occasion, I phoned two different rental car offices (each was a nationally recognized agency) and asked the cost to rent a car in Pittsburgh, for noon on the following Wednesday, returning the car to the airport at 6:00 P.M. the following Friday. I asked each company for the least expensive car rental.

By the time I added the base per-day cost for the car, the collision waiver charge, the gas charge, and tax, I ended up with a price of

$140.15 for one company and $136.88 for the other. I then continued working with the lower estimate. To that charge I had to add the following:

Rental Car Quote for Pittsburgh, Pennsylvania
Wednesday to Friday
(Two Days)

Lowest price, including CDW, initial gas, and tax	$136.88
Parking at my hotel for two nights	15.00
Minimum other parking fees (estimated)	5.00
Tips to valet parking attendants (total)	5.00
Gas during the two days	5.00
Total cost	$166.88

This total does not account for any problems I might have with the car. It is based on typical charges, not including additional tips or daily parking, which could easily run $10 for the two days.

Compare the fee structure just listed with the fees for the alternative transportation:

Limousine, round trip, Airport/Town/Airport	$ 20
Tip driver $2 each way, or a total of	4
Four cab rides for each day in Pittsburgh, at an average estimated cost of $6 per fare	48
Tips to cab drivers	6
Total cost	$ 78

If you substitute a cab ride, round trip to and from the airport, add another $30 to the total cost, based on a per-trip charge of $25	30
Total cost using cabs throughout	$108

Of course, if you will be staying at a hotel that offers free airport pickup and delivery, you could save $50 on the above charge.	−50
Total cost using free airport rides	$ 68

Just about any way you slice it, the alternative charge is much lower than the charges you would pay for using a rental car.

Planning Is the Key to Saving Big

If you are familiar with the city you are traveling to and you know the travel alternatives (and their costs), you can make a fairly good estimate of what you might save with alternate transportation methods compared to a car rental. I went to Washington, D.C., not long ago for a one-day trip and had decided in advance that I would not need a rental car. I decided I could take cabs or the subway to get wherever I needed to go. However, I hadn't anticipated some of the delays in getting to the subway stations. I ended up taking more cabs than I had planned. By the end of the day, I was exhausted both physically and financially.

TIP

International rental charges can often be reduced when you cross borders into another country but return the car in the original country. Ask in advance if the high sales tax charged will be waived during the time you—and the car—are out of the country. I discovered this technique last year in Austria when I traveled to Czechoslovakia. All that was required was a stamp placed on a certain document at the Austrian border, showing I was leaving Austria, and then another stamp upon my return to Austria. Because the tax in Austria is 25 percent of the total rental charges, I saved considerably.

When It Pays to Rent

If you need to travel great distances, need the comfort of your own car, and require the privacy of traveling on your own terms—and if you love to drive—renting a car can be a good and even thrifty experience.

Two weeks before writing this, I visited Spain and rented a car for one week at a total cost (including gas, insurance, tax, unlimited mileage, and all the other extras) of $255. By the end of the week, I had driven more than 2000 miles in the car and had accomplished all my business, in my own time and with plenty of privacy. I could never have had this experience had I taken cabs, limos, buses, trains, or any other form of available transportation. And I saved money over these other modes of transportation, too.

How to Survive the High Cost of Rental Cars

Keep in mind that expense is a relative concept and has to be weighed against other priorities, such as time and comfort. Sometimes, you just have to spend more to receive what you want or need. Nevertheless, these 10 basic concepts represent ways to keep your rental car costs down.

1. Plan ahead
2. Join an association
3. Understand the contract
4. Avoid the insurance rip-off
5. Don't buy the agency's gas
6. Shop around
7. Reserve least expensive
8. Do not "buy" upgrades
9. Check local agencies
10. Avoid drop-off charges

Plan Your Trip to Avoid Excess Charges

When you rent a car, the time of day that you log the car out will establish the "required check-in time." For example, if you pick up the car at 1:00 P.M. and expect to have the car for two days, your return time will be 1:00 P.M. two days later. Sometimes, the rental car company will give you an hour or so grace period—but don't count on it. Ask to be sure. If you keep the car for a few extra hours past the check-in time or the grace period, the extra charge can quickly add another full day to the bill.

The added expense for missing the rental agency's deadline will include all of the extra charges for each day—taxes, the insurance waiver, and so on. If you had rented the car for a period that happened to be discounted or have a larger car due to a special promotion for a weekend rate, your penalty for missing the deadline can be as large as the total rental for your discount package.

If you anticipate the need for a car for only one day, you might save by taking advantage of the hotel's free transportation from the airport in the morning. Then, rent a car later in the day and return the car at the airport the following afternoon. By doing this, you can avoid being charged for a second day.

Association Discounts

Many organizations, associations, and companies have negotiated with rental car agencies to provide rental discounts for their members. You may already belong to one such group or organization without being aware of this benefit.

Some frequent flyer programs also offer special rates or discounts on car rentals, and many international airlines have developed special programs that allow passengers to rent cars at their destinations at very attractive rates.

If you work for a large company, find out whether the company has a special corporate rate with any car rental agencies. It is important to remember, though, that rental car agencies, like airlines, offer special promotions from time to time. These promotional rates might be lower than any special deals you could get with your company or another association.

TIP

Trade-offs and hidden costs often exist with special "deals." For example, 100 to 150 free miles per day provided with one category of rental price might provide you with more than enough free miles for your needs. If so, there is no need to pay for the more expensive "unlimited mileage" category.

On the other hand, if you will be driving quite a lot, and, in fact, aren't sure exactly how many miles you will travel in the rental car, then the unlimited mileage rate can be the only way to go.

Read and Understand Your Rental Agreement

Have you ever taken the time to read a rental agreement in its entirety? Most people haven't, although you would probably be unpleasantly surprised to learn the details involved in such agreements.

If you read the contract, you will discover several elements that do not seem logical. For example, many rental companies offer very low weekly rentals. It is possible to rent a car, in some states, for less than $80 per week. Assume you sign for this category of rental. Four days into the rental agreement, you discover you need to return home. When you return the car, you may find that, because you have not kept the car for a full week, you are charged for the daily rate, and end up actually paying double or triple for the vehicle. You might even be charged mileage, even though the weekly rate had unlimited miles.

Avoiding the Insurance Rip-Off

When you rent a car, you will probably be given the option to waive or accept several separate parts of the agreement. Most of them concern collision and damage liability.

Understanding the Collision-Damage Waiver

Many business people who rent cars nearly everywhere they travel say they *never* agree to the collision-damage waiver. Their justification is, "Why should I pay up to $15 per day when my own PAP (personal auto policy) will cover me?" But because most people pay for rental cars by credit card, the rental agency allows them to take the car without paying the CDW charge; in essence, the agencies hold the credit card hostage. If the renters drive the cars and incur or cause any damage, the rental car company is apt to charge the repairs to the travelers' cards—and get away with it, too.

Try renting a car sometime without paying by credit card. If you don't want the CDW and do not have a credit card, most car agencies require you to put up a sizable deposit (as much as $400 for some companies) before you can have the car.

Say you rent a car using your credit card and do not sign the CDW because you are covered for rental car damages by your own personal insurance. Then you get into an accident with the rental car. Your expectation is that you should be able to just tell the rental car company to contact your insurance company, right? The more likely scenario is as follows:

1. The damage occurs. It may not matter who is at fault.
2. You call the rental car company.

3. The agency representative picks up the car (if and when the agency can).
4. The agency discovers you have not initialed the CDW.
5. You are requested to file a report with your insurance company.
6. The information you need to report the accident is in the glove compartment of the rental car, wherever it now is.
7. You eventually get the information, file the report, and then meet the insurance adjuster. Now you discover you have a $500 deductible and the damage is $499.50, so there is nothing the adjuster can do for you. Or you discover that the damage is $4000 and you still have to pay the first $500.
8. You return home and try to clear up the mess that now exists between the car rental company, the repair people, your own insurance company, and the credit card company, which has put a hold on your card.

All of these steps assume that nobody was injured or arrested, which would compound your problems.

Apply for a Credit Card That Covers You Automatically for Collision

With many major credit and charge cards, collision coverage is free. If you have a major credit card and rent cars on a regular basis, you should call the customer service number and ask about this provision. If your card does not offer this service, apply for one that does.

I rent cars on an average of 135 days per year. With a minimum cost of $8 per day for CDW charges, I save $1080 in one average year by charging my rental cars with my American Express card.

The program seems to actually work, too. I was in a minor accident when someone ran into

me in Madrid not long ago. I filled out the usual
accident forms, was contacted by a service company about a month later to review the details,
and that was that, with zero cost and only a few
minutes of detail work for me.

Never Rely on Your Own PAP

Complications can grow when you rent a car with
additional drivers, and these other drivers are not
insured under the same plan as you are. You
might have paid with your credit card (one that
doesn't pay for collisions and damages), but the
other person was driving, and guess what? He
doesn't even own a car and certainly doesn't have
any personal coverage. Guess who gets stuck
now? The bottom line: If you do not have a credit
card that covers you in case of an accident, you
should always pay the CDW. But get a better
credit card soon!

Personal Accident and Personal Effects Coverage

If you have personal auto coverage at home, then
you are probably covered under this policy, although the coverage might not be adequate. You
may be surprised to discover (too late) that your
coverage is limited. Deductible, exclusions, and
the like can come into play.

Read your policy and, if necessary, call your
insurance agent to find out the extent of your
rental car coverage. If you have reasonable coverage, it probably provides greater protection
than a rental car company's CDW. Decline the
CDW if you feel sure you have adequate coverage
under your personal policy.

Liability Insurance

Liability insurance is a must for business travelers who drive (and is required by law in many
states). If you have PAP, you most likely have a
reasonable amount of liability insurance, too.
However, is a reasonable amount enough? Con-

sider whether, during your travels, you sometimes have passengers in the car. If you are in an accident, and your business associates are injured, your liability could be substantial—in the hundreds of thousands of dollars.

Also find out whether your company offers separate coverage for employees who drive rental cars. If such a policy exists, find out just how much coverage is extended to you when you are away from home (and the office) on business. Do not assume anything, and ask questions of your insurance agent.

Copy the list in Figure 14-1 and send it to your insurance agent. Ask for a reply.

Responding to this bill of goods is a tough assignment for any insurance agent, and I was surprised to discover that some of the coverage

---

1. What coverage does my PAP provide for rental cars, as it relates to
   (a) Collision damage
       i. deductible
       ii. how to report
       iii. geographic limitations
   (b) Personal accident and personal effects
       i. deductible
       ii. how to report
       iii. geographic limitations
       iv. exclusions
   (c) Liability insurance
       i. maximum amount per accident
       ii. maximum amount per person
       iii. legal defense
       iv. geographic limitation to where legal action is filed
2. What are the steps required to handle each of the potential problems given in item 1? Include phone numbers for worldwide use.
3. What additional insurance do I (my company) need to adequately protect myself and the firm? At what cost?
4. What kinds of rental vehicles are excluded from my present PAP (or my company's auto coverage)?
5. What would happen if I rented a car in . . . (select five cities that you frequently visit).

Figure 14-1 *Questions for the Insurance Agent About Rental Cars*

I thought I had was either less effective or non-existent as soon as I left the United States.

Liability insurance, for example, rarely provides for your defense unless you are sued within the United States. Say you rent a car in Jamaica, have an accident, and get sued there. Your insurance company will write you, saying, in effect, "Sorry pal, get them to sue you in Miami."

Naturally, people who will sue you want the "home-court" advantage. They aren't going to file litigation in the United States if they live elsewhere. The moral: When in Rome (or any other place outside the United States), purchase local liability insurance—unless you know for certain that your own insurance company will come to your defense.

The High Cost of Rental Agency Gas

The standard industry attitude has been, "You have a full tank now, so when you return the car, make sure the tank is full or we'll charge you." What the agency doesn't tell you is that "its gas" is often twice the standard market price. Again, the rental car agency makes a nice profit on your lack of knowledge about the car rental business's tactics.

Alamo, one of the newer companies in the industry, came up with a novel idea. It went like this: "The tank is nearly empty. Please bring the car back with an empty tank, because we will not give you any credit for the gas you put in our car." Well, after Alamo had to deal with thousands of cars running out of gas a few blocks from the return station, the agency changed its corporate tune; Alamo now offers the regular full-tank deal like everyone else. It also provides you with the option to rent the car with a partial tank, for which the agency charges you something on the order of $1.80 per gallon and allows you to return the car with an empty tank at no additional charge.

Best Price Chicago, Worst Price California

The car renter who is loyal to one rental company is sure to pay too much somewhere along the way. Just about all the major rental car companies have their version of the airlines' frequent flyer program. In some cases, you can actually pick up mileage for your favorite airline frequent flyer account. As is the case with the airlines, car rental companies provide their "frequent driver" programs to keep you from renting elsewhere.

Although I recommend belonging to any and all frequent anything programs, as long as they cost you nothing, you *must* shop around whenever you are going to rent a car. Rental car companies do not have a "set" price that applies nationwide. Local competition, or lack of it, may account for fluctuations in a company's rate schedule from location to location. Seasonal differences in climate might also make some areas more expensive than others at certain times of the year. In any case, never assume that, just because Avis had the lowest rental price in Chicago last week, Avis will be the lowest price in Los Angeles this week.

Rental car companies are always expanding into more cities and countries. There are plenty of newcomers to this playing field. Competition does affect the rental car market, but as is true with the airlines, the let's-see-what-the-customers-will-let-us-get-away-with mentality also plays a big role. The result is that special deals can be made from time to time, especially when one company makes a sudden shift in marketing strategy and "tests" a new kind of approach in one area of the country, or even in just one city. If that city is where you need a car rental and you are able to rent from that car agency, you (or your travel agent) have played the game skillfully.

What Class of Car Should You Rent?

Unless I have a very specific need for a larger car, I always reserve the least expensive car possible. Note that I said "least expensive," not smallest. A rental agency might happen to have an abundance of cars in a particular rental class—perhaps midsize. To keep these cars on the road, the agency might charge you less for that class than for a smaller car. Also, if you are renting over a weekend, you may find that the rental car company has a weekend special for a larger car.

When you reserve the least expensive car and arrive at the rental agency to discover it is out of that car, the common practice is for the agency to give you a larger car, at the price you were quoted for the least expensive car. Whereas the actual inventory for different rental fleets will vary, there are times of the year in certain cities when a certain class of car is most likely not available. If you frequent a city several times, ask that same smiling rental agent who greets you from time to time: "When would I likely get an automatic upgrade due to inability to meet my reservation for the least expensive car?" You might be surprised to discover that you are given a truthful answer.

WARNING: Be aware of the *special upgrade* that might be offered when you check in. The offer goes like this: "Mr. Cummings, we have a special promotion today. For $5 more per day I can give you a full-size car. Shall I put you down for one?"

If I say "Yes," there is a chance that I will be paying $5 for the same car I would get if I had said "No." Why? Simply because that location might already be out of the least expensive car I reserved.

This scheme isn't the same as the usually above-board upgrades provided by frequent flyer clubs and other group affiliations. But don't be too quick to slap your upgrade coupon on the

counter or "pay" for that special upgrade. If the company is out of the car you have reserved, and is about to give you a larger car anyway, then your coupon for a larger car should upgrade you to an even larger vehicle. If it doesn't, save the coupon for another trip. If you are offered an upgrade at a slight extra cost, ask the agent if you could see the kind of car you reserved in comparison to the one they want you to upgrade to. They may suddenly remember that you would get a free upgrade because they are out of the class of car you reserved.

If You Upgrade, Make Sure None of the Other Costs Go Up

Upgrades might increase some of the other costs of the rental, and you should be sure that a "free upgrade" does not cost you an additional 50 cents a mile, extra insurance charges, and so on—in addition to twice the gas consumption of the adequate, although smaller, reserved car.

Local Rental Car Companies— Are They Any Good?

Many local rental car companies give the national companies a real run for their money—and offer you a break for yours. But just because the rental company is local, and even situated off the airport, does not mean it will be the least expensive. The best way to get long-term benefits from car rentals is to determine which cities you frequent the most, then ask your travel agent to study the local market to determine how the smaller local companies compare with the national rental car companies.

If you frequent a particular branch of your own company, the local people might be able to negotiate with one or more of the in-town rental car companies for a reduced price that even includes special services, like airport pickup and delivery, delivery to the hotel, and longer grace periods for drop-off and check-in.

I have rented cars from local rental car companies for years and have had both unexpectedly pleasant and unabashedly horrifying experiences with them. The most common unpleasant are mechanical problems I've had with cars rented from a local agency. Of course, I have had some horrible experiences with the national companies, too. But as a rule of thumb: Never rent from a local company if you are going to take the car more than two hours away from their location.

Avoid Drop-Off Charges

Drop-off charges are often hidden, so you have to ask about them specifically. The actual charge will vary widely from place to place. A company might assess a ridiculously high drop-off charge in one city, and none at all in another.

There are ways to avoid drop-off charges, and in fact get a free car at the same time. Most agencies end up with cars that belong to other locations and have to return the cars to those other locations. They return the cars by having someone drive them (unless they load a bunch on a transport van), and actually pay individuals to transport the car to the original location. If you find that you frequently drive from one city to another, you should contact some of the rental car companies that have locations in each city and see if you can work out a deal where you rent a car in each city, then do them a favor by taking a car "for them" between the cities.

Look in local newspaper classifieds under "Car Transport" or "Transportation." You will often discover companies that are looking for drivers to take cars from one city to another. Sometimes these companies contract out to the rental car companies. In other situations, the companies simply handle car shipments for people who do not like to drive across country when they move or visit their seasonal home for holidays. A perusal of the Yellow Pages under these same headings, or "Auto Delivery," might lead you to other such companies. Usually, these transport companies will give you a gas allowance, as well as a certain number of days to travel from Point A to Point B. Often, the deal includes a one-way airplane ticket to return home.

WARNING: Although you can still rent a car with unlimited mileage offered, many car rental agencies are shifting to a new strategy. They offer cars with "free mileage." Each company at each location may have a different formula, which makes direct comparisons of rentals difficult. For example, the same midsize car could be $35 and 100 free miles at one agency, and $40 and 150 free miles at the other. The moment you use up the free miles, you begin to pay exorbitant charges for each additional mile. Many people are used to renting cars with unlimited mileage and don't realize that they are being taken advantage of.

TIP

Do you have a complaint about your last car rental? Follow these steps:

1. Write a letter explaining very briefly what happened.
2. Attach a copy of your agreement, if available.
3. State what you want to have happen (be reasonable).
4. Send one copy to your travel agent; another to the Car Agency Home Office—Attention PRESIDENT OF THE COMPANY— URGENT; and another copy to the American Car Rental Association, 2011 Eye

Street, N.W., Fifth Floor, Washington, DC
20006, or call 1-202-223-2118.

Car Rental Companies You May Want to Know About

The following is a fairly representative list of
rental car companies in the United States and
abroad. Remember that off-airport locations
often rent for less than airport agencies, but the
savings may not match the inconvenience required to get to and from the off-airport agency
location.

Advance Car Rentals
Minneapolis, Minnesota
612-591-0076
800-328-6262 reservations

Affordable Services (Limo)
Los Angeles, California
213-622-9787

Agency Rent a Car
Salon, Ohio
216-349-1000
800-221-8666 reservations

Alamo Rent a Car
Fort Lauderdale, Florida
305-522-0000
800-327-0400 except FL
800-327-9633 FL only

All Star Limousine
Long Island City, New York
718-784-7766
800-999-7766 reservations

Alpha Rent-a-Car
Miami, Florida
305-871-3432

American Intl. Rent a Car

Dallas, Texas
800-225-2529

Auto-Europe

Camden, Maine
800-223-5555 reservations
800-458-9503 Canada only

Avis Rent a Car System

Garden City, New York
516-222-3175 office
800-331-1212

Budget Rent a Car Corp.

Chicago, Illinois
312-580-5000 office
800-527-0700 world reservations

Budget Rent a Car Canada

Toronto, Ontario
416-486-2919
800-268-8900 reservations
800-268-8970 Quebec
112-800-268-8900 B.C.

Budget Rent a Car Hawaii

Honolulu, Hawaii
800-922-7221
800-527-0700

Carey Intl. Limousine

Washington, D.C.
800-336-4646

Connex Intl. European Car Rentals, Ltd.

Peekskill, New York
800-333-3949 USA
800-843-5416 Canada

Dollar Rent a Car
Los Angeles, California
213-776-8100 office
800-421-6878 USA
Honolulu, Hawaii
800-367-7006 HI only

Enterprise Rent a Car
St. Louis, Missouri
314-863-7000 office
800-325-8007 except MO
800-392-0248 MO only

Europe by Car
New York, New York
212-581-3040 office
800-252-9401 CA only
800-233-1516 except CA

General Rent a Car
Hollywood, Florida
305-926-1700 office
800-327-7607 reservations

Hertz Corporation
New York, New York
212-980-2121 office
Domestic Reservations
800-654-3131 except OK
800-522-3711 OK only
800-268-1311 Canada
800-654-8200 AK and HI
Intl. Reservations
800-654-3001

Kemwel Group
Harrison, New York
914-839-5555 office
800-678-0678 reservations

Kenning Car Rental
Chesterfield, England
800-227-8990 USA and Canada
0-246-20-8888 UK

Marsans International
New York, New York
212-239-3880 office
800-223-6114 reservations

National Car Rental
Minneapolis, Minnesota
612-830-2121 office
800-328-4300 reservations

Payless Car Rental System
St. Petersburg, Florida
813-381-2758 office
800-541-1566 reservations

Renault USA, Inc.
New York, New York
212-532-1221 office
800-221-1052 reservations

Sears Rent a Car
Chicago, Illinois
312-580-5000 office
800-527-0770 except TX
800-442-0770 TX only

Showcase Rental Cars and Limousine Service
Los Angeles, California
213-670-7002 office
800-421-6808 reservations

Snappy Car Rental
Beachwood, Ohio
216-831-6340 office
800-321-7159 except OH
800-669-5252 OH only
800-633-6533 Canada

Thrifty Car Rental
Tulsa, Oklahoma
918-665-3930 office
800-367-2277 reservations

≡ 15
Some Tips on Tipping

How Much to Tip in the United States

A surprising number of adults in the U.S. don't know how to tip for basic services in their own country. Many people don't tip certain types of service workers because they either do not know whether they should or are afraid that they'll tip the wrong amount.

As a basic guide, Table 15–1 shows the generally accepted minimum tip for many service workers in the United States.

Table 15–2 provides a brief description of the service rendered by each type of service worker and the reasons for the tip provided.

International Tipping

Although tipping is pretty much a universal phenomenon, the way you tip and the amounts you give differ from country to country. Unless I've

Table 15-1 *Customary Tips for Services*

Person or Service	Usual Minimum Tip
AAA VIPs	Modest personalized gift
Bar bill	10 to 15%
Bartenders—Barmaids	0 to 10% in addition to above
Bellmen (hotels)	$1 minimum plus 50 cents per bag
Cab drivers	10%, minimum 30 cents
Chef	Praise
Delivery people	$1
Doormen	$1
Elevator operators	50 cents (optional)
Head waiter	$5 in addition to restaurant bill (optional)
Hotel maid	$1 per person per day
Hotel manager	Specialty gift (optional)
Limousine drivers	$5 minimum plus $5 per hour
Maitre d'	$5 each couple to get a good table (optional)
Massage staff	$5 for each massage
Parking attendants	$1 per service
Porters	50 cents per bag, minimum $1
Restaurant bill	10 to 20%, includes waiter/bus boy
Room service	$1 plus 5%
Secretary	Gift
Shoeshine person	20%
Travel agent	Gift (optional)
Waiter	*See* Restaurant bill

indicated otherwise in this chapter, you should tip in the currency for the country you are in.

Tips in Developing and Eastern European Countries

When you are traveling in developing countries or in Eastern or Central Europe, reduce the percentage by about 75 percent—if you tip in hard European or U.S. currency, the tipping guide can be thrown out the window or at least cut to a quarter of its value. The reason is that the street market value for hard currency is double or triple the official rate. With this in mind, when you travel in these countries, carry a good supply of $1 and $5 bills and you'll be treated like royalty when you tip.

Table 15–2 *Description of Tipping Strategy*

Person or Service	Description of Tip or Variation
AAA VIPs	These are people in a responsible position at restaurants, hotels, and so on, and are people whom you will want to be friendly with in case you need something special. You do not give these people money; bring a more personal gift. Sometimes a small item, such as a bottle of perfume or Havana cigars, will endear you to these individuals for quite some time. This gift is given even though you received zero service this time. You are paving the way for something better next time. But if you do not get better treatment on your next visit, taper off rather than add to the value of the gift.
Bar Bill	Tip 10% to 15% to your bar bill for normal service. Should the bartender provide special service that you feel warrants additional reward, then feel free to leave something extra on the bar, but do not add it to the bill.
Bartenders-Barmaids	*See* Bar Bill
Bellmen	Never tip less than 50 cents for each bag they bring to your room, with the minimum being $1. If you arrive by cab or car and you are greeted by the doorman and bellmen, tip only the doorman at the door and only the bellmen who bring up your bags.
Cab Drivers	10%, with 30 cents being the minimum unless some tour guiding and other interesting conversation was involved.
Chef	Praise to a chef is worth a million dollars.
Delivery People	$1 is generally enough unless what they brought was extra heavy, extra important, or extra valuable.
Doormen	$1 is maximum unless you are trying to impress someone.
Elevator Operators	50 cents, and only in unusual situations.
Head Waiter	A $5 tip is minimum *if you are going to tip a head waiter.* You do not have to tip the head waiter at all, but if you plan to frequent this restaurant, it is a good idea to set your own stage and let the waiter know who is the producer.

continued

Person or Service	Description of Tip or Variation
Hotel Maid	This depends on how many nights you are going to stay in this hotel. If you are staying only one night, then it is not necessary to tip the maid. For stays of more than one night, a tip of $1 per day would be reasonable. If she does something really nice, tip accordingly.
Hotel Manager	I make it a habit to bring something special to the hotel managers of those hotels I frequent. By doing this I am able to ensure that I get unique and specialized service and that nothing due me is overlooked (messages, mail, or services).
Limousine Drivers	The absolute minimum is more than enough. Calculate $5 plus $5 per hour—and do not be surprised if the driver pulls you aside to suggest more money is merited. If the driver becomes insistent, smile and tell him you have to cash a money order and you will be right back, but don't return.
Maitre d'	If you are going to tip the maitre d', slip him nothing smaller than a bill. This may not do anything for you if this is your first night at the restaurant, but build on that. After a short while, you will be offered the best tables.
Massage Staff	A $5 tip is enough no matter how magnificent the massage was.
Parking Attendants	$1 per car per park. This is a maximum anywhere in the world, and is over and above the actual parking fee for the lot.
Porters	No matter where a porter hails from, tip 50 cents per bag with a minimum of $1.
Restaurant Bill	The minimum tip to be added on any restaurant bill is 10% of the total cost of the meal. The maximum is 20% unless something very special occurred. Examine your bill before you tip to make sure this restaurant does not automatically add, say, 15% to the tab for service. If a restaurant does this (it should say so somewhere on the menu), you are under no obligation to tip. And if you think the

continued

Person or Service	Description of Tip or Variation
	service was very poor, ask for that automatic 15% to be removed or reduced.
Room Service	$1 plus a maximum of 5% of the total bill for the items ordered.
Shoeshine Person	A flat 20% is plenty, unless the person has told you the funniest story you've ever heard.
Travel Agent	A small item brought back from your travels will surprise and endear you to your travel agent, so there's no need to be more extravagant than that.
Waiter	When you have a good one, try to keep him by returning to that same restaurant and that same waiter. Tip well. An additional 5% directly to the waiter (not added to the bill) and in addition to the normal service tip will be more than enough.

In the Soviet Union, the official line is not to allow tipping. In reality, you will find that a well-intended tip, given without public display, will be accepted gratefully and even more so if it is hard currency.

Hungary is a bit more cosmopolitan about tipping. There you can tip just as you would in most Western European countries. U.S. dollars are well received in Hungary, Czechoslovakia, Poland, and other Eastern Bloc countries.

China is also in a whirlwind of change, and no matter what you see other people doing, you should limit your tips to expressions of thanks and small, nonmonetary gifts. Tour guides are an exception. Tip your guide the equivalent of $1 per person per day (or per tour if it is less than a day). In China, tip in U.S. currency or with a personal item, like a pair of blue jeans.

In the Third World and countries known to have a low annual wage and/or high unemployment, tips may be the major source of income for the people you come in contact with. You may find that for $7, which may be double or triple the average daily wage, you can hire someone to follow you about town all day carrying your camera equipment. However, make sure you hire someone your hotel or tourguide vouches for, or someone you can outrun.

When Is It Impolite to Tip?

This question perplexes many people, but the answer is pretty simple. It is impolite to tip only if you are dealing directly with the owner, or a member of his or her family. Other offers to tip may be rejected even after your first or second insistence. Never insist more than twice, because it is rude to persist in this manner and may even be interpreted as an insult.

Tipping Customs in Major Business Countries

Argentina—Argentina is probably the most European of Latin American countries. There is a noticeable Italian flair to much of life in the big cities, as well as a strong mixture of German and English backgrounds. Tips are expected and are most appreciated when given separately and directly to the person you want to tip, rather than adding it to the bill.

Australia—Australians and neighboring New Zealanders do not tip, so they are not accustomed to receiving them. Exceptions can be found in major tourist areas where the locals have grown to expect tips. However, I suggest you stick to a sincere show of appreciation, a warm "Thank you very much," and if you feel overwhelmed by some excellent service, leave a modest tip.

Austria—As is true throughout much of Europe, most restaurants and hotels automatically add 10 to 15 percent to the bill for service. If you ask whether the tip is included, the answer will probably be "No," because there is a difference between the service charge and a tip. Phrase your question this way: "Does this price include service?" If so, you should add to this only if the service was at least above average. Your tip will be most appreciated when given directly to the person you wish to tip, because he or she may never see it otherwise.

Belgium—Tip according to the U.S. schedule, except for restaurants and hotels where a substantial add-on is included for service. In these cases, tip only for exceptional service and then do so modestly.

Brazil—As with most of South and Central America, tipping is an important aspect of Brazilian life, because the people count on the extra income. No matter what the restaurant may add to the bill as a service charge, you should tip above that. When walking or driving through the cities, you may discover you are surrounded by children asking for money or trying to do something for you (clean the window of your car, carry your bags, and so on). Do not give money unless they actually do something for you. If you want to give the others something, have some hard candy that you can pass around.

For your more important events, an up-front tip of $5 (at most) works wonders throughout Latin America and should be given with a smile as you begin the task at hand (getting a good table at a restaurant, checking in to your hotel or airline flight, renting a car, and so on).

Canada—Follow the U.S. schedule, only be sure to tip in Canadian dollars.

Caribbean—Follow the U.S. schedule for all major cities in the Caribbean. If you are staying at a full-service facility that provides an American or Modified American Plan, the hotel will likely explain their policy for tips. Do tip the reception person (once you are sure who that is) $5 before you request your room to ensure that your stay will be as pleasant as possible.

Colombia—Colombia has a rather unique law. If a restaurant has added a service charge, and the service is horrible, the customer can request that the meal charge be removed. If the establishment does not oblige, a heavy fine can be imposed. Because of this law, it is unusual for people to tip above the added service charge. Where there is no added charge, such as for cabs, guides, room service, and so on, follow the U.S. schedule. If you are driving a car, you will quickly discover that almost wherever you park someone will come up asking for a tip to watch your car. Never give more than $1, but do give something; otherwise, the car may not be there when you return, or it may lack its wheels.

Denmark—As with all of Scandinavia, tipping is rare even for outside services such as cabs. However, do tip bellmen, porters, and other people who do physical work at your service. If you receive exceptional service in a restaurant or bar, ask to see the owner and tell him or her how much you enjoyed the meal and the service.

Egypt—Be ready to see palms turned toward you in search of *baksheesh*. Give generously (the equivalent of 25 cents would be a generous tip) to anyone who performs a service for you in any way. You will need to carry around a lot of small denominations, because you may be tipping for everything, including people who open doors, people who close doors, elevator operators, people holding fans, and so on.

Finland—*See* Denmark.

France—Look for the words *service compris* or *service en sus*, both of which indicate there has been a service charge added to the final bill. Do not ask if the tip is included—the French consider a tip to be something over and above the service charge. In these establishments you need not tip unless the service was exceptional. For services provided outside a restaurant, follow the U.S. schedule.

Germany—Throughout Germany, tip just as you would in the United States, even if a service charge has been added.

Greece—Even though restaurants and hotels include a service charge (generally 15 percent), you should tip in addition to this, and always directly to the person you wish to tip and in local currency. Tip on the modest side of the U.S. schedule.

Hong Kong—Never tip more than 10 percent, but always in cash given directly to the person you want to tip. Add a warm "Thank you" and some praise to the owner or manager for such excellent service—if you were especially pleased.

Iceland—You may actually offend someone by tipping here, so limit tips to exceptional service, tour guides, and if you return to the same hotel time and again, a gift for the manager.

India—Pay $5 up-front, during check-in at your hotel, and you will have opened several doors to excellent service. To some degree, India will appear as impoverished as Egypt, so plan to tip along the way and tip with small amounts of money to anyone who does something for you. To determine how much extra tip you should leave at a restaurant, check whether a service charge has been added; it is not a uniform custom to add service charges. Do not tip the outstretched palm of anyone who has not been of assistance to you.

Ireland—Do not tip unless you received exceptional service. If your money is refused, quickly retract the tip and exchange it for a warm "Thank you" and some praise. Exceptions will be cab drivers, porters, and guides; tip them according to the U.S. schedule.

Israel—Although tipping is relatively new in Israel, it has come to be expected. In fact, you may be verbally abused if you tip stingily or not at all. Ask if there is a service charge added to your bill and tip no more than 5 percent above that. Where no service charge is included, tip according to the U.S. schedule.

Italy—Once you are sure there is a service charge added, you can limit your tip to an extra 5 to 10 percent of the bill. If there is no service charge, tip 10 to 20 percent of the bill. Outside restaurants and hotels, tip according to the U.S. schedule.

Japan—In general, tipping is not a common practice. Give small gifts for people who serve you on a frequent basis. An up-front tip in the equivalent of $5 to the service person at a Japanese inn may be expected. Carry your predetermined tips in small white envelopes and never hand cash directly to anyone unless it cannot be avoided; for cab drivers and porters, however, you should tip according to the U.S. schedule.

Mexico—Mexicans have been through many ups and downs in dealing with American tourists. For now, the relationship is excellent. The people are friendly and their service can be the best in Latin America. Tip them accordingly using the U.S. percentages as your guide.

Netherlands—If you think about the saying, "Let's go Dutch," you'll begin to realize what it must be like to live on tips in Holland. Refer to the listing for Belgium for information on tipping in the Netherlands.

New Zealand—Don't plan on tipping much. New Zealanders don't do it, so they don't expect it. But when you get that exceptional service, open your wallet a little.

Norway—*See* Denmark.

Portugal—Portugal is a wonderful place to visit, and the prices are so reasonable that even a 15 percent tip added in is still a bargain. But tip only modestly when service is added to the bill and never more than 15 percent when it is not.

Spain—Spain has some magnificent hotels and wonderful restaurants. But bargain prices no longer exist. Tip according to the U.S. schedule. However, be alert to the 15 to 20 percent service charge at most restaurants and tip only for exceptional service above that.

Sweden—As in all of Scandinavia, the locals hardly ever tip. The best advice here is to add a maximum of 5 percent to the bill. Because Swedes take great pride in what they do and believe their wage to be enough, praise works wonders here.

Switzerland—Follow the standard for Sweden, except when you are in the Italian sector near Como and Lugano, where you should follow the tips shown for Italy.

Turkey—Follow the suggestions for Egypt, except bear in mind that the Turks expect up-front tips for special services. A bellydancer will expect to be paid and tipped in advance of her performance if you have hired her for a private party. She will also expect to receive tips during her performance. Turks are not overly gracious in the way they accept tips, but do not hold this against them.

United Kingdom—The English are not well known for their generous tipping. However, if you are not a native of the United Kingdom, you will never offend anyone by following the U.S. schedule.

How to Give the Right Business Gift

When you give a gift to a client or associate, for any business reason, it should not have a promotional aspect to it. Flowers sent to show your respect for a wedding, funeral, or as a thank you for a social evening or event you were invited to are okay. In this last situation, excellent gifts include a travel book containing photographs or candy, which you present personally when making an appearance at the home of the client or associate.

Only in rare instances is it essential for a gift to be expensive, and unless the occasion is unique, a maximum of $50 should be set as a standard policy. Most of the time, half that amount suffices.

Try to Be Unique and Thoughtful in Your Selection of a Gift

If you want to make a lasting impression, you may find that a practical gift, like a paperweight that says "To Harry from Jack," will be appreciated (in the United States only, though). If the person you wish to give a gift to is in another area of the country, you may consider sending something indigenous to the area you live in, such as a box of local fruits, maple syrup, local handicraft, or a book of photography of your area.

Giving Gifts on an International Scale

Keep in mind that you do not have to go to Korea to give a gift to a Korean. There are plenty of Asian and Asian-American businesspeople in the

United States who maintain strong ties to their culture.

For Table 15-3 (on pages 302–307) I have selected some of the major business centers around the world and described the business gifts that would be ideal for each region. The gifts are divided into two categories: business gifts, which you give at the end of a meeting, and social gifts, which you give at the start of the event.

Special Things to Remember About Giving and Accepting a Gift

1. To be safe, hand the wrapped gift with your right hand or with both hands, but never with your left hand alone.
2. Accept a gift with both hands.
3. Never urge someone to open the gift you just gave. This would serve to embarrass the recipient or other guests who have not brought a gift.
4. Never open a gift that has been given to you unless urged to do so (and only when you will not embarrass others present who have not given you a gift or whose gift may not measure up to the standards of the one you may open).
5. Always follow up any gift-giving event with a card of thanks.
6. When in doubt, give candy and/or flowers, which you send in advance of your arrival.
7. Appreciate the religious nature of your host or client and never give a gift that would be obviously wrong in the setting. Arabs may drink alcohol when away from home, but do not assume they will appreciate a bottle of brandy given to them when they are at home—in front of other members of their family who are devout Moslems.

Table 15–3 Preferred Gifts Around the World—and Ones Not to Give

Country or Region	What to Give or Avoid Giving—
Europe	**Business**—Give a bottle of American whiskey or wine, or some other American product only if you know it is something the person likes. Photographic books of the United States or pen sets *without your company logo* are also thoughtful gifts. Avoid giving cigarettes unless they are requested (except when given to your private hotel staff). **Social**—Flowers or fine chocolates taken to the home are a nice gift. Avoid chrysanthemums and lilies, because these flowers are most often reserved for funerals; also avoid giving roses, which are for lovers.
Germany	**Business**—A sample of your product, a pen set, photographic book of the United States, or American whiskey is appropriate. **Social**—Flowers are best (no red roses, though); candy second; and a fine German calvados, French cognac, or American whiskey will also do nicely.
Greece	**Business**—Give a bottle of a fine Greek brandy or some unique American product for which there is no Greek counterpart (maple syrup, for example) or photographic books of the United States. A decorator box filled with American cigarettes is okay. **Social**—Flowers are a good choice, but tell the local florist the occasion and have the manager suggest the best kind of arrangement for you to send ahead. An American fruitcake is a good choice if your visit will be near the Christmas holidays.

Ireland
Business—Modest gifts such as a collection of U.S. stamps or American bourbon or wine will do.
Social—Flowers, chocolate, maple syrup, cane sugar, cheese, or a good bottle of wine, American bourbon, or something for the children will be appreciated.

Israel
Business—Photographic or other books are the best gift, unless you have advance knowledge of the preference of your client.
Social—Chocolate would be at the top of my list; second would be flowers, but only if you explain the occasion to a florist and let the florist select the arrangement. Never send flowers to a funeral.

Italy
Business—Fine French brandy, American bourbon, Swiss chocolates, and U.S. commemorative stamps are my choices, in that order.
Social—Any flowers except chrysanthemums and lilies, and flowers must be an odd number; as an alternative, any of the usual business gifts will do nicely. Do not give roses, unless you are a Romeo sending a gift to your Juliet.

Netherlands
Business—Give U.S. commemorative stamps, American bourbon or blended whiskey, or other items you know will be appreciated, such as a recent novel or other book.
Social—Flowers or local chocolates only. Be sure to ask the florist for suggestions.

Norway
Business—Photographic or other interesting books about the United States, or U.S. stamps, but avoid giving any alcoholic beverage.

continued

301

Country or Region	What to Give or Avoid Giving—
	Social—Flowers, chocolates, or some small item from the United States, such as maple syrup or American candy not likely to be found in Norway (peanut brittle, turtles, and so on).
Poland	Business—U.S. stamps, photographic books of the United States, American bourbon, French brandy, and pen sets—in that order.
	Social—Flowers (not red roses or lilies) or chocolates and seasonal pastries.
Portugal	Business—A photographic book or pen set.
	Social—If time permits a reciprocal invitation is best; if not, then have a florist prepare appropriate flowers.
Spain	Business—A box of fine cigars (Havana or Canary Island have the best), American whiskey, or a fine Scotch malt will do nicely.
	Social—Chocolates, a box of marzipan, small pastries, a bottle of fine Spanish wine or brandy, and, last on my list, flowers (but never dahlias, chrysanthemums, or lilies).
Switzerland	Business—Give a box of fine cigars (see Spain), U.S. commemorative stamps, or a personalized sample of your product—without a commercial logo.
	Social—Flowers and chocolates or other candies are fine, but avoid red roses.
Africa	Business—Unless you know the person and can bring items that you know will be accepted and appreciated, stick to very simple gifts that are obviously business in nature, such as a pen set

with the company logo or an engraved placard showing your appreciation for their help or service.

Social—Do not take a gift for the wife (or wives) of the house, except in Egypt or Uganda, or where you socially know the wife and know she will be there. Candy or a small item of glass crystal would be a good choice.

South Africa

Business—A personalized sample of your product, pen set, American whiskey, box of fine cigars, book of photography, and stamp sets are all good choices.

Social—Candy, flowers (no red roses or funeral flowers), recent best-selling novel (as long as it is not about South African political issues), and a bottle of fine wine are all good selections.

Middle East

Business—Gold (gold-plated is okay) items are appreciated, and a pen set (fountain pens only) would be a nice gift. A placard of appreciation following a successfully concluded business deal would be nice, too. A photographic book is okay, but make sure there are no photographs of women. Never give alcoholic beverages or tobacco, even if you know the person uses the item.

Social—Candy or a stamp collection for children are fine, but do not offer a gift or ask about the wife or wives. Avoid being too complimentary over any possession that an Arab has, because he might feel obliged to give it to you out of courtesy.

China

Business—Give only very modest gifts, such as a small photographic book, American stamp collection, fountain pen set, or something you know will be appreciated and acceptable.

continued

Country or Region	What to Give or Avoid Giving—
India	**Social**—Present flowers or fruit that have been prepared by your hotel, provided the hotel's preparer understands the nature of the social visit. A more personal item may follow on a later visit, such as copies of photographs you have taken of your guests.
	Business—Try a pen set, maple syrup, or a personalized sample of your product or a framed placard of thanks. **Social**—A gift that can be shared by the children, or a photographic book of the United States; fruit or candy is equally acceptable, as are copies of photographs taken on previous visits.
Asia Japan	**Business**—Gifts that come in pairs are thought to be special, so a pen set (two items), cuff links, a box with two bottles of brandy or wine, and so on, are excellent gifts. **Social**—French brandy, malt Scotch, a box of chocolates, candy, or small cakes are fine social gifts; avoid giving flowers, except for funerals. As with business gifts, make sure the present is professionally wrapped in a pastel-colored paper. You cannot do this at home and expect it to look nice when you arrive at your host's; let your hotel arrange for the wrapping.
South Korea	**Business**—Pen sets, American stamps, a book of photography, or a personalized sample of your product are all good ideas. **Social**—Flowers (explain the situation to a local florist), or a small glass crystal gift or candy will be good. Except for flowers, any gift should be wrapped.

304

Taiwan

Business—Pen sets, American stamps, American whiskey, or a personalized sample of your product or a placard showing your appreciation for past hospitality.
Social—A basket of fruit, or candy, or small sweets that are locally in season would be ideal. Have your hotel arrange the gift.

Latin America

Business—On the first encounter, your parting gift may be a personalized pen set or a personalized sample of your product. If you know something about the person ahead of time and can bring something more useful, then do so. On a subsequent meeting, you can bring gifts such as Havana cigars, American whiskey, and the like. Begin your meetings by giving the gift.
Social—If you are invited to a social event at the home of your host and have time, send flowers scheduled to arrive the day of the event prior to your arrival. If you are unable to send in advance, take flowers and/or chocolates. Once you know the people you can bring more personal items that you know they would like, such as alcoholic beverages they prefer, perfume, gifts for the children, and so on. A thank-you note and follow-up flowers sent a few days after the social event will separate you from the crowd.

Other Parts of the World

Look at the fundamental background of the people you are to visit. It is likely they will have originated in one of the places already mentioned. You should be safe following the suggestions already given.

8. In Western Europe, business gifts should be limited to your second visit. Company promotional material, if in good taste, is okay. Exceptions to this include Spain and Italy, where a gift at the end of the meeting is okay when a social event is involved (a lunch or party); even then, the gift should be separate from any social gift you may have tendered.

9. In Eastern Europe, expect to be given gifts and expect to give them on your first visit. French wine and brandy, or American or Scotch whiskey are good choices; they will soon disappear, so there is no evidence left for embarrassment. Do expect to be a bit more extravagant than your Eastern European hosts. You might even find that they are overly generous considering what they can reasonably afford.

10. If you are a businesswoman, your gift giving should be kept to very simple items that are of an obvious business nature. Commemorative stamp sets, pen sets with the company name, a framed placard honoring the respective company, a personalized sample of your product, and the like, are okay. Send social gifts following your visit, except when you are in Spain and Latin America, where they should precede your visit, but only if you know that the woman of the house will be present at the social event. If not, a thank-you card after the event is enough. Women must avoid any possible inference that the gift is a personal invitation to something more than business. What you might think is clearly a simple business matter can be grossly misinterpreted.

11. No matter where you are in the world, one obvious and well-accepted gift is the return of a social event. Make sure, however, that you do not try to outdo the dinner, lunch, cocktail party, banquet, or other event

hosted for you during your visit. When in foreign lands with confusing customs, seek help from your hotel or from the social attache at the nearest American or Canadian Embassy.

12. Never attempt to be funny or think your good humor will be understood or appreciated. One person's joke is another's insult.

16
Using Tax Laws to Your Advantage

Which travel deductions will Uncle Sam allow, and which ones will he frown on? And what will the repercussions be if Uncle Sam frowns on *your* tax return?

Such questions are the stuff of nightmares for business travelers. You've heard it said probably hundreds of times: "I'm innocent until proven guilty." Americans are proud of this high standard of justice. But the IRS has gotten this standard backward. If you're hauled in for an audit of your federal tax returns, the burden of proof is on *you* to prove that you are *not* guilty. If you're a frequent traveler and you take deductions on your travel expenses, the burden of proof can become quite heavy.

Extensive travel deductions often are a red flag to IRS auditors, who frequently catch leisure travelers trying to claim vacation expenses as business deductions. Even if your business travel deductions are legitimate, you might be the one to pay the price for all those vacationers who have stuck it to Uncle Sam.

Dealing with your travel deductions doesn't have to trigger nightmares. You can protect yourself from the IRS's brand of justice by following two rules:

☐ Know how the tax laws affect you.

☐ Know how to document your business expenses.

This chapter shows how to legally take advantage of the tax code that affects business travel. Along the way, I'll explain how to simplify the business of keeping records that the IRS will accept as "proof."

The information in this chapter has been reviewed by the Fort Lauderdale office of Millward & Co., Certified Public Accountants. Their associate, Robert L. Ricci, has assured me that the contents of this chapter are accurate—and in accordance with the current tax code (Internal Revenue Code 1800) as of January 1991.

WARNING: I need to issue one *caveat* before delving into the tax code. The IRS does not make the laws that govern taxation; however, the IRS is given a great deal of latitude in interpreting tax laws. In other words, you and the IRS may differ on the way a law should be interpreted. If you and a federal auditor differ regarding your travel deductions, and you take your case to tax court, the odds are good that you will lose. It is always wise to have a certified public accountant (CPA) either prepare or review your tax returns. A CPA who has experience dealing with IRS auditors (or who may even have been one) is in a good position to know how your deductions will be interpreted.

Understanding the Two-Percent Rule

The "two-percent rule" is a government creation designed to stick it to the salesperson. The two-percent rule applies if your company does not reimburse you for travel expenses—that is, if they are out-of-pocket expenses that you claim as deductions on your tax return. Specifically, the two-percent rule says that, for individual employees, two percent of an employee's adjusted gross income must be subtracted from allowable travel expenses.

Consider: Virginia owns a company that requires her to be on the road frequently. Since she owns the company, all her travel expenses are paid with company funds. Her company, in turn, takes a 100-percent deduction on these expenses because they are operational expenses.

Virginia then decides to sell the business, but stays on as an employee. She still travels frequently, but now must pay her travel expenses out of her own, personal income. All of the expenses that she deducts are legitimate; she deducts only for money spent on travel—including plane fare, accommodations, laundry, and other reasonable personal expenses incurred during travel.

However, under the two-percent rule, Virginia can no longer take her deductions the way a company does—income, less operational expenses. Instead, she must subtract two percent of her adjusted gross income from her total travel expenses before she lists them as a deduction.

Yes, Virginia, There Is a Loophole

As I've indicated, the two-percent rule applies to employees, but not employers. If your company will reimburse you directly for your travel expenses, follow that route. You will be reimbursed fully for your expenses *and* you won't have to worry about reporting the expenses on your federal tax return (unless your total deductions exceed what your company is willing to reimburse you for). Keep in mind that your company may insist on strict recordkeeping for all expenses you submit for reimbursement. However, who would you rather report to—your company's accountant or the IRS?

The only other way to sidestep the two-percent rule is to go into business for yourself. Independent contractors are allowed to take a full deduction for travel expenses. There are pros and cons involved in becoming an independent contractor, so it's wise to hire an attorney or CPA before you make such an important decision.

Understanding the 20-Percent Rule

When I discussed the two-percent rule, you may have noticed that I made no mention of meals and entertainment expenses. The government is 10 times stingier when it comes to these expense categories.

The "20-percent rule" states that you must subtract 20 percent from the total cost for meals and entertainment *before* you can apply these expenses as a deduction. For example, if you take a client to lunch and pick up the tab ($100), the most you can deduct is $80 (subtracting 20 percent of the total). Unlike the two-percent rule, the 20-percent rule applies to employers as well as employees. The 20-percent rule covers any form of entertainment that is primarily intended to develop business relations with parties outside the company. The rule does not apply to social events that have no business connection.

Combining the Two-Percent Rule and the 20-Percent Rule

If you are entertaining a client in your home city, the 20-percent rule applies. If you are traveling, the two-percent rule applies to expenses that you will deduct. But if you entertain a client when you are on the road, do you apply the two-percent rule *or* the 20-percent rule?

Unfortunately, *both*.

In fact, in this situation, you first must apply the 20-percent exclusion to your meals and entertainment expense total, then apply the two-percent rule. Only then can you deduct the amount of expenses remaining from your adjusted gross income. I realize this is a bit confusing, so consider the following scenario.

Charles is a salesman for a tele-fax company and is frequently on the road calling on clients. He is paid a salary plus a bonus and is reimbursed by his company for the following expenses:

☐ Car allowance (a specified amount per mile)

☐ A per-diem meal allowance (only while he is out of town)

☐ Hotel accommodations (up to a specified amount per night)

Charles frequently incurs other expenses that are a necessary part of doing business. These other expenses are not reimbursed by the company. Also, Charles sometimes exceeds the allowances specified by the company for his car, meals, and hotel accommodations. For example, this year Charles incurred heavy expenses on his car for repairs and for taking several trips out of town to be interviewed by a prospective new employer.

When Charles and his accountant figure his tax for the year, Table 16–1 shows what they dis-

Table 16–1 *Charles' Expenses and Reimbursements*

Item	Amount Paid by Charles	Amount Reimbursed by Company	Excess Deductible Expenses
Car	$ 4,500	$ 3,200	$1,300
Meals	3,900	2,800	1,100*
Hotel	6,000	5,100	900
Entertainment	1,400	0	1,400*
Other	1,050	0	1,050
Totals	$16,850	$11,100	$5,750

*20 percent must be excluded from the deduction for this expense.

cover. After the company reimburses Charles for the allowable $11,100, he has an out-of-pocket expense total of $5,750. Of this total, 20 percent must be subtracted from the excess Meals and Entertainment amounts shown in Table 16–1 ($1,100 plus $1,400 is $2,500, less 20 percent is $2,000). This reduces the total deductible amount to $5,250 ($2,000 + $1,300 + $900 + $1,500).

Assume that Charles' CPA has calculated his adjusted gross income as $62,500. The CPA then applies the two-percent rule, which means that two percent ($1,250) of Charles' adjusted gross income must be subtracted from the total deductions amount. After this subtraction is made ($5,250 minus $1,250), Charles' allowable deduction is $4,000. Here are the final calculations:

Deductions not reimbursed by the company:	$ 5,750
Application of 20-percent exclusion rule:	− 500
Deductions allowable and subject to two-percent rule:	$ 5,250
Adjusted gross income:	$62,500
	×0.02
Two percent of adjusted gross income:	$ 1,250
Amount of allowable deduction:	$ 4,000

If Charles' company does not reimburse him for any expenses, his tax return will look different. His gross expense will be $16,850, and he will have to apply the 20-percent exclusion to the meals and entertainment portion of this expense amount. This leaves him with $15,740 in allowable expenses, from which he still has to deduct two percent of his adjusted gross income. His final allowable deduction will be $14,490.

TIP

If your company reimburses you fully for meals and entertainment, the 20-percent rule is applied to your company's return, not yours. If at all possible, encourage your company to pay for *at least* this portion of your expenses.

TIP

The 20-percent exclusion makes no distinction between meals and entertainment expenses incurred while you are in town and those incurred on the road. However, in your recordkeeping, you should separate expenses incurred on the road from those incurred while in your home city. This separation will simplify your year-end accounting by making clear which expenses are subject to the two-percent rule. For the same reason, be sure to separate your expenses clearly into categories (meals, entertainment, plane fare, and so on).

Seven Common Deductible Business Travel Expenses

The seven travel expense categories mentioned in the following list are obviously deductions; however, there are some special tips worth mentioning for each:

☐ *Airplane tickets.* If your company prohibits reimbursement for any travel class more expensive than coach, book in *Y* (coach) class. Then pay the upgrade to business class or first class yourself. In many cases, this is a nominal charge. By doing this, you will at least be reimbursed for most of your air fare.

☐ *Train tickets.* Although a plane might get you to your destination faster than rail travel, it is worth comparing the fares if you have the extra travel time. If you book in a sleeper car, you might arrive at your destination more refreshed than if you had dealt with the hassle of airports and air travel.

☐ *Ship tickets.* If your tickets are for an American-registered ship that stops at American ports, you can deduct up to $2000 of the ticket cost—provided you are attending a convention on board. If you travel by ship to your destination (regardless of the ship's port of registry), you can deduct no more than double the per-diem allowable to U.S. government employees. (The per diem paid to government employees changes, so check with your accountant for the correct rate.) Meals that are included in the gross price of the ticket are not subject to the 20-percent rule.

☐ *Rental cars.* Keep thorough records of any "extra" charges you incur while driving a rental car. Extra charges are those that do not appear on a rental agreement, such as parking fees, gas, and oil. These are bona fide deductible expenses—but the IRS may disallow them if you do not document them carefully.

☐ *Hotel accommodations.* How do you deduct a room charge if you travel with a spouse or friend, and that person is not essential to business? You could deduct half the cost of a double room. However, you may also deduct the actual charge that would have applied to a single room, which is usually more than half the cost of a double room. Make sure you substantiate the single-room charge. Ask the reservation clerk to make a note on the statement, when you check out, indicating the single-room charge, including tax and other charges that would normally be applied.

☐ *Taxis, airport vans, and limousines.* Reasonable tips are allowable deductions for taxis and other vehicle transportation services. However, if you are traveling with your spouse or a friend, the cost of a taxi will be the same as it would be if you were traveling alone. Vans and limousine services, on the other hand, usually involve a per-person charge. When you take into account the tax deduction involved, the slightly added cost of taking a taxi is usually offset.

☐ *Meals.* "Reasonable" meal costs are fully deductible; however, you and the IRS might disagree about what is and is not "reasonable." Because the IRS can disallow a deduction in its entirety if there is a disagreement, it is best to avoid lavish meals. In other words, don't try to claim a $250 deduction for dining alone unless you have full backup data.

Six Frequently Overlooked Travel Expenses

These next six travel expenses all are legitimate and deductible, but are often overlooked or not documented by business travelers. The few extra minutes required to document these expenses can be well worth the effort when it is time to total your deductions.

☐ *Phone calls.* You can deduct the cost of making business phone calls while you are traveling. Legitimate deductions include calling your office, checking on your reservations, calling clients, and making any arrangements essential to your travel. Keep a record of each phone call and its purpose. If you are audited, the auditor may ask whether phone calls that appear on your hotel bill are personal or business in nature.

☐ *Business supplies.* Strictly speaking, the purchase of business supplies while you are on the road is not a travel expense; however, these purchases can be legitimate business expenses. The purchase of pens, pads of paper, computer disks, and other supplies all should be recorded. Your accountant can later determine how and whether to apply these expenses as deductions on your return. (Your company might also be willing to reimburse you for these items, provided you have receipts.)

☐ *Postage.* Postage is also technically not a travel expense, but is a legitimate business expense. Record postage costs for all letters and packages that you send while you are on the road. You should also record postage costs for items that you send from home but that contain follow-up information or material for clients you have visited.

☐ *Personal expenses.* Dry cleaning and ironing costs, and purchases for personal hygiene (deodorant, shampoo, soap, and so on) are all legitimate travel expenses. Record these expenses when you are on the road.

☐ *Parking and other out-of-pocket costs.* Parking meters, parking garages, and any other out-of-pocket costs that relate to business travel can be deducted.

☐ *Newspapers, subscriptions, and other reading material.* You can deduct the cost of any business-related reading material that you purchase while traveling. The material must contain necessary information that pertains to the business you are conducting while you are away from home.

Surviving a Tax Audit

The key to faring well during a tax audit is to provide plenty of documentation. Auditors—whether they work for the IRS or a private company—love paper trails. If an IRS auditor questions you regarding a deduction, written documentation is far more convincing than some rambling explanation. Keep in mind that you are likely to be at least a little nervous during an audit. Your ability to remember or explain an expense might be hindered by your emotional state. If you have kept all receipts and recorded all expenses in a journal, you can let your written documentation speak for you.

Three Major Benefits of Thorough Recordkeeping

Every taxpayer keeps some records. But if you claim business deductions, you need to go a few steps beyond "some records." Your recordkeeping needs to be *thorough*. As I'll explain later, that does not necessarily mean "complex" and "time consuming." You can develop thorough recordkeeping habits with just a bit of time and effort. The payoff includes these three major benefits:

☐ You will begin to notice and record expenses that once seemed "too insignificant" to bother with. When you begin to record everything that you believe might represent a deduction, you'll see how rapidly seemingly trivial expenses add up.

☐ Your money-management habits will become more professional. This added touch of professionalism is bound to be noticed by clients and associates. As you begin to match your knowledge of IRS regulations with documentation and receipts, you will grow increasingly better at maximizing your deductions.

☐ You build a strong defense against an IRS auditor's inquiries. An auditor will quickly notice the detail involved in your recordkeeping and that you can support each answer with documentation. The more questions you can answer successfully by providing documentation, the less likely it will be for an auditor to spend a great deal of time on your audit.

Taking Advantage of the $25 Rule

For single payments of less than $25, you do not need to produce receipts. However, it is important that you record each expense. Write down a brief description and the amount of each purchase, along with the reason you made the purchase. Make sure the reason you provide indicates clearly that the purchase was related to business. Also note when and where you made the purchase.

If you plan to pay for items with cash and do not want to keep receipts, a good approach is to split the items into separate purchases that total less than $25. For instance, you could pay for drinks separately, then pay for dinner, bringing both payments under $25.

TIP

Frequent business travelers might want to open a separate checking account for business expenses. Whenever you pay cash for a business expense, note the expense in a diary. Then, use your business checking account to pay yourself back for cash expenses over $25. This gives you a detailed check register of all purchases that require receipts. In many audits, an auditor will want to see only your business records, not your personal receipts. Why call into question your personal financial records if it isn't necessary to do so?

You may also wish to apply for a credit card that you use only for business expenses. Similar to the business checking account, this helps keep your personal charges separate from business charges.

How to Make Recordkeeping Simple Yet Thorough

I have seen dozens of "easy-to-record" expense folders and booklets. Quite frankly, I think all of these preprinted documents are a waste of time and money. Each page is prelined into categories; many are never used. And many expenses don't fit well into any of the provided categories.

I use a simpler approach—one that you might find useful. I purchase a daily diary at the start of each year. Most business supply stores carry them. The most convenient ones are in book form (just about any size will do), with each page left blank except for a date printed on the page. To use the daily diary, just write on the appropriate page the actual expenses that you incur for that day of the year.

Another advantage of the daily diary over the prelined versions is that you can use this same book to enter appointments and other information about your business activity.

Use Your Diary as a Defense During an Audit

Remember, auditors love paper, and a daily diary automatically provides you with 365 organized, carefully documented pages of material—probably containing far more information than an auditor will want to review. At minimum, consider the following diary entries to be essential:

☐ *The date.* If the diary you purchase does not have a date printed on each page, spend about 30 minutes marking the date at the top of each page—until you have filled all pages for a calendar year (be sure to include weekends).

☐ *Your location.* When you are on the road, write the name of the city you are in at the top of each relevant page. If no city name has been entered on a page, assume you were in your home town that day. This approach makes it easy to identify pages with travel expenses.

☐ *Appointments.* The first entry I usually make on a page is a list of business appointments that I have scheduled for that day. If a meeting is canceled or postponed, make a note of this fact.

These entries help an auditor to recognize the nature of your business and your level of business activity. For each appointment, note the following information in the diary:

    a. Location of the meeting
    b. Scheduled attendees
    c. Purpose of the meeting
    d. Results of the meeting

☐ *Meals.* Note any meals that involve business or that you take while out of town. Provide the following information for each meal:

    a. Location of the meal
    b. Names of guests or associates who ate with you
    c. Business topic(s) discussed at the meal
    d. Cost of the meal, with itemized entries for food, beverages, and entertainment

☐ *Auto-related expenses.* Note these expenses whenever you purchase gas, pay for a car repair, take a cab, pay bridge and road tolls, pay parking meters, and just about any other expense that involves a vehicle you are using for business purposes. If you are driving out of town, log the mileage near the top of the page. This serves as a notice to an auditor that the car was used extensively during that day. In the body of the diary for that day, also describe the purpose of the trip.

☐ *Flight and other travel information.* You shouldn't need to write your full travel itinerary in your diary, because you already have a travel itinerary prepared by your travel agent or secretary before you leave town. However, it is a good idea to note where you will be traveling to and from each day. If your plans change, your printed itinerary may become incorrect. Let your diary be your most accurate record.

☐ *Incidental business expenses.* Ask yourself whether you purchased anything during the day that *might* be a business expense. If the answer is "Yes" or even "Maybe," describe the purchase in your diary. Let your accountant determine later whether what you've written is a legitimate business expense.

☐ *Multiple business dealings.* If on a given day, you engage in several different business meetings, possibly with different clients, clearly note in your diary that these meetings have separate purposes.

☐ *Credit card charges.* Note each expense that you charge on a credit card, and be sure to note which card you used. This notation serves as supporting documentation if a receipt or other item is questioned during an audit. You can also use these notations to double-check your monthly credit card statements.

☐ *Gifts.* If you give something away—regardless of what the gift is or to whom it is given—make a note of it. If it is not a business gift, your accountant might determine it to be a legitimate charitable contribution.

The IRS is basically distrustful of business travel deductions and other business expense deductions claimed by individuals. You want to avoid suspicion wherever possible. Because the burden of proof regarding deductions is on you, *provide plenty of proof.* It really isn't that much of a burden. Just a few minutes each day will provide enough time to record your business activities and expenses thoroughly.

17

Information for 25 U.S. Metropolitan Areas

If you travel on business frequently, you probably have visited some of the metropolitan areas mentioned in this chapter. You have probably also encountered congested airports, unreasonable transportation fares, and unacceptable accommodations and meals. This chapter presents information and tips that can help you to eliminate many of these travel problems. For each of the 25 U.S. metropolitan areas mentioned in this chapter, you'll find information on airports, taxis and other transportation services, hotels, restaurants, weather, and more.

Metropolitan areas are categorized alphabetically by city name and by region—Eastern, Midwestern, Southern and Southwestern, and Western. To find information for a particular city, look up the appropriate region first, then search alphabetically for the city name. The 25 cities or metropolitan areas mentioned in this chapter are

Eastern
Baltimore, Boston, New York, Pittsburgh, Washington, D.C.

Midwestern

Chicago, Cincinnati, Cleveland, Detroit, Minneapolis/St. Paul, St. Louis

Southern/Southwestern

Atlanta, Dallas/Fort Worth, Fort Lauderdale, Houston, Las Vegas, Miami, New Orleans, Orlando, Phoenix

Western

Denver, Los Angeles, Salt Lake City, San Francisco, Seattle

TIP

Whenever you enter a taxi, regardless of the city, have the driver answer these questions: Is there a flat rate into town, and if so, what is the rate? What is the usual charge (to your destination)? If the taxi ride is priced by meter, always make sure the meter starts at $0.00.

Eastern Metropolitan Areas

BALTIMORE

Area Code: 301
Estimated Population: 1.9 million
Altitude: 489 feet
Time Zone: Eastern
Airport to City: 10 miles
Rental Cars at Airport: Avis, Budget, Dollar, Hertz, National
Newspapers: The Sun, The News American, The Evening Sun
Convention Center(s)/Information: Baltimore Office of Promotion & Tourism, 34 Market Place, Suite 310, 752-8632

Transportation into Town

Allow 30 to 40 minutes to downtown Baltimore from Baltimore-Washington International Airport, by taxi, for around $15. A bus into Baltimore, with stops at major hotels, departs the airport approximately every 30 minutes from 5 A.M. to midnight; the fare is $5 per person. ABC Limo (859-3000) travels to most downtown hotels for a fare of $5 per person.

Airport Information

Baltimore-Washington International Airport serves both Baltimore and Washington, D.C.

Suggested Dining

The Brass Elephant, 924 North Charles Street, 547-8480, specializes in Northern Italian food.

Phillip's Harborplace, 301 South Light Street (in Light Street Pavilion), 685-6600. Other restaurants and eateries are also in the Light Street Pavilion.

Tio Pepe, 10 E. Franklin Street (between Charles Street and St. Paul Place), 539-4675, serves Spanish cooking.

Suggested Lodging

EXPENSIVE

Hyatt Regency Baltimore, 300 Light Street, Inner Harbor, 800-228-9000 or 528-1234.

Peabody Court, 612 Cathedral Street, at Mt. Vernon, 800-732-5301 or 727-7101.

MODERATE

Days Inn Inner Harbor, 100 Hopkins Place, 576-1000 or 800-325-2525.

Suggested Nightlife

The Owl Bar at Belvedere Hotel, 1 E. Chase Street.

Places to Visit

Harborplace, a collection of shops, restaurants, and market stalls at the Inner Harbor. Dozens of quaint towns and historical sites (including Annapolis and Fort McHenry) are a short distance from downtown Baltimore.

Weather Information

Baltimore weather is influenced by the Chesapeake Bay, the Atlantic Ocean, and more critically the Bermuda High, which draws hot, humid low pressure systems from the South and into Baltimore. This tends to create a mild but often damp winter, and humid stormy summers.

Average Temperatures

	J	F	M	A	M	J	J	A	S	O	N	D
Avg. High	41	43	53	65	75	83	87	85	79	68	56	43
Avg. Low	25	26	32	42	52	62	66	65	58	46	36	26

BOSTON

Area Code: 617
Estimated Population: 4 million (includes suburbs)
Altitude: Sea level to slightly over 300 feet
Time Zone: Eastern
Airport to City: 4 miles to the center of Boston
Rental Cars at the Airport: Alamo, American Intl., Ajax, Avis, Budget, Dollar, Hertz, National
Newspapers: Boston Globe, Boston Herald
Convention Center(s)/Information: Boston Convention and Visitors Bureau, Prudential Plaza, P.O. Box 490, 536-4100

Transportation into Town

A 30-minute drive from Logan International Airport, by taxi or bus, will take you to the center of the city. Taxi fare is about $10; share-a-cab is available at Terminal D (3:30 P.M. to 11 P.M.). Airways red-white van is about $6.50 and operates hourly from 8 A.M. to 10 P.M., on the hour (267-2981). A 10-minute boat trip across the harbor via the free van (departing the airport every 15 minutes to Logan boat dock) arrives at Rowe's

Wharf next to Boston Harbor Hotel. The $5 boat ride operates from 6 A.M. to 8 P.M. weekdays, and from noon to 7:45 P.M., every 30 minutes, on weekends.

Airport Information
Logan International Airport is a major international gateway to Europe and points around the United States and Canada. Shuttle flights from Logan to New York City are convenient; however, Logan Airport frequently is fogged in during midwinter, early morning, and late evening.

Suggested Dining
Anthony's Pier Four, 140 Northern Avenue, 423-6363, specializes in seafood and a harbor view.

Cafe Budapest, located in the Copley Square Hotel, 47 Huntington Ave.

Grill 23, 161 Berkely Street, 542-2255, is stylish and attracts a young, lively crowd.

Bay Tower Room, 60 State Street, 723-1666, is known for its harbor view and rack of lamb.

Suggested Lodging
EXPENSIVE
Ritz-Carlton, 15 Arlington Street, 536-5700, is only steps from the Newbury Street Shops.

The Meridian, 200 Franklin Street, Post Office Sq., 800-223-9918 or 451-1900, is a transformed 1922 Renaissance-designed Federal Reserve Bank Building, in the heart of the financial district.

The Bostonian, at Faneuil Hall Marketplace, 800-343-0922 or 523-3600.

MODERATE
57 Park Plaza Hotel Howard Johnson's, 200 Stuart Street, 800-654-2000 or 482-1800. Provides free parking.

Sheraton Commander, 16 Garden Street, Cambridge, 547-4800.

Chandler Inn, 26 Chandler Street, 482-3450, is small but charming.

Suggested Nightlife
Joe's American Bar, 279 Newbury Street, 536-4200.

Places to Visit
Try the well-marked Freedom Trail walk on a nice day. Pick up a *Freedom Trail Guide,* which provides information on important colonial and revolutionary sites along the trail. Allow at least two hours for the walk. Faneuil Hall Market Place is a renovated wharf area with many shops and restaurants.

Weather Information
Boston has a reputation for cold and wet winters. Fog and snow can cause delays in and out of Logan. Spring and autumn provide the best weather for visitors.

Average Temperatures

	J	F	M	A	M	J	J	A	S	O	N	D
Avg. High	36	37	45	53	67	77	81	79	72	63	51	39
Avg. Low	22	23	31	41	50	59	65	63	57	47	39	27

NEW YORK CITY
Area Code: 212
Estimated Population: 17 million (includes suburbs)
Altitude: Sea level to 415 feet
Time Zone: Eastern
Airport to City (to central areas):
Approximately 18 miles from JFK, 9 miles from La Guardia, and 12 miles from Newark
Rental Cars at the Airport: Avis, Budget, Dollar, Hertz, National
Newspapers: New York Times, Daily News, New York Newsday, Wall Street Journal

Convention Center(s)/Information: The New York Convention and Visitors Bureau, 2 Columbus Circle, 397-8222

Transportation into Town

Allow 60 minutes, by taxi, from JFK, at a fare less than $50; allow 40 minutes, by taxi, from La Guardia, at an approximate fare of $25 to $30; allow 60 minutes, by taxi, to and from Newark, at an approximate fare of $45. Ask the airport dispatcher about "share a ride," which can cut cab fares to less than $10. During peak driving times, add 15 minutes. Bus service to and from each airport is provided at the 42nd Street bus terminal opposite Grand Central Station and is an inexpensive way to get into town, provided you can spare the extra time required. Your best bet is Newark by bus to and from the Port Authority at 44th and 8th; it's cheap and fast.

Airport Information

New York City is serviced by three major airports, yet only John F. Kennedy (JFK) is a major international airport. Both JFK and La Guardia are located within the borough of Queens, New York; Newark International is across the Hudson River in New Jersey.

Suggested Dining

Excellent ethnic food and American cuisine are available at hundreds of excellent spots. The following are some of the more well-known restaurants.

The Ballroom, 253 West 28th Street, 244-3005, has a dining room with a cabaret revue.

Russian Tea Room, 150 West 57th Street, 265-0947, is next to Carnegie Hall.

The Oyster Bar and Palm Court are both at the Plaza Hotel, 59th Street and 5th Avenue, 759-3000.

The Algonquin, 59 West 44th Street, 840-6800, is a favorite of the literary set.

Gallagher's, 228 West 52nd Street, is known for its prime rib.

The Palm, 837 Second Avenue, 687-2953, and **The Palm Too,** 840 Second Avenue, 687-5198 (across the street from each other) are unpretentious but not inexpensive.

Cafe Luxembourg, 200 West 70th Street, 873-7411 (very crowded late in the evening).

Kabuki, 115 Broadway, 962-4677, is in 1 World Trade Center. This Japanese restaurant is a good lunch spot.

Suggested Lodging
EXPENSIVE

Grand Hyatt, Park Avenue and Grand Central (on 42nd Street), 883-1234 or 800-228-9000.

Marriott Marquis, 1535 Broadway, 398-1900 or 800-228-9290.

Manhattan East Hotels, with several to choose from, are small suite hotels located throughout Manhattan, 800-637-8483.

Waldorf-Astoria, 301 Park Avenue, 355-3000.

MODERATE

Days Inn, 440 West 57th Street, 581-8100 or 800-325-2525, is newly remodeled and reasonable.

Gorham, 136 West 55th Street, 245-1800, is centrally located.

Howard Johnson's, 851 8th Avenue, corner of West 51st, 581-4100 or 800-654-2000.

Suggested Nightlife

Maxwell's Plum, 1181 1st Avenue, 628-2100.

Roebling's, at the south end of Street Seaport, 227-9322.

Odeon, 145 West Broadway, 233-0507.

Places to Visit
The Empire State Building, although no longer the tallest building in the world, still offers great views of the city. Location is West 34th Street and 5th Avenue, 736-3100.

Broadway theater shows often have to be reserved weeks or months in advance; however, two half-price sales offices (one at Broadway and 47th Street and the other at 2 World Trade Center) offer tickets for matinees and for same-day performances.

Carnegie Hall is renowned for its excellent acoustics; phone 247-7800. For operatic performances, call the Metropolitan Opera, at Lincoln Center, 362-6000.

The diamond district, located along 47th Street between 5th and 6th Avenues, is a good place to window shop.

Weather Information
Weather systems that affect New York City typically come from the west, which leads to cold winters (but infrequent snowstorms) and hot summers.

Average Temperatures

	J	F	M	A	M	J	J	A	S	O	N	D
Avg. High	38	49	48	61	71	80	85	83	77	67	54	41
Avg. Low	26	26	34	44	53	63	68	66	60	51	41	30

PITTSBURGH
Area Code: 412
Estimated Population: 2.5 million (includes suburbs)
Altitude: 700 feet to 1400 feet
Time Zone: Eastern
Airport to City: Greater Pittsburgh International Airport is located about 20 miles from most central Pittsburgh areas.

Rental Cars at the Airport: Alamo, Avis, Budget, Hertz, National, Payless, Snappy, Thrifty

Newspapers: Post-Gazette, Press

Convention Center(s)/Information: Greater Pittsburgh Convention and Visitors Bureau, 4 Gateway Center, 281-7711

Transportation into Town

Allow 45 minutes, by taxi, during normal business hours, at a fare of less than $30 into most central areas of Pittsburgh. Limousine service into town or Oakland is available for about $10— allow about one hour. Add 30 minutes to your transportation time during rush hour and poor weather.

Airport Information

Greater Pittsburgh International Airport is less than well designed; consequently, the terminal and surrounding area are in a near-constant state of reconstruction.

Two major roads are used to travel to and from the airport. Both roads are major rush-hour arteries; delays can be lengthy during rush hour and during other congested periods. The nearby Ohio, Allegheny, and Monongahela rivers tend to stimulate fog and damp snow during winter, adding to traffic and air travel delays.

Suggested Dining

Back Porch, 114 Speers Street, 483-4500, is located out-of-town, but is an excellent historic dining location if you have the time to visit.

Christopher's, 1411 Grandview Avenue, on Mt. Washington overlooking Pittsburgh, 381-4500.

Grand Concourse, 1 Station Square, 261-1717, is across the Monongahela River in a beautifully restored railroad station.

Poli's, 2607 Murray Avenue, take Squirrel Hill exit from Rt. 376, past Oakland. This is an unelegant local landmark featuring seafood.

Suggested Lodging
EXPENSIVE
Hyatt at Chatham Center, 112 Washington Place, 471-1234 or 800-228-9000.

Sheraton Inn, 7 Station Square, 261-2000 or 800-325-3535, is across the Monongahela River, near Duquesne University.

MODERATE
Holiday Inn-Medical Center, next to University of Pittsburgh, 682-6200 or 800-465-4329, is a newly opened hotel only three miles from the center of Pittsburgh.

Suggested Nightlife
Grand Concourse (*See* Suggested Dining).

Places to Visit
Carnegie-Mellon Theater Co., at Kresge Theatre, is located on the campus of Carnegie-Mellon University on Forbes, next to Schenley Park, 578-2407.

The Pittsburgh Symphony Orchestra performs from September through May in Heinz Hall, 600 Penn Avenue, 281-5000. Many summer programs of jazz abound in the parks in and around Pittsburgh. For information, call 255-2390.

Weather Information
Winter storms move into Pittsburgh from Canada, which makes for a cloudy, wet, and cold winter. Pittsburgh is hilly, so expect travel delays and problems during and following winter storms. Spring and fall weather is mild; summers are somewhat humid.

Average Temperatures

	J	F	M	A	M	J	J	A	S	O	N	D
Avg. High	35	37	47	61	71	79	82	81	75	64	49	37
Avg. Low	21	21	29	39	48	58	61	59	53	42	33	24

WASHINGTON, D.C.

Area Code: 202
Estimated Population: 3.5 million
Altitude: Sea level to 418 feet
Time Zone: Eastern
Airport to City: National Airport is about 6 miles from most central D.C. areas. Dulles International is in Northern Virginia, approximately 30 miles from the center of town.
Rental Cars at the Airport: Alamo, Avis, Budget, Dollar, General, Hertz, National
Newspapers: The Washington Post, The Washington Times
Convention Center(s)/Information: The Washington Convention and Visitors Association, 1575 I Street, NW, Washington, D.C., 789-7000. The International Visitors Information Service, 733 15th Street, NW Suite 300, 783-6540

Transportation into Town

Taxis in Washington, D.C., operate on a zone basis; fares from the airport into town range from about $8 to $15. From Dulles, a taxi into town can cost $35 and may take one hour or longer during the morning rush hour, and one hour from town to Dulles during the afternoon rush hour. Vans into town are available at both airports, although you will not save much on van fare compared with cab fare if you are traveling from National. From Dulles to town, van fare is about one-third the cost of a taxi. Allow 30 to 45 minutes in a van from National and 60 to 90 minutes from Dulles, depending on your destination.

The Metro rail system, with a station at National Airport, is a clean, safe, and rapid way to travel into Washington, D.C., and to outlying suburbs. The fare from the airport into town is about $1.

Airport Information

Three major airports serve Washington, D.C.: National, Dulles International, and Baltimore-Washington International. National Airport is closest to the city (about 5 miles to the Capitol building). Dulles is about 30 miles from the city, located in Virginia, and Baltimore-Washington International is about 40 miles to the northeast, near Baltimore, Maryland.

Suggested Dining

Broker, 713 8th Street, SE, 546-8300, features wild game dishes.

Dominique's, 1900 Pennsylvania Avenue, NW, 452-1126.

El Bodegon, 1637 R Street NW, 667-1710, features Spanish fare, with occasional flamenco guitar and dance entertainment.

La Chaumiere, 2813 M Street, NW, 338-1784, is in Georgetown, site of many fine restaurants and lounges.

Suggested Lodging

EXPENSIVE

The Ritz-Carlton, 2100 Massachusetts Avenue, NW, 293-2100 or 800-424-8008.

Willard Intercontinental, 1401 Pennsylvania Avenue, NW, 628-9100 or 800-327-0200, is near the State Department and other government offices.

MODERATE

Lombardy, 2019 I Street, NW, 828-2600 or 800-424-5486, contains apartments and suites at a very reasonable price, and is located near the George Washington University.

Howard Johnson's Downtown at Kennedy Center, 2601 Virginia Avenue, NW, 965-2700.

Suggested Nightlife

F. Scott's, 1232 36th Street, NW, 965-1789, in Georgetown.

Paper Moon, 1073 31st Street, NW, 965-6666, in Georgetown.

Places to Visit

The Kennedy Center, off Virginia Avenue, NW, is host to numerous theater productions and concerts throughout the year. Call 254-3600 for information.

The Mall, a two-mile-long park, begins at the Lincoln Memorial and ends at the Capitol Building. Other memorials and tourist sites along the mall include the Vietnam Veterans Memorial, the reflecting pool and Washington Monument, and the Smithsonian Institution museums.

Gray Line (479-5986) and **Tourmobile Sightseeing** (554-7945) both offer several daily tours designed to fit a variety of schedules and interests.

Weather Information

Washington experiences sudden summer thunderstorms and heavy damp winter snows from time to time. Early spring is host to the annual cherry blossom festival.

Average Temperatures

	J	F	M	A	M	J	J	A	S	O	N	D
Avg. High	47	52	60	72	79	87	93	93	85	75	61	50
Avg. Low	26	30	37	50	58	67	71	70	62	51	38	29

Midwestern Metropolitan Areas

CHICAGO

Area Code: 312
Estimated Population: 8 million (includes suburbs)
Altitude: 580 to 672 feet
Time Zone: Central
Airport to City: The distance from O'Hare to downtown Chicago is 25 miles; the distance from Midway to downtown is 10 miles.
Rental Cars at the Airport: Avis, Budget, Dollar, Hertz, National

Newspapers: Sun-Times, Chicago Tribune
Convention(s)/Information: Chicago
Convention & Visitors Bureau, McCormick
Place-on-the-Lake, 567-8500

Transportation into Town

Allow at least an hour to downtown Chicago from
O'Hare, by taxi, for about $20 to $25. Allow
about 30 minutes to downtown from Midway, by
taxi, for about $10 to $15.

Continental Airport Express vans depart
from O'Hare every 30 minutes on weekdays (less
frequently on weekends) and cost less than $10
one way and less than $17 round trip to most
areas in town. The same company has van service
from Midway to downtown Chicago, with the
fare for this trip about $8 one way and $14 round
trip. For information, call 454-7800.

The CTA (subway-elevated train) departs
from inside O'Hare direct to the downtown
Loop. The 35- to 45-minute ride costs only $1.

Airport Information

O'Hare International is one of the world's busiest
airports. Constant expansion can be anticipated
through the year 1992. Because O'Hare is a major
hub for several airlines, traffic and flight delays
are frequent, especially during winter.

Midway Airport is much smaller and handles
chiefly regional air traffic (no nonstop international traffic). Midway is the preferred destination airport for Chicago if your business is downtown or on the east or south side.

Suggested Dining

Ambria, 2300 North Lincoln Park West, in the
Belden-Stratford Hotel, 472-5959, is a popular
French restaurant. Ask for the fixed price menu
(around $45), 472-5959.

Cafe Ba-Ba-Reeba, 2024 North Halsted Street,
serves Spanish cuisine, 935-5000.

Shaws Crab House, 21 East Hubbard Street, 527-2722, is a relatively new addition to Chicago's fine seafood establishments.

House of Hunan, 535 North Michigan Avenue, 329-9494, serves spicy Chinese cuisine.

Suggested Lodging
EXPENSIVE
The Ritz-Carlton, 160 E. Pearson, 266-1000, begins at the 12th floor of the Water Tower Place shopping center.

The Westin, 909 North Michigan Avenue, is one block south of the Ritz-Carlton, 800-228-3000.

The Drake, 140 E. Walton Place, 787-2200.

MODERATE
Allerton Hotel, 701 North Michigan, 440-1500, is an older, renovated hotel in the same district as the more expensive hotels.

Blackstone Hotel, 636 South Michigan Avenue, 427-4300.

Suggested Nightlife
Lion Bar, at The Westin, 909 North Michigan Avenue, 943-7200, is popular with the local businesspeople.

Places to Visit
The Chicago Mercantile Exchange and International Money Market, 30 South Wacker Drive, 930-8249.

Museum of Science and Industry, South Lake Shore Drive at 57th Street, 684-1414.

Weather Information
The incoming winds from Lake Michigan make Chicago winters cold, wet, and blustery and help create humid summers. Temperatures are hot from mid-June to early September; Chicago also gets most of its precipitation during this period. During winter, check weather forecasts for the

Chicago area before you commit to flights into O'Hare or Midway.

Average Temperatures

	J	F	M	A	M	J	J	A	S	O	N	D
Avg. High	31	35	45	59	70	81	84	83	76	65	48	35
Avg. Low	17	20	29	40	50	60	65	54	56	46	33	22

CINCINNATI

Area Code: 513
Estimated Population: 1.5 million (includes suburbs)
Altitude: 430 to 970 feet
Time Zone: Eastern
Airport to City: 15 miles into the center of town
Rental Cars at the Airport: Avis, Budget, Dollar, Hertz, National
Newspapers: Cincinnati Enquirer, Cincinnati Post
Convention(s)/Information: Cincinnati Convention Center, 525 Elm Street, 352-3750; Greater Cincinnati Convention and Visitors Bureau, 300 W. 6th, 621-2142

Transportation into Town

Allow 30 to 40 minutes to downtown from the airport (which is actually in Northern Kentucky), by taxi, at a flat rate under $18. Phone 241-2100 for taxi service.

The Jet Port Express departs from the airport every 30 minutes from 6 A.M. (8 A.M. on Saturdays and Sundays) until 11:30 P.M., with stops at The Westin, Hilton, Clarion, Hyatt Regency, and Netherland Plaza. Fares are $8 one way and $12 round trip. Allow a one-way travel time of one hour or longer, depending on your destination and traffic conditions.

Suggested Dining

Mount Adams, in an area called Cincinnati's Montmartre, has many shops and restaurants along quaint narrow streets.

Maisonette, 114 E. Sixth Street, 721-2260, serves world-famous French cuisine.

Pigall's Cafe, 127 West Fourth Street, 651-2233, casual dining.

Top of the Crown, at the 32nd floor of the Clarion Hotel, 141 West Sixth Street, 342-2160.

The Sovereign, 810 Matson Place, 471-2250.

Suggested Lodging

EXPENSIVE

Omni Netherland Plaza, 35 W. Fifth Street, 421-9100, is connected to the Convention center by skywalk. Ask for information about the Executive Service Plan.

The Hyatt Regency, 151 W. Fifth Street, 579-1234.

The Cincinnatian, which reopened in 1987, is a restored century-old landmark, 601 Vine Street, 381-3000.

MODERATE

Holiday Inn-Downtown, 800 West Eighth Street, (8th and Linn), 241-8660 or 800-HOLIDAY.

Vernon Manor, 400 Oak Street, 800-543-3999, is an Elizabethan-style hotel.

The Clarion, 141 West Sixth Street, 352-2100.

Suggested Nightlife

The Precinct, 311 Delta Avenue, is a well-known sports bar.

Joe's Bar at the Terrace Hilton, 15 West Sixth Street.

Places to Visit

Try the Ohio River Cruise, where you'll travel on a boat called the Huck Finn.

Riverfront Stadium, home of the Cincinnati Reds during baseball season.

Weather Information

In general, the climate is moderate throughout the year, with autumn providing perhaps the best weather and colorful surroundings. Cincinnati winters average about 100 days at freezing temperatures or below, whereas summer has fewer than 30 days above 90 degrees. Rain produces occasional flooding, especially during summer months.

Average Temperatures

	J	F	M	A	M	J	J	A	S	O	N	D
Avg. High	40	43	52	66	75	84	87	86	80	69	53	42
Avg. Low	24	26	33	45	54	62	66	54	57	47	36	27

CLEVELAND

Area Code: 216
Estimated Population: 2.3 million (includes suburbs)
Altitude: 570 to 1060 feet
Time Zone: Eastern
Airport to City: 15 miles to downtown
Rental Cars at the Airport: Avis, Budget, Dollar, Hertz, National, Snappy, Thrifty
Newspapers: The Cleveland Plain Dealer
Convention(s)/Information: Convention and Visitors Bureau of Greater Cleveland, 1301 E. 6th Street, 621-4110; also, Cleveland Convention Center, 1220 E. 6th Street, 348-2200

Transportation into Town

Allow 30 to 40 minutes from Hopkins International Airport into Cleveland, by taxi, for under $20.

The Regional Transit Authority (RTA) operates a train that travels to the downtown Terminal Tower for $1. Actual time en route is about the same as a cab ride, but you may have to transfer when you arrive at the Terminal Tower.

Airport Information

Hopkins International Airport lacks the services of most larger airports. Passing through Customs is generally quick, but in peak periods it can take up to an hour.

Suggested Dining

Watermark, 1250 Old River Rd., is in The Flats on the Cuyahoga River's East bank, 241-1600.

Pier W, 12700 Lake Avenue, in Lakewood, 228-2250, is west of the city but has a fine view of the skyline and is known for its seafood.

Sammy's, at 1400 West 10th Street, phone 523-5560, is another chic place with a very "in" crowd.

Suggested Lodging

EXPENSIVE

Bond Court, 777 St. Clair Avenue, 771-7600, is a luxury hotel overlooking Lake Erie and is convenient to the convention center.

Stouffer's Inn on the Square, 24 Public Square, 696-5600.

MODERATE

Hollenden House, East 6th Street and Superior Avenue, 621-0700.

Beryl's Gold Coast Inn, 11837 Edgewater Drive, is about seven miles from the center of town, off U.S. Rt. 6, 226-1616.

Suggested Nightlife

Stagedoor Johnnie's, Prospect Avenue between East 14th and 24th Streets.

Sweetwater Cafe, 1320 Huron Road, at Playhouse Square, 781-1150.

Places to Visit

The Food Market, with hours on Monday, Wednesday, Friday, and Saturday, opens its doors at 7:00 and becomes crowded quickly. Located across the river from downtown, at W. 25th

Street and Lorraine Avenue, this is one of the best open-air markets in the country.

Cleveland Museum of Art, 11150 East Blvd. at University Circle, 421-7340, is free to visitors (closed Mondays). The museum features medieval and Oriental art.

The Fine Arts Gardens of Wade Park, next to the Cleveland Museum of Art (see above) is noted for its seasonal flower displays.

Cleveland Health Education Museum, 8911 Euclid Avenue, 231-5010, houses an unusual exhibition of the functions of the human body.

Weather Information
Cold weather from Canada passes through Cleveland, which creates long, cold winters. Spring comes and leaves quickly. Summer is brief and mild. Fall is the ideal season for this part of the country.

Average Temperatures

	J	F	M	A	M	J	J	A	S	O	N	D
Avg. High	33	35	44	58	68	78	82	80	74	64	49	36
Avg. Low	20	21	28	38	48	57	61	60	53	44	34	24

DETROIT
Area Code: 313
Estimated Population: 4.5 million (includes suburbs)
Altitude: 575 to 675 feet
Time Zone: Eastern
Airport to City: About 22 miles to central Detroit
Rental Cars at the Airport: Alamo, Avis, Budget, Dollar, Hertz, National, Payless, Snappy, Thrifty
Newspapers: Detroit Free Press, Detroit News, Royal Oak Tribune, Oakland Press

Conventions: The Metropolitan Detroit Convention and Visitors Bureau, 2 Jefferson Avenue, 567-1170

Transportation into Town
Allow one hour into town from Wayne County Airport. Taxi fare to Detroit is less than $30; bus fare is less than $10 per person. Taxi fare to Ann Arbor is less than $40 and to Dearborn costs approximately $20.

Airport Information
Detroit Metropolitan Wayne County Airport serves Detroit and surrounding metropolitan areas; however, Windsor Airport is also available and is across the Detroit River in Windsor, Ontario (Canada). Consider using the less-crowded Windsor Airport, especially if you are returning to Detroit from Europe.

Suggested Dining
The Caucus Club, 150 West Congress Street, 965-4970.

Elaine's, in the Pontchartrain Hotel, 2 Washington Blvd., 965-0200.

Van Dyke Place, 649 Van Dyke, 821-2620, is in a restored mansion.

Suggested Lodging
EXPENSIVE
The Omni International, adjoining the Millender Center, 333 East Jefferson Avenue, 222-7700. Ask about the Executive Service program.

The Pontchartrain Hotel, at 2 Washington Blvd., 965-0200, was recently remodeled.

MODERATE
The Botsford Inn, 28000 Grand River Avenue, in Farmington Hills, 474-4800.

The Hilton International Windsor, in Windsor, Ontario, 519-973-5555 or 800-HILTONS.

Suggested Nightlife
Galligan's, 51 East Jefferson, 963-2098, is located across from the Renaissance Center.

Places to Visit
Greenfield Village is a 260-acre indoor/outdoor museum complex in Dearborn.

The Renaissance Center, in Detroit's inner city, has several fine restaurants and shops.

Weather Information
Detroit is cloudy nearly 300 days of the year. Winters are cold and damp. Summers are warm and relatively sunny with frequent but brief showers.

Average Temperatures

	J	F	M	A	M	J	J	A	S	O	N	D
Avg. High	32	34	44	58	69	79	83	82	75	64	79	35
Avg. Low	17	19	27	37	47	57	61	59	52	42	32	21

MINNEAPOLIS/ST. PAUL

Area Code: 612
Estimated Population: 2 million
Altitude: 687 to 1058 feet
Time Zone: Central
Airport to City: Located to the south of both Minneapolis and St. Paul, Hubert H. Humphrey Airport is about 10 miles from most central locations in either city.
Rental Cars at the Airport: Alamo, Avis, Budget, Dollar, Hertz, National
Newspapers: Minneapolis Star-Tribune, St. Paul Pioneer Press/Dispatch
Convention(s)/Information: The Greater Minneapolis Chamber of Commerce and Convention and Tourist Commission, 81 South 9th Street, Minneapolis, 370-9132; the St. Paul Convention Bureau, 445 Minnesota Street, St. Paul, 292-4360

Transportation into Town

Allow 30 minutes during uncongested traffic periods, by taxi, from the airport to most central areas in either city. Taxi fare is under $20 to most areas in Minneapolis and under $15 to St. Paul.

An airport limousine service to Minneapolis and St. Paul operates from 5:30 A.M. to midnight. To Minneapolis, the fare is less than $8 one way and $11 round trip, per person; the limo drive to St. Paul's hotels (ask first to make sure the limo stops at your hotel) is quick and costs about $5 one way.

Airport Information

The Hubert H. Humphrey Airport is a modern facility and is easily reached from either Minneapolis or St. Paul. Minnesotans are adept at managing life in cold, snowy weather. Despite heavy winter snowstorms, you should encounter few if any major air or ground traffic delays into or out of the airport.

Suggested Dining in Minneapolis

Anthony's Wharf, 201 S.E. Main Street, 378-7058, is located under the 3rd Avenue Mississippi bridge.

501 Restaurant, 510 Groveland Avenue, 874-6440, is next to the Guthrie Theatre.

The Fifth Season, at the Marriott City Center, 30 South Seventh Street, 349-4000.

Suggested Dining in St. Paul

The Blue Horse, 1355 University Avenue, 645-8101.

The Lexington, 1096 Grand Avenue, 222-5878.

Suggested Lodging in Minneapolis

EXPENSIVE

Hyatt Regency, 1300 Nicollet Mall, 370-1234 or 800-228-9000.

Marriott City Center, 30 South Seventh Street, 349-4000 or 800-228-9290.

MODERATE
Marriott, 1919 East 78th Street, 845-7441 or 800-228-9290.

Howard Johnson's, 7801 Normandale Road, 835-7400 or 800-654-2000.

Suggested Lodging in St. Paul
EXPENSIVE
St. Paul, 350 Market Street, 292-9292, is also the home of the classic restaurant L'Etoile.

MODERATE
Holiday Inn-Town Square, 411 Minnesota Street, 281-8800 or 800-HOLIDAY.

Sheraton Midway, 400 Hamline Avenue North, 642-1234 or 800-325-3535.

Suggested Night Life in Minneapolis
Loon Cafe, 500 North First Street, 332-8342.

Figlio, Calhoun Square, 3001 Hennepin at Lake Street, 822-1688, offers sidewalk tables during the summer.

Suggested Night Life in St. Paul
Cafe Latte, 850 Grand Avenue, 224-5687.

Places to Visit
The Guthrie Theatre, in Minneapolis, is host to one of the best repertory companies in the United States. Performances usually are from May to February, but concerts and special productions are presented year-round. Phone 377-2224 for tickets and information.

St. Paul's Cathedral, in St. Paul, is a replica of St. Peter's in Rome and is noted for its 175-foot dome.

Fort Snelling State Park is on the way to or from the Airport. This is the oldest landmark for the Twin Cities, located on a high bluff, and overlooks the meeting place of the Mississippi and Minnesota rivers. Phone 726-9430 for information on special events.

Weather Information

Expect a wide range of temperatures and weather conditions. The flat topography and numerous lakes help create long, windy winters with plenty of snow, and hot, humid summers with plenty of mosquitoes.

Average Temperatures

	J	F	M	A	M	J	J	A	S	O	N	D
Avg. High	21	26	37	55	68	77	82	81	71	61	41	27
Avg. Low	3	7	20	34	46	57	61	60	49	39	24	11

ST. LOUIS

Area Code: 314
Estimated Population: 600,000
Altitude: 472 feet
Time Zone: Central
Airport to City: 17 miles to most central parts of St. Louis
Rental Cars at the Airport: Alamo, Avis, Budget, Dollar, Hertz, National
Newspapers: St. Louis Globe Democrat, St. Louis Post-Dispatch
Convention Center(s)/Information: A. J. Cervantes Convention and Exhibition Center, 801 Convention Plaza, 342-5000; St. Louis Convention and Visitors Commission, South Broadway, Suite 300, St. Louis, 421-1023 or 800-325-7962

Transportation into Town

Allow 30 to 45 minutes from Lambert-St. Louis Airport into town, by taxi, for less than $20 to most central areas.

The Jet Port van departs from the airport every 20 minutes, 6:30 A.M. to 10:30 P.M. The fare is less than $8 one way and $15 round trip to most areas. For taxi and van service, allow about an hour travel time to your destination. Allow two hours or more during rush hour or in bad winter weather.

Airport Information

Lambert-St. Louis International Airport is un-congested and generally easy to use; however, the airport has five terminals that stem from the main terminal, which makes for potentially long walks if you must connect to a flight located in a distant terminal. Consider taking only carry-on luggage if you will have to catch a connecting flight with an hour or less layover.

Suggested Dining

Anthony's, 10 South Broadway, 231-2434, serves excellent Italian cuisine.

Tony's, 826 North Broadway, 231-7007, also serves wonderful Italian food.

Catfish & Crystal, 409 North 11th Street, 231-7703.

Top of the Riverfront, at the Clarion Hotel, 200 South 4th Street, 241-9500, has window tables that provide a panoramic view of the city.

Suggested Lodging

EXPENSIVE

Marriott Pavilion, home of the 1964 New York World's Fair Spanish Pavilion, is in the heart of St. Louis, at 1 Broadway, 421-1776 or 800-228-9290.

Doubletree Hotel, 16625 Swingley Ridge Road, 523-5000, has tennis, swimming, and golf.

Sheraton St. Louis, 910 North 7th Street, 231-5100 or 800-325-3535, is on the Mississippi.

MODERATE

Holiday Inn-Riverfront, 200 North 4th Street, 621-8200 or 800-HOLIDAY, caters to the business traveler.

Howard Johnson's North, 9075 Dunn Road, in Hazelwood, 895-3366 or 800-654-2000.

Suggested Nightlife

The Grand Hall Bar at the Omni International Hotel, Union Station at 1820 Market Street, 241-6664.

Houlihan's, in the Union Station complex, 436-0844.

Places to Visit

Anheuser-Busch Brewery, 610 Pestalozzi Street, 577-2626, conducts free tours on weekdays.

St. Louis is a sports town and plays host to the St. Louis Cardinals (baseball) and the Blues (hockey), and other teams. Check at your hotel desk for sporting events taking place during your stay.

Weather Information

Long, hot, humid summers are the rule, with infrequent severe thunderstorms. Winter produces little snow; however, because much of the air traffic connects from neighboring regions that have poor winter weather, winter flight delays are routine in St. Louis.

Average Temperatures

	J	F	M	A	M	J	J	A	S	O	N	D
Avg. High	40	44	53	67	76	85	88	87	80	70	54	43
Avg. Low	23	26	33	46	55	65	69	67	59	48	36	26

Southern/Southwestern Metropolitan Areas

ATLANTA

Area Code: 404
Estimated Population: 2 million (includes suburbs)
Altitude: 1050 feet
Time Zone: Eastern

Airport to City: 12 miles
Rental Cars at the Airport: Alamo, Avis,
Budget, Dollar, General, Hertz, National
Newspapers: Atlanta Constitution, Atlanta
Journal
Convention Center(s)/Information: Chamber of
Commerce: 1300 N. Omni International, 521-
0845; Convention and Visitors Bureau, 235
Peachtree Street, N.E., Suite 1414, 521-6633

Transportation into Town
Allow approximately 30 minutes to town from
Hartsfield International Airport, by taxi, at a flat
fare of $15.

The Airport Shuttle stops by the terminal
every 20 minutes from 5 A.M. to midnight; the
fare is $7 one way, $12 round trip. The bus from
the airport to town is $6 to $10, depending on
destination.

MARTA (rail transit system) departs from
the airport terminal and travels into Atlanta; fare
is usually less than $1; travel time is approxi-
mately 20 minutes to Peachtree Center (center
of town).

Airport Information
Hartsfield International is one of the world's largest airports and serves as a hub for much of the
air traffic that passes through the South.

Suggested Dining
The Ritz Carlton, 181 Peachtree Street North,
659-0400, has two fine restaurants: The Dining
Room and The Cafe.

The Fish Market, 3393 Peachtree Road, Northeast, 262-3165.

Pano's & Paul's, 1232 West Paces Ferry Road,
261-3662 (dinner only, from 6 P.M., Monday to
Saturday).

Nikolai, at the rooftop of the Atlanta Hilton, 659-
2000 (elegant dining).

The Coffee Shoppe at the Hilton.

Suggested Lodging
EXPENSIVE

Marriott Marquis, 265 Peachtree Center Avenue, N.W., 800-228-9290.

Ritz Carlton, 181 Peachtree Street N.E., 800-241-3333.

Hilton and Towers, 255 Courtland Street, 659-2000 or 800-HILTONS.

MODERATE

Courtyard by Marriott, several locations, 800-321-2211.

Howard Johnson's Motor Lodge, several locations, 800-654-2000.

Suggested Nightlife
Peachtree Cafe, 286 East Paces Ferry Road Northeast.

Places to Visit
The Cyclorama, a painting and sculpture 400 feet in circumference and complete with sound and lights, portraying the battle of Atlanta during the American Civil War.

Other recreational areas include Piedmont Park; the Atlanta Botanical Garden; and Six Flags Over Georgia, which features the Scream Machine, the fastest, longest, and tallest roller coaster in the United States

Weather Information
Winter is brief and mild, and summer is long and hot. Atlanta experiences about 50 thunderstorms each year, most of which occur during the spring and midsummer. Flight delays are commonplace during these thunderstorm seasons.

Average Temperatures

	J	F	M	A	M	J	J	A	S	O	N	D
Avg. High	51	54	61	71	79	84	86	86	81	72	61	52
Avg. Low	33	35	41	50	59	66	69	68	63	52	40	34

DALLAS/FORT WORTH

Area Code: Dallas—214; Fort Worth—817
Estimated Population: Dallas, 3 million
(includes suburbs); Fort Worth, 1 million
(includes suburbs)
Altitude: 450 to 750 feet
Airport to City: Dallas/Fort Worth Airport is
located equidistant between Dallas and Fort
Worth (about 25 miles from each city); Love
Field is only seven miles northwest of Dallas
but more than 40 miles from Fort Worth.
Rental Cars at the Airport: Alamo, American
International, Avis, Budget, Hertz, National,
Thrifty (Dallas-Fort Worth); Avis, Budget,
Hertz, National (Love Field)
Newspapers: Dallas Times Herald, Dallas
Morning News, The Dallas Observer, The Fort
Worth Star-Telegram
Convention Center(s)/Information: Dallas
Convention and Visitors Bureau, 1507 Pacific,
954-1111; Fort Worth Convention and Visitors
Bureau, 700 Throckmorton, 336-8791

Transportation into Town

From Dallas/Fort Worth Airport: Allow up to 45
minutes to central locations in either city, by taxi,
at a flat fare (including tip and toll) of less than
$25.

Bus transportation takes slightly longer and
costs about $10 per person.

Allow about an hour to most hotels if you
are traveling by van; the TBS, Bluebird, and VIP
vans stop at major hotels and cost under $10 to
most locations.

From Love Field: Allow about 30 minutes (in
light traffic, longer during rush hours) to most
central areas in Dallas, by taxi, with a fare of
about $12.

A bus into town departs from Love Field
every 10 minutes, with a travel time of 30 to 60
minutes; the fare is less than $1.

Airport Information

The Dallas/Fort Worth Airport is one of the world's largest airports (in area). Love Field is much smaller and handles chiefly local air traffic and smaller commercial carriers.

Suggested Dining in Dallas

Atlantic Cafe, 4548 McKinney Avenue, 960-2233, specializes in seafood.

The Hofbrau, 3205 Knox, 559-2680, is a well-known steak house.

Routh Street Cafe, 3005 Routh Street, 871-7161, has Southwestern fare.

Suggested Dining in Fort Worth

The Balcony, 6100 Camp Bowie Blvd., 731-3719, serves from a continental menu.

The Crystal Cactus Room, at the Hyatt Regency Hotel, 815 Main Street, 870-1234, specializes in seafood and Texas steaks.

Suggested Lodging in Dallas
EXPENSIVE

Dallas Marriott Mandalay, 221 S. Las Colinas Blvd., in Irving, is located between the Dallas airport and town, 800-228-9290 or 559-2100.

Plaza of the Americas, 650 North Pearl Blvd., at Bryan Street, 800-223-5672 or 979-9000, offers free limousine service into town.

MODERATE

Embassy Suites, 2727 Stemmons Expressway, 630-5332, or 800-362-2779, is an all-suite facility.

La Quinta Motor Inns (several to choose from), call 800-531-5900.

Suggested Lodging in Fort Worth
EXPENSIVE

Stockyards, at 109 East Exchange, 625-6427, is a renovated, historic hotel.

Worthington, 200 Main Street, 870-1000, is a European-style facility across from Sundance Square.

MODERATE
Fort Worth Hilton, 1701 Commerce Street, 335-7000, or 800-HILTONS, is in the center of town and near the Convention Center.

Holiday Inns (several to choose from), call 800-HOLIDAY.

Places to Visit
Age of Steam Museum, located on the Midway in Dallas, 421-8654, provides replicas and history about steam-engine trains and other steam engines.

The John F. Kennedy Memorial, at Main and Market streets, marks the location where President Kennedy was assassinated.

Six Flags Over Texas is located in Arlington, equidistant from Dallas and Fort Worth. The park is not open all year. Call first for information, 640-8900.

Amon G. Carter Museum of Western Art, in Fort Worth, 3501 Camp Bowie Blvd., 738-1933, is best known for its paintings by Frederic Remington and Charles M. Russell.

Weather Information
Weather in the Dallas-Fort Worth area is humid and subtropical, with hot summers. This part of Texas is subject to thunderstorms during late spring. The heaviest rains occur in April and May. July and August are typically dry months.

Average Temperatures

	J	F	M	A	M	J	J	A	S	O	N	D
Avg. High	56	60	67	76	83	91	95	96	88	79	67	59
Avg. Low	34	38	43	54	62	70	74	74	67	56	44	37

FORT LAUDERDALE

Area Code: 305
Estimated Population: 1 million (includes all of
Broward County)
Altitude: Sea level to 20 feet
Time Zone: Eastern
Airport to City: 10 miles to the center of Fort
Lauderdale, plus 10 miles to many hotels
located north of the city.
Rental Cars at the Airport: Ajax, Alamo,
American International, Avis, Budget, Dollar,
Enterprise, General, Hertz, National, Payless,
Snappy, Thrift
Newspapers: Fort Lauderdale Sun-Sentinel
Convention Center(s)/Information: Broward
County Tourist Development Council, 201 S.E.
8th Avenue, 765-4466

Transportation into Town

From Fort Lauderdale/Hollywood International
Airport, allow 20 minutes to the beach and the
center of town, 10 minutes to Port Everglades,
and an hour to Miami. Taxi fare to most areas
will be less than $15, and not more than $25 to
Pompano Beach and Hollywood Beach. Limousine and van service is available to most areas
in and near Fort Lauderdale for about $10, and
about $15 to $20 to Boca Raton or Miami.

Airport Information

Modernization work has recently been completed on Fort Lauderdale/Hollywood International Airport, although no shuttle service is
available between terminals. Plan on a 15- to 20-
minute walk if you are catching a connecting
flight at a distant terminal.

Suggested Dining

La Ferme, 1601 E. Sunrise Blvd., 764-0987, is a
country-style French restaurant.

Il Giardino's, 609 E. Las Olas, 763-3733, serves
Italian fare.

Suggested Lodging
EXPENSIVE
Marriott has three locations in the Fort Lauderdale area: in Harbour Beach, 3030 Harbour Dr.; at 17th Street and the Intracoastal; and at Cypress Creek. Phone 800-228-9290 for information and reservations for all three locations.

MODERATE
Embassy Suites has several locations in the area. Call 800-362-2779 for information.

Ireland's Inn, 2220 North Atlantic Blvd., 565-6661, is on the beach.

Suggested Nightlife
Stan's Lounge, 3300 East Commercial Blvd. and the Intracoastal west of Waterway, 772-3700.

Shooters, at the Intracoastal and East Oakland Park Blvd. east of Waterway, 566-2855.

Places to Visit
The Jungle Queen scenic cruise departs at Bahia Mar, one of the area's best known marinas, and is across from the beach on A-1-A.

Several gambling sports are located in the Fort Lauderdale area, including dog racing, jai alai, horse racing, and trotter racing.

The beach at Fort Lauderdale is known for its beauty.

Weather Information
The coastal area from Palm Beach south to Miami (known as the Florida Gold Coast) has a subtropical climate controlled by warm gulfstream air. Summers are long and warm, with ample rainfall. Winter is mild and relatively dry. Rain is heavier and frequent a few miles inland from the Atlantic coast. Hurricane potential is high in September and October, although the hurricane season does not end until mid-November.

Average Temperatures

	J	F	M	A	M	J	J	A	S	O	N	D
Avg. High	76	77	79	83	85	88	89	90	88	85	80	77
Avg. Low	59	59	63	67	71	74	75	76	76	71	64	60

HOUSTON

Area Code: 713
Estimated Population: 3 million (includes suburbs)
Altitude: 50 to 60 feet
Time Zone: Central
Airport to City: 25 miles from most commercial areas to Houston Intercontinental Airport; 12 miles to Hobby Airport.
Rental Cars at the Airport: Agency, Avis, Budget, Dollar, General, Hertz, National, Snappy, Thrifty (Houston Intercontinental and Hobby airports); Holiday, Payless (Houston Intercontinental only)
Newspapers: Houston Chronicle, Houston Post
Convention Center(s)/Information: Greater Houston Convention and Visitors Council, 3300 Main Street, 523-5050

Transportation into Town

Driving time from Intercontinental Airport into downtown Houston can take up to 1 hour, 30 minutes, and up to 1 hour from Hobby to downtown Houston. Taxis charge a flat rate, about $26, to and from Intercontinental Airport; meters are used to and from Hobby, with fares averaging about $17. A helicopter service shuttles passengers to downtown Houston from Intercontinental Airport, for about $50. Van services depart frequently from both airports, with fares averaging about $10 per person.

Airport Information

Houston's Intercontinental Airport is a large hub and serves as a connection point for many flights to and from the Southwest and Mexico. Roads into and out of the airport are limited, which leads to frequent traffic problems. Avoid traveling to or from the airport during rush hours.

Although Hobby is closer to downtown Houston than Intercontinental Airport, traffic flow into and out of Hobby is almost always poor; Hobby is recommended if your destination is southeast of town.

Suggested Dining
Birraporetti's, 500 Louisiana Street, next to the Alley Theatre, 224-9494, serves moderately priced Italian fare.

Brennan's, 3300 Smith Street, 522-9711.

Ninfa's, 2704 Navigation, 228-1175, serves reasonably priced Mexican food. This is a chain, with other locations in and around Houston.

Suggested Lodging
EXPENSIVE
La Colombe d'Or, Montrose Blvd., is a converted mansion next to Saint Thomas University in the Montrose area.

Inn on the Park, in the Riverway complex, at Post Oak Lane and Woodway Drive, 871-8181.

Hyatt Regency, 1200 Louisiana Street, 654-1234 or 800-228-9000.

MODERATE
Hilton, with several locations to choose from. Call 800-HILTONS for reservations and information.

Holiday Inn, with several locations to choose from. Call 800-HOLIDAY for reservations and information.

Suggested Nightlife
Rockefeller's, 3620 Washington, 864-9365, has jazz groups regularly.

Nash D'Amico's Pasta and Clam Bar, 2421 Times Blvd., 521-3010.

Places to Visit

Lyndon B. Johnson Space Center is a 1620-acre facility used to train NASA astronauts. The Space Center is located approximately 25 miles south of Houston. Call 483-4321 for information.

Astrodome, hundreds of professional sporting events throughout the year, 799-9544.

Weather Information

Warm moist air from the Gulf of Mexico helps create mild winters and hot, humid summers. Houston averages only 24 days of freezing weather per year.

Average Temperatures

	J	F	M	A	M	J	J	A	S	O	N	D
Avg. High	63	66	72	79	86	91	94	94	90	83	73	66
Avg. Low	41	45	50	59	65	71	73	72	68	58	49	43

LAS VEGAS

Area Code: 118
Estimated Population: 500,000 (includes outlying areas)
Altitude: 2050 feet
Time Zone: Pacific
Airport to City: Slightly less than 10 miles.
Rental Cars at the Airport: Ajax, Alamo, American International, Avis, Budget, Dollar, Enterprise, General, Hertz, National, Payless, Snappy, Thrifty
Newspapers: Review Journal, Las Vegas Sun
Convention Center(s)/Information: Las Vegas Convention and Visitors Authority, Convention Center, 3150 Paradise Road, 733-2323

Transportation into Town

Allow 30 to 45 minutes, by taxi, to outlying areas of Las Vegas, and slightly less to the Strip; in peak traffic times, add another 15 minutes. Fare to the Strip is less than $15 and into town, less than $20. Gray Line Airport Express charges $5 to $7 to the Strip and town locations; however, add 40 minutes travel time for this service.

Airport Information
McCarran International Airport has recently been expanded, with some operational rough spots still apparent. In traveling to the airport, expect long walks from the taxi drop-off point to ticket counters and gates.

Suggested Dining
Good, fast, and inexpensive food can be found at most casino lunch buffets.

Battista's Hole in the Wall, 4041 Audrie, 732-1424, specializes in pasta.

Tillerman, 2245 East Flamingo, 731-4036, specializes in fish and steak served in an oasis-like setting.

Vineyard, 3630 Maryland Parkway, 731-1606, is in a mall and is inexpensive.

Suggested Lodging
EXPENSIVE
Bally's Grand, 3645 Las Vegas Blvd., 739-4111.

Caesar's Palace, 3570 Las Vegas Blvd., 731-7110.

MODERATE
The Mint, 100 East Fremont Street, 385-7440.

Circus Circus, 2880 Las Vegas Blvd., 734-0410.

Best Western Inns, with several locations to choose from. Call 800-528-1234 for reservations and information.

Suggested Nightlife
Las Vegas never sleeps, and gaming activities are numerous both on the Strip and off, 24 hours per day.

Botany's, 1700 East Flamingo, 737-6662, is an informal disco.

Places to Visit
Hoover Dam and Lake Mead, 30 minutes south of Las Vegas; phone 293-4041 for information on Hoover Dam and 293-4041 for information about Lake Mead.

The Strip features 24-hour gambling, stage shows and revues, and lounge and club activity. Death Valley requires a full day for the drive and the visit. Many tour-guide companies in Las Vegas offer tours.

Weather Information
Las Vegas is in the middle of a vast desert surrounded by mountains that have elevations from 2000 to 10,000 feet above the desert floor. The mountain protection helps create a relatively mild climate much of the year, although summers are very dry and can be hot.

Average Temperatures

	J	F	M	A	M	J	J	A	S	O	N	D
Avg. High	56	61	68	77	87	97	104	101	95	81	66	57
Avg. Low	32	37	42	50	59	67	75	73	65	53	41	34

MIAMI

Area Code: 305
Estimated Population: 3 million (includes suburbs)
Altitude: Sea level to 34 feet
Time Zone: Eastern
Airport to City: Miami International Airport is only five miles from downtown Miami, and about ten miles from many beach locations. Fort Lauderdale/Hollywood International is about 25 miles from the center of Miami, but is a convenient airport for travelers destined for North Miami areas.

Rental Cars at the Airport: Alamo, Avis, Budget, Dollar, General, Hertz, National, Value

Newspapers: Miami News, Miami Herald, El Diario (Spanish)

Convention Center(s)/Information: Greater Miami Convention and Visitors Bureau, 701 Brickle Avenue, 539-3000

Transportation into Town

Allow 20 to 30 minutes to most downtown areas, and an additional 10 minutes to beach locations. Taxi fares are under $20 to most Miami locations. Red Top Vans provides service to most in-town areas for under $8 per person, and to northern areas, as far north as Fort Lauderdale, for about $15.

Airport Information

Miami International Airport is a major gateway to the Caribbean, to Central and South America, and to many European cities. Because there is only one Customs area, international passengers can experience delays of one hour or longer; aliens may encounter delays of two hours or longer.

Suggested Dining

Brasserie de Paris, 244 Biscayne Blvd., in the Everglades Hotel (downtown), 379-5461, serves authentic French cuisine.

Casa Juancho, 2436 Southwest Eighth Street, in Little Havana, 642-2452, serves Spanish cuisine, but Cuban style.

Kaleidoscope, 3112 Commodore Plaza, 446-5010, in Coconut Grove.

Suggested Lodging

EXPENSIVE

Mayfair House, 3000 Florida Avenue, 441-0000 or 800-433-4555, is in the remodeled Coconut Grove.

Omni International, 1601 Biscayne Blvd., 374-0000, is close to town and to the port of Miami.

MODERATE

Days Inn has several new ones to select from, in convenient locations. Call 800-325-2525 for reservations and information.

Holiday Inns are numerous in the area. Call 800-HOLIDAY for reservations and information.

Suggested Nightlife

Daphne's, 3900 N.W. 21st Street, 871-3800, is near the airport at the Sheraton River House.

Most of the discos and lounges in the area provide free buffet meals during Happy Hour.

Places to Visit

Hialeah is one of the world's most beautiful race tracks. If you go, plan to leave prior to the final race to avoid extremely heavy exit traffic.

Coconut Grove, a small village near Miami, is designed for walking and has many shops and restaurants.

Miami Seaquarium, located on Rickenbacker Causeway, is the world's largest tropical aquarium. Open year-round.

Deep-sea fishing outings are available through several charter-boat companies at many Miami-area marinas. Call several locations for competitive estimates.

Weather Information

The coastal area from Palm Beach south to Miami (known as the Florida Gold Coast) has a subtropical climate controlled by warm gulfstream air. Summers are long and warm, with ample rainfall. Winter is mild and relatively dry. Rain is heavier and frequent a few miles inland from the Atlantic coast. Hurricane potential is high in September and October, although the hurricane season does not end until mid-November.

Average Temperatures

	J	F	M	A	M	J	J	A	S	O	N	D
Avg. High	76	77	79	83	85	88	89	90	88	85	80	77
Avg. Low	59	59	63	67	71	74	75	76	76	71	64	60

NEW ORLEANS

Area Code: 504
Estimated Population: 1.3 million (includes suburbs)
Altitude: Sea level to 26 feet
Time Zone: Central
Airport to City: 15 miles to most areas in central New Orleans
Rental Cars at the Airport: Alamo, American International, Avis, Budget, Dollar, Enterprise, Hertz, National, Payless, Snappy, Thrifty
Newspapers: The New Orleans Times-Picayune, The States-Item
Convention Center(s)/Information: Greater New Orleans Tourist and Convention Commission, 1520 Sugar Bowl Drive, 566-5011

Transportation into Town

Allow 45 minutes to and from most areas in town, and slightly more during rush hour. Taxi services charge a flat rate—less than $20—into town. Van transportation to downtown hotels is available for about $8, but can take as long as an hour. Another lengthy approach is to take the airport-downtown bus, which travels to and from the intersection of Loyola and Tulane avenues, for about $1 each way.

Airport Information

Moisant Airport is a relatively small and problem-free urban airport. However, the increasing hub traffic may lead to expansion in the near future.

Suggested Dining

New Orleans is known for its hundreds of world-class restaurants. The ones listed here are only a small sampling.

Brennan's, 417 Royal, in the French Quarter, 525-9711, specializes in breakfast, but is extremely crowded on weekends.

Fitzgerald's, at West End Park overlooking Lake Pontchartrain, 282-9254, serves excellent seafood.

Felix's, 739 Iberville, 522-4440, is known for its oysters.

K-Paul's Louisiana Kitchen, 500 Mandeville Street, 947-6712, is the headquarters for Paul Prudhomme, who helped make "cajun" and "blackened redfish" household expressions.

Chart House, 801 Chartres Street, is known for its steak, crab, and other seafood specialties. Ask for a balcony table with a view of Jackson Square.

Suggested Lodging

EXPENSIVE

Omni Orleans, 621 St. Louis Street, 529-5333, is also home of the locally popular Esplanade Lounge.

Windsor Court, at 300 Gravier Street, 523-6000, is an English-style hotel.

Inter-Continental New Orleans, 444 St. Charles Avenue, 525-5566 or 800-327-0200, is in the middle of the business district.

Royal Orleans, 621 St. Louis Street, 529-5333 or 800-843-6664, is in the French Quarter.

MODERATE

Cornstalk, 915 Royal Street, 523-1515, is a small, Victorian-style home.

Holiday Inn-East, 6324 Chef Menteur Highway, 241-2900 or 800-HOLIDAY, is perhaps the best of several Holiday Inns in the area.

Quality Inn Midtown, 3900 Tulane Avenue, 486-5541 or 800-228-5151, is well located and has an excellent restaurant.

Suggested Nightlife
Touche-Bar, 621 St. Louis Street, in the Omni Royal Orleans, 529-5333.

Flagon's, 3222 Magazine, 895-6471, is one of New Orleans' first wine bars.

Places to Visit
A river tour on the Mississippi is a treat, even if you only take the ferry across to Algiers. Several tour boats are available. One of the more popular tours on weekends is on *The President,* which leaves from the end of Canal Street. Phone 586-8777 for information.

Moon Walk, named after Moon Landrieu, a former mayor of New Orleans, is an interesting promenade along the Mississippi.

Bourbon Street is the home of New Orleans Jazz. Most clubs are open 24 hours, 7 days per week, although evenings are best for music.

Weather Information
The abundance of water—Lake Pontchartrain to the north, the Mississippi River to the east and south, the nearby Gulf of Mexico, and several local marshes—creates hot and humid weather with frequent rains and heavy thunderstorms, from mid-June through September. Winter rains, when they occur, can continue uninterrupted for days. Winter rains and spring fog tend to disrupt both air and ground traffic. New Orleans is also the target of hurricanes, with late summer being the primary hurricane season.

Average Temperatures

	J	F	M	A	M	J	J	A	S	O	N	D
Avg. High	62	65	70	78	85	90	90	91	87	80	70	64
Avg. Low	43	46	51	59	65	71	73	73	70	60	50	45

ORLANDO

Area Code: 407
Estimated Population: 800,000 (including Walt Disney World)
Altitude: 110 to 150 feet
Time Zone: Eastern
Airport to City: The center of Orlando is about 15 miles north of Orlando International Airport. The convention center on International Drive is about 12 miles west of the airport. The Walt Disney complex is past the convention center, about 8 miles to the south.
Rental Cars at the Airport: Alamo (the largest rental car facility in the world—and one of the most congested), American International, Avis, Budget, Dollar, Hertz, National, Payless, Snappy, USA
Newspapers: Orlando Sentinel
Convention Center(s)/Information: Orlando Chamber of Commerce, 75 East Ivanhoe Blvd., Orlando, 425-1234; Orlando Convention and Visitors Bureau, 7680 Republic Drive, Orlando, 345-8882; Walt Disney World Co., 824-4321

Transportation into Town

Many of the Disney World hotels are close to the airport but can be found from the airport to near the entrance of Disney World. A taxi into Orlando is less than $20 and takes about 30 minutes. A taxi to Disney World costs about $35, but expect to pay half this amount to most of the hotel areas near the airport. Allow 20 minutes by taxi to the convention center. Limousine vans into town are about $10 one way, $15 round trip, and $10 each way to and from Disney World.

Airport Information

Orlando International Airport includes modern Disney-like monorail trains that transport passengers from the main terminal to one of two outer arrival and departure terminals. The airport has lots of room to grow, which it surely will. This airport has excellent in-terminal services, including fine restaurants.

Suggested Dining

La Normandie, 2021 East Colonial Drive, 896-9976, specializes in lunch for the business community and serves dinner for special events.

Charlie's Lobster House, 2415 Aloma Avenue, in Winter Park, 677-7352.

Barney's Steak House, 1615 East Colonial Drive, 896-6864, features quiet dinner music and a reasonably priced menu.

Empress Room, in Walt Disney World village, on the Empress Lilly riverboat at Lake Buena Vista. Call 828-3900 for a reservation, at least one week in advance, if possible.

Orient IV, 130 Altamonte Avenue, in Altamonte Springs, is inexpensive and serves excellent Chinese cooking.

Suggested Lodging

EXPENSIVE

Hyatt Regency Grand Cypress, 1 Grand Cypress Blvd., Lake Buena Vista, 800-228-9000, is near the convention center and the Disney complex.

Marriott's Orlando World Center, World Center Drive, Orlando, 239-4200 or 800-228-9290, is also near the convention center.

MODERATE

The following all have several locations to choose from:

Holiday Inn, 800-HOLIDAY for reservations and information.

Howard Johnson's, 800-654-2000 for reservations and information.

Ramada Inn, 800-2-RAMADA for information and reservations.

Days Inn, 800-325-2525 for reservations and information.

Suggested Night Life

Rosie O'Grady's Good Time Emporium, 129 West Church Street in Orlando. (Several other establishments are nearby.)

Park Avenue, 4315 North Orange Blossom Trail, in Winter Park, 295-7350.

Places to Visit

Walt Disney World is a must, of course. However, Orlando also offers several excellent tennis facilities and golf courses.

Several places to eat, enjoy good music, and watch people can be found in the 100 block of West Church Street in Orlando.

Walt Disney World Shopping Village now encompasses Pleasure Island and is home to many fine shops, restaurants, and bars in a lakeside setting. Call for reservations for most restaurants.

Weather Information

The swampy land and many lakes in the area help create high humidity throughout the year. The heaviest rains fall from June through September, although thundershowers occur throughout the year. Winter days are mostly sunny, though, with warm, pleasant temperatures.

Average Temperatures

	J	F	M	A	M	J	J	A	S	O	N	D
Avg. High	70	72	76	81	87	89	90	90	88	82	76	71
Avg. Low	50	51	56	61	66	71	73	73	72	66	57	51

PHOENIX

Area Code: 602
Estimated Population: 1 million (includes suburbs)
Altitude: Approx. 1150 feet

Time Zone: Mountain Standard (does not switch to Daylight Savings Time)
Airport to City: Distance to many commercial areas of Phoenix is 8 to 10 miles.
Rental Cars at the Airport: Ajax, Alamo, American International, Avis, Budget, Dollar, General, Hertz, National, Payless, Value
Newspapers: Arizona Republic, Phoenix Gazette, Tribune Newspapers
Convention Center(s)/Information: Phoenix and Valley of the Sun Convention and Visitors Bureau, 505 North Second Street, Suite 300, 254-6500; Phoenix Civic Plaza, 225 East Adams Street, 262-6225

Transportation into Town

A taxi ride into downtown Phoenix is less than $12 and takes about 25 minutes. Taxi service to Scottsdale is only slightly more expensive and a few minutes longer. Supershuttle and other limousine and van services charge under $7 to most areas of Phoenix, and less than $15 to Sun City, Mesa, and other outlying areas.

Airport Information

Sky Harbor has four somewhat disjointed terminals, which can create difficulty for passengers trying to make connecting flights. Although a bus service is available for travel between terminals, allow extra time between connections for interterminal transportation.

Suggested Dining

Avanti's of Phoenix, 2728 East Thomas Road, 956-0900, serves Northern Italian fare.

Compass, at 122 North Second Street, phone 252-1234, is a 24th floor, revolving dining room atop the Hyatt Regency.

Pointe in Tyme, 11111 N. 7th Street, 866-7500 is part of The Point resort.

The Velvet Turtle, 3102 East Camelback Road, 957-7180, specializes in beef Wellington.

Suggested Lodging
EXPENSIVE

Arizona Biltmore, 24th Street and Missouri, 955-6600.

Phoenix Hilton, Central and Adams, 800-HIL-TONS.

Embassy Suites has several locations. Call 800-362-2779 for reservations and information.

MODERATE

Holiday Inn and Holidome Corporate Center, 2532 West Peoria Avenue, 943-2341 or 800-HOLIDAY, includes a health center.

Sheraton Greenway Inn, 2510 West Greenway Road, 993-0800 or 800-325-3535, has tennis as well as golf privileges.

Suggested Nightlife
Oscar Taylor's, in the Biltmore Fashion Square, 956-5705.

Pop's Restaurant and Market Place, 4510 North Scottsdale Road, in Scottsdale, 945-7677.

Places to Visit
Desert Botanical Gardens, in Papago Park off the Galvin Parkway, 941-1217.

Heard Museum, 22 East Monte Vista, 252-8848, has regional archeological treasures, including artifacts from ancient Native American civilizations. The museum includes a Native American jewelry and craft gift shop.

Desert tours are offered by several tour companies. Gray Line, 254-4550, offers one of the more popular tours.

Weather Information
Phoenix is a desert valley, surrounded by mountains, which makes for a dry climate with occasional and severe thunderstorms in July and August. Summers are very hot, with low humidity in early summer. Winters are warm and dry.

Average Temperatures

	J	F	M	A	M	J	J	A	S	O	N	D
Avg. High	65	69	75	84	93	101	105	102	98	87	74	66
Avg. Low	38	41	45	52	60	68	77	76	69	57	45	38

Western Metropolitan Areas

DENVER

Area Code: 303
Estimated Population: 1.5 million (includes suburbs)
Altitude: 5130 to 5470 feet
Time Zone: Mountain
Airport to City: 9 miles to most areas in downtown Denver
Rental Cars at the Airport: Alamo, American Intl., Avis, Budget, Dollar, General, Hertz, National, Payless, Snappy, Thrifty, Western
Newspapers: Denver Post, Rocky Mountain News
Convention Center(s)/Information: Denver Metro Convention and Visitors Bureau, 225 W. Colfax Avenue, 892-1112

Transportation into Town

Anticipate no more than a 30-minute drive into town, unless traffic is heavy or a winter storm is in process. Taxi fare into Denver is less than $15 and slightly less than $40 into Boulder. Limousine service is available to most major hotels in Denver, usually for less than $8 per person. An express bus into downtown Denver also is available for less than $2.

Airport Information

Stapleton International Airport is one of the highest airports in the world, and is a growing hub for carriers that serve western and southwestern cities.

Suggested Dining

Baby Doe's Matchless Mine, 2520 West 23rd Avenue, 433-3386, is a replica of the Matchless Mine in Leadville.

Manhattan Cafe, 1620 Market Street, 893-0951, is also home to a piano bar named Ivory's.

Tante Louise, 4900 East Colfax Avenue, 355-4488, serves French cuisine in an unpretentious atmosphere.

Suggested Lodging

EXPENSIVE

Marriott City Center, 1701 California Street, 297-1300 or 800-228-9290, is located in the Arco Tower in the center of town.

Radisson, 1550 Court Place, 893-3333 or 800-228-9822, has a winter ice rink that converts into a summer terrace.

MODERATE

Denver Inn-Downtown, 321 17th Street, 296-0400, serves a complimentary breakfast.

La Quinta, 3500 Fox Street, 458-1222.

Suggested Nightlife

Ironworks Sports Bar and Restaurant, 25 Larimer Street, 825-4901, serves very spicy food.

Places to Visit

The United States Mint, located on Delaware Street between Colfax and 14th, 844-3582, offers free admission.

The State Capitol is near the U.S. Mint and has a rotunda similar to the Capitol building in Washington, D.C. The rotunda in Denver is coated with gold leaf valued at more than $50,000.

Larimer Street has many interesting shops, restaurants, and bars.

Weather Information

Denver has a mild, sunny, semiarid climate. Sudden cold fronts from Canada can disrupt this mild climate, however. Autumn is pleasant and spring weather tends to be stormy.

Average Temperatures

	J	F	M	A	M	J	J	A	S	O	N	D
Avg. High	43	46	50	61	70	80	87	86	78	67	53	46
Avg. Low	16	19	24	34	44	52	59	57	48	37	25	19

LOS ANGELES

Area Code: 213 (818 in the San Fernando Valley and parts of the San Gabriel Valley)
Estimated Population: 10 million (includes suburbs)
Altitude: Sea level to about 5000 feet in mountain areas
Time Zone: Pacific
Airport to City: Los Angeles is a sprawling metropolitan area with three major airports. The following distances are to downtown Los Angeles: 15 miles from Hollywood-Burbank Airport; 17 miles from Los Angeles International Airport; 22 miles from Long Beach Airport.
Rental Cars at the Airport (Los Angeles International): Alamo, Avis, Budget, Dollar, General, Hertz, National
Newspapers: Los Angeles Times, Los Angeles Herald-Examiner
Convention Center(s)/Information: Greater Los Angeles Visitors and Convention Bureau, 515 South Figueroa Street, 624-7300

Transportation into Town

Los Angeles International (recently renamed Tom Bradley International Airport) is near the Pacific Ocean and the city of Santa Monica. Taxi fare to downtown Los Angeles is about $30, with a driving time of about 45 minutes—longer during rush hour. The bus system is good, with a bus ride taking about one hour to downtown Los Angeles at a fare of about $2. Van service is provided by Super Shuttle (800-554-6458 or 800-554-0279 in California); use the courtesy phones in the luggage claim area to summon a Super Shuttle van; the fare is less than $15 to most central locations; advance reservations are required for a return trip to the airport.

If your destination is Hollywood, Burbank, Glendale, or Van Nuys, Hollywood-Burbank Airport is a closer and less congested alternative.

Airport Information

Los Angeles International Airport (Tom Bradley International) is one of the largest and most congested airports in the United States. Hollywood-Burbank and Long Beach airports offer less crowded alternatives.

Suggested Dining

Simply Blues, 62900 Sunset Blvd. at Vine, 466-5239, offers live jazz many nights.

The Mandarin, 430 North Camden Drive, 272-0267, serves Chinese fare.

Mischa's Restaurant and Cabaret, 7561 Sunset Blvd., 874-3467, is Russian both in menu and atmosphere. Entertainment is provided most evenings.

Suggested Lodging

EXPENSIVE

Bel-Air, 701 Stone Canyon Road, Los Angeles, 472-1211.

Beverly Hills Hotel, 9641 Sunset Blvd., Beverly Hills, 276-2251, is also home to the famous Polo Lounge.

Beverly Hilton, 9876 Wilshire Blvd., Beverly Hills, 274-7777 or 800-HILTONS.

Sheraton hotels are located throughout the Los Angeles area. Call 800-325-3535 for reservations and information.

MODERATE
Mikado Best Western, 12600 Riverside Drive, 763-9141 or 800-528-1234, is located near Hollywood.

Holiday Inn-Crowne Plaza, 5985 Century Blvd., 642-7500 or 800-HOLIDAY.

Suggested Nightlife
Rangoon Racquet Club, 9474 Little Santa Monica Blvd., in Beverly Hills, 274-8926.

Scandia, 747 North La Cienega, 652-9998.

Cutters, 2425 Colorado Avenue, Santa Monica, 453-3588.

Places to Visit
The Farmers' Market, located at West 3rd Street and Fairfax, is a large, open-air market.

Many television shows are filmed in the Los Angeles area and they admit audiences. For general information, call the Los Angeles Visitors Center, 624-7300. The Tonight Show is the most requested—call 818-840-3537 for information about this show and for NBC studio tours.

The Burbank Studios, although dwarfed by the Universal Studios Tour, is excellent and much less crowded (only a few people are permitted to tour the studio at one time). Call 818-954-6000 for reservations (required) and information.

The *Queen Mary* is docked at Long Beach Harbor and includes a 300-room hotel. Phone 213-435-3511 for hotel reservations.

The Spruce Goose, located next to the *Queen Mary* in Long Beach, is the world's largest all-wood aircraft, designed and owned by Howard Hughes.

The Los Angeles area is home to dozens of excellent theaters. If you plan to attend a show during a visit to Los Angeles, purchase a copy of *The Los Angeles Times* to examine theater listings. Many shows require reservations several weeks in advance.

Weather Information

Los Angeles is blessed with mild weather throughout the year. Days are warm, with cool nights, even during summer. Rain is infrequent. However, the surrounding mountains trap warm air in the San Fernando and San Gabriel Valleys, creating smoggy unhealthful air, especially during summer.

Average Temperatures

	J	F	M	A	M	J	J	A	S	O	N	D
Avg. High	63	64	64	66	68	70	75	76	76	73	70	66
Avg. Low	45	47	49	52	55	59	62	63	62	57	51	47

SALT LAKE CITY

Area Code: 801
Estimated Population: 800,000 (includes suburbs)
Altitude: 4200 feet to 8000 feet
Time Zone: Mountain
Airport to City: Salt Lake City International Airport is located 7 miles west of the city.
Rental Cars at the Airport: Ajax, Alamo, American International, Auto Express, Avis, Budget, Dollar, Freedom, General, Hertz, National, Payless, Snappy
Newspapers: Salt Lake Tribune, Deseret News
Convention Center(s)/Information: Salt Lake Convention and Visitors Bureau, 180 South West Temple Street, 521-2822; Salt Lake Area Chamber of Commerce, 175 East 400 Street, 364-3631.

Transportation into Town

Allow at least 30 minutes to most downtown locations, by taxi, at a fare of less than $15. Allow at least 60 minutes to downtown locations by bus or van. Van fare is less than $12 into town. For destinations outside of Salt Lake City, it is advisable to rent a car at the airport.

Airport Information

Salt Lake City International Airport is a two-terminal facility, which can create problems for travelers who must make a connecting flight at a different terminal. The airport is expanding rapidly; expect to encounter changes in facilities and services in the future.

Suggested Dining

La Fleur de Lis, 165 South West Temple, 359-5753, serves French cuisine.

Log Haven, 3800 South Millcreek Canyon, 272-8255.

Market Street Grill, 48 Post Office Place, 322-4668, offers mesquite-grilled fare and French-style pastries.

The Roof, in the Westin Hotel, 531-1000, has an outstanding view of the Mormon Temple.

Suggested Lodging

EXPENSIVE
Salt Lake Marriott, 75 South West Temple Street, 531-0800 or 800-228-9290.

MODERATE
Little America, 500 South Main Street, 363-6781 or 800-435-9450.

Perry, 110 West 3rd South, 521-4300, is one of the oldest hotels in the city, but renovation was completed in 1985. This hotel fills up quickly, so book rooms as far in advance as possible.

Suggested Nightlife

NOTE: Utah law requires a $5 two-week visitor membership for entry to most clubs in the state.

D.B. Cooper's, 19 East 200 South, 532-2948.

The piano bar at the Salt Lake Hilton, 150 West 5th South, 523-3344.

Places to Visit

The Great Salt Lake is 73 miles from the city. Although this is a popular tourist attraction, the water teems with billions of brine shrimp and the shores are often heavy with flies; beaches are more for observing than for sunning or swimming.

Temple Square is the headquarters for the Mormon Church (formally called The Church of Jesus Christ of Latter Day Saints). The Square is home to the Mormon Tabernacle Choir and the Church Office Building, which houses the world's largest genealogical library.

Weather Information

Spring weather is often stormy, and summers are hot and dry. Winters are snowy and cold, but also sunny—ideal for skiing.

Average Temperatures

	J	F	M	A	M	J	J	A	S	O	N	D
Avg. High	37	43	51	62	72	81	93	90	80	66	50	39
Avg. Low	18	23	28	36	44	51	60	59	43	38	28	21

SAN FRANCISCO

Area Code: 415
Estimated Population: 5 million (includes Oakland and suburbs)
Altitude: Sea level to 1000 feet
Time Zone: Pacific
Airport to City: 16 miles from San Francisco International Airport to most central business

areas in San Francisco; the distance from Oakland International Airport to downtown San Francisco is about the same, although travel time to San Francisco is usually longer from Oakland International.

Rental Cars at the Airport: Alamo, Alpine, American International, Apple, AVCar, Avis, Budget, Dollar, General, Hertz, National, Payless, RPM, Snappy, Thrifty

Newspapers: San Francisco Chronicle, San Francisco Examiner

Convention Center(s)/Information: San Francisco Convention and Visitors Bureau, 1390 Market Street, 391-2000

Transportation into Town

From San Francisco International, allow about 30 minutes to downtown—slightly longer during rush hour. From Oakland International, allow about 45 minutes to downtown San Francisco, and at least 1 hour during rush hour. By cab, travel time between the two airports is about 1 hour.

Taxi fare into San Francisco is usually under $30. A van into town can take up to 1 hour, at a fare less than $8. The Bus-BART connection takes about one hour, at a fare less than $2 each way, but waiting times at airport bus stops can be as long as 30 minutes.

Airport Information

San Francisco International Airport is still undergoing some renovation—both within the terminal and on access roads.

Oakland International Airport is much smaller than San Francisco International, and may be more convenient than San Francisco International for some destinations. Avoid traveling between Oakland International and downtown San Francisco during rush hour.

Suggested Dining

Ernie's, 847 Montgomery Street, 397-5969, is popular with local celebrities.

Mandarin, 900 North Point Street, in Ghirardelli Square, 673-8812, has a unique Chinese menu.

Tarantino's, 206 Jefferson Street, 775-5600, is at Fisherman's Wharf.

Suggested Lodging

EXPENSIVE

Fairmont Hotel and Tower, at California and Mason Streets, 772-5000 or 800-527-4727.

Mark Hopkins Intercontinental, 1 Nob Hill, 392-3434 or 800-327-0200.

Hyatt on Union Square, 345 Stockton Street, 398-1234 or 228-9000.

MODERATE

Galleria Park, 191 Sutter Street, 781-3060 or 800-227-4248 is in the heart of the financial district.

Howard Johnson's at Fisherman's Wharf, 580 Beach Street, 775-3800 or 800-654-2000.

Suggested Nightlife

Perry's, 1944 Union, 922-9022 (several other clubs are located along Union).

Places to Visit

Fisherman's Wharf (to Pier 39) offers seafood restaurants, lounges, shops, harbors, boats, and people watching. Start at Ghirardelli Square at Polk and Larkin, and continue east along Embarcadero.

Chinatown, with the main entrance on Grant near Union Square, offers unique shops, restaurants, and cultural experiences. Japan Center, at Gary Blvd. and Larson Street, is not as famous as Chinatown, but unique nevertheless.

The Golden Gate Bridge, with the best view available from the other side of the bridge, look-

ing toward San Francisco, is especially beautiful
at sunset.

Weather Information

The San Francisco Bay is a major contributing
factor to the weather, tempering both the summers (rarely hot) and the winters (cool but rarely
as cold as other northern areas). Rainfall is scarce
between June and October, and minimal during
other months. Heavy early morning and evening
fogs are frequent and can disrupt both auto and
air traffic.

Average Temperatures

	J	F	M	A	M	J	J	A	S	O	N	D
Avg. High	55	59	61	63	67	70	71	72	74	70	63	56
Avg. Low	41	44	45	47	50	53	54	54	54	52	47	43

SEATTLE

Area Code: 206
Estimated Population: 500,000
Altitude: Sea level to 170 feet
Time Zone: Pacific
Airport to City: 15 miles from the Seattle/
Tacoma airport to the center of Seattle.
Rental Cars at the Airport: Alamo, Avis,
Budget, Dollar, Hertz, National, Pacific,
Payless, Thrifty
Newspapers: Seattle Daily Journal of
Commerce, Seattle Post-Intelligencer, Seattle
Times
Convention Center(s)/Information: Seattle
Center, 305 Harrison Street, 625-4234; Seattle
Trade Center, 2601 Elliot Avenue, 625-5641;
Seattle Visitors Bureau, 1815 7th Avenue, 447-
7273

Transportation into Town

Allow 40 to 60 minutes into downtown Seattle
or Tacoma, by taxi, at a fare of $30 or slightly
less. Gray Line Express provides bus service into

downtown Seattle and centrally located hotels, for about $5 one way and $9 round trip, and departs the airport every 30 minutes from 6 A.M. to midnight; a transfer to Vancouver, British Columbia, also is available for an additional $30.

Airport Information

The Seattle/Tacoma International Airport is a major point of departure for cities in the Orient. The central terminal has four concourses; however, many international carriers operate from the North Satellite or the South Satellite terminals, both of which can be difficult and time-consuming to travel to from another terminal. Allow 30 to 60 minutes additional time for switching terminals if you are connecting to an international destination.

Suggested Dining

The Brasserie Pavillion, 206 1st Avenue South, 623-4167, is known for its salmon.

F. X. McCrory's Steak, Chop and Oyster House, 419 Occidental Avenue South, 623-4800, provides a 1920s atmosphere.

Le Provencal, 212 Central Way, in Kirkland, 827-3300.

Suggested Lodging

EXPENSIVE

Sorrento, 900 Madison Street, 622-6400 or 800-426-1265.

Westin Seattle, 1900 5th Avenue at Westlake, 728-1000 or 800-228-3000, is also the home of Trader Vic's restaurant.

MODERATE

Best Western inns are numerous in the Seattle and Tacoma areas. Call 800-528-1234 for reservations and information.

Quality Inn at Sea-Tac, 3000 South 176th Street, 246-9110 or 800-228-5151, is at the airport.

Suggested Nightlife
The Duke's Yacht Club, 1111 Fairview Avenue North, 622-0200 (other excellent clubs are within walking distance).

Places to Visit
Seattle Center is the site of the 1962 World's Fair and offers many restaurants.

Weather Information
Rains are extremely frequent, but not heavy. However, severe snow storms can move into the area suddenly during the winter months, creating air and ground traffic delays. Summer and autumn both offer mild, pleasant weather.

Average Temperatures

	J	F	M	A	M	J	J	A	S	O	N	D
Avg. High	43	48	51	57	64	69	75	74	69	59	50	45
Avg. Low	45	36	36	40	45	50	54	54	59	45	39	35

Index

Accidents, weather-related airline 173, 207–9
AIDS, danger from, 159
Air Traveler's Fly Rights, 120
Airdata, Inc. and weather information, 19
Air-Evac International, 163
Airline Reporting Corporation (ARC), 53
Airline Transportation Association, directing safety complaints to, 190
Airlines, 169–90
  accidents on commuter, 173
  avoiding stop overs or changing planes on, 176–77
  booking flights on, 11–13
  bumping passengers from, 1, 119, 120–21
  business-class service on, 75, 78, 79, 82, 84–88
  check in, early, 118–19
  choosing commuter, 175–76
  coach-class service on, 82–83
  commuter, 175–76
  competition among, 71–73
  complaints to, 127, 190
  computer reservation system of, 103–4
  crew mutinies on, 177–79
  dealing with terrorism on, 183–90
  discount fairs on, 83
  earaches from travel on, 149–51
  false claims by, 1
  first-class service on, 74–79
  frequent flyer programs of, 106–14
  higher fares for business travel on, 67–69
  in-flight malfunctions on, 179–80
  in-flight safety precautions on, 181–83
  last minute charges on, 125–26
  liability for lost and damaged luggage of, 45–46
  list of frequent flyer programs for, 107–12
  list of meal service on, 76–77
  loss leader fares by, 70–71
  lost tickets, 16
  luggage handling by, 20–21, 22–23, 43–48, 124–25
  malfunctions prior to departure on, 169–71
  negotiation of discounts with, 61
  not arriving at destination, 182–83
  overbooking by, 120–24
  passenger rights on, 117–18, 120
  preparation checklist for travel on, 10
  reservations on, 24–25
  seat selection on, 114–16
  seating on, 12
  special meals on, 14–15
  tickets as tax deductible business expense, 315
  toothaches from travel on, 151–52
  travel agent bookings on, 54–56
  weather and, 19, 171–75
Airports
  avoiding stopovers at congested, 176–77
  looking for alternative destinations, 100
  luggage thieves in, 23–24
Alcohol
  effect of on travel, 140–41
  as a gift, 299, 300–305
  and intestinal gas, 155
  and jet lag, 133
  and travel, 159
Allergies
  and in-flight earaches, 149
  and medical alert medallions, 11, 32
Altitude sickness, 137–39
American Car Rental Association, directing complaints to, 281–82
American Express Card and weather information, 19
American Express travelers checks
  acceptance of, 248

emergency contact phone
  numbers for, 257
  See also Travelers checks
American Society of Travel
  Agents (ASTA), 53–54
  complaints to, 127–28
Amsterdam, discount tickets to,
  106
Anxiety, effects, 141, 144–45
Around-the-world fares, 96–97
ATA Carnet and custom duties
  on trade show displays,
  241–42
Atlanta information on, 352–55
Audit
  surviving IRS, 318–19
  travel diary as defense
    against IRS, 321–23

Baltimore, information on,
  326–28
Bank of America travelers
  checks, 257. *See also* Travelers checks
Banks, cashing of travelers
  checks by, 250–51
Barclays/Visa travelers checks,
  257. *See also* Travelers
  checks
Boarding, early, 118–19
Boarding pass and overbooked
  flights, 121
Boston, information on, 328–30
British Airways, around-the-
  world fare on, 96
Bumping by hotels and airlines,
  1, 120–21
Burn out, 1, 5
Buses
  liability for lost and damage
    luggage, 46
  motion sickness on, 147
Business
  airline competition and fares,
    71–73
  and discounts offered by
    travel agents, 60–62
  higher air fares for, 67–69
  and loss leader air fares, 70–
    71
  travel expense diary and
    taxes, 17
  travel expenses in, 2
Business-class seats
  on airlines, 75, 78, 79, 82
  availability of and amenities
    of, listed by airlines, 84–88
  not bumped, 119
  listing of, 84–88

Car
  carrying auto insurance infor-
    mation, 31–32

motion sickness in, 144–45,
  147
recording location of, 31
Car rental(s), 13
  avoiding drop-off charges
    with, 280–81
  breakdown, 209–13
  complaints about, 281–82
  cost varies by locality, 277
  deciding whether to use, 263–
    64, 269
  as deductible business ex-
    penses, 315
  determining real cost of, 264–
    65, 267
  discounts for frequent flyers
    listed, 107–12
  high costs of, 269–79
  insurance for, 31
  insurance rip-off on, 266–68,
    272–76
  listed, 282–85
  local companies in, 279–80
Carnet. *See* ATA Carnet
Centers for Disease Control,
  163
  *Health Information for Inter-
    national Travel*, 159
Chartered flights, risks of, 124
Check in, do it early, 118–19
Chicago, information on, 338–
  41
Children not bumped, 119
Choking, reaction to, 200–202
Cincinnati, information on,
  341–43
Citicorp travelers checks, 257.
  See also Travelers checks
Citizenship, lack of proof of,
  242–45
Cleveland, information on,
  343–45
Clothes
  to bring on trip, 22, 38–40
  cleaning of after motion sick-
    ness, 149
  comfortable, motion sickness
    and, 145
  for flying, 34
  as tip to robbers, 219
  as tip to terrorists, 186, 188
Coach-class service on airlines,
  82–83
Collision and damage waiver
  (CDW), 266–68, 272–74
Commuter airlines
  choosing among, 175–76
  weather-related accidents on,
    173
Complaints about car rentals,
  212–13, 281–82

about reservation problems, 216
where to send, 128
Consolidators, *See* Ticket consolidators
Constipation remedies, 154–55
Credit cards
acceptance of, 247–48, 252
bonus mileage for charging airline tickets with, 107–13
buying airline tickets with, 90
and car rental insurance, 273–74
charges on as tax receipts, 323
as collateral for lost travelers checks, 254
insurance on and car rentals, 211
lost or stolen, 11
and purchase of airline tickets from consolidators, 79
record numbers of, 30
tips for safekeeping, 258–62
what to do if refused, 216–19
Crime
and hotel robberies, 224–28
luggage thieves, 23–24
preventing robbery and mugging of travelers, 219–28
tips for preventing pickpockets, 259–62
Crisscross strategies and super saver tickets, 90–93
Customs, 235–36
coping with a search by, 236–39
duty charges listed, 240
and imitation brands, 239
and trade show display items, 241–42

Dallas, information on, 355–58
Daylight savings time, 24–25
Dehydration
from air travel, 139–40
prevention of while flying, 34
travel diarrhea and, 153–54
Delta Airlines, special rate first class service on, 75
Denver, information on, 375–77
Depression from traveling, 130, 157–59
Detroit, information on, 345–47
Diarrhea, 129, 130, 152–54
Diary of travel as defense in IRS audit, 321–23
Documents
keeping extra copies of, 30

given to family member, 11, 17
Driver's license records, 30
Drug smuggling and strict customs procedures, 236
Dublin, where to obtain discount tickets to, 105
Duties. *See* Customs

Earaches, 130, 149–51
Edinburgh, discount tickets to, 106
Ehret, Charles F., 133–34
Electric converter, 27
Electric extension cord, packing, 26, 27
Emergencies, travel, 199–233
accidents, 207–9
airline crew mutinies as, 177–79
arrests as, 204–7
customs search as, 236–39
fires as, 228–33
foreign medical treatment sources listed, 167–68
in-flight malfunctions as, 179–80
list of medical agencies for, 163–65
lost and stolen travelers checks as, 252–55
sudden medical, 200–204
political unrest as, 191–94
refusal to accept credit cards as, 216–19
robbery as, 219–28
safety precautions on airlines to handle, 181–83
terrorism as, 183–90
tips for safekeeping cash, travelers checks, and credit card in case of, 258–62
U.S. citizenship, lack of proof of, 242–45
U.S. Foreign Service Offices listed, 165–67
Enterovioform, caution against taking, 153
European Assistance Worldwide Service, 163–64
Exercise as preventive for motion sickness, 145
Eye drops, 28–29

Fares, airline, 67–73. *See also* Tickets
Federal Aviation Administration (FAA) and airline maintenance, 171
Film, safeguarding, 34–35
Fires, escaping from, 228–33

First-class seats
  not bumped, 119
  and terrorism potential, 186
First-class service
  on airlines, 74–79
  listing for airlines, 84–88
Food poisoning, 158–59
Foreign travel
  acceptance of travelers checks
    in, 248, 249, 250–51, 252
  accident insurance for, 207–8
  arrests during, 205–7
  auto insurance for, 31–32,
    276
  avoiding political unrest dur-
    ing, 191–94
  computer reservation system,
    103–5
  customs during, 235–45
  excess weight luggage in, 44
  giving and accepting gifts on,
    298–307
  hiding American nationality
    during, 21
  illness prevention before,
    161–63
  lost and stolen travelers
    checks during, 254
  medical emergencies during,
    204
  planning car rentals for, 268
  proving U.S. citizenship dur-
    ing, 242–45
  reservations, confirming, 214
  sources of emergency medical
    treatment listed, 165–68
  surviving being taken hostage
    during, 195–97
  taxes on car rentals, 265
  tipping in, 288–98
  U.S. Foreign Service Offices
    listed, 165–67
  viruses and food poisoning
    from, 158–59
Fort Lauderdale, information
  on, 358–60
Fort Worth, information on,
  355–58
Frequent Flyer, 10, 12–13
  airline travel, 112–14
  availability on airlines listed,
    76–77
  business-class seats listed by
    airline, 84–88
  and clearing wait lists, 73
  programs listed, 106–13
  upgrades on Delta and TWA,
    75

Gasoline and rental cars, 276
Gifts

  acceptance of, 299, 306–7
  appropriateness of by coun-
    try, 298–307
  selection of, 298–99
  taxes on, 323
Glasgow, discount tickets to,
  106

Handicapped travelers not
  bumped, 119
Health care abroad, 164–68
Health Information for Interna-
  tional Travel, 159
Hijacking, surviving, 184–88
Hostage, survival tips, 195–97
Hotels. See Lodging
Houston, information on, 360–
  62
Hubs and price of airline tick-
  ets, 99, 104

Illness. See sickness
Immunization status, 161
Insurance, 11
  and accidents while traveling,
    207–9
  and bonds payment of cus-
    toms duties, 242
  and car rentals, 31, 211, 266–
    68, 272–76
  carrying information on auto,
    31–32
  claims after robbery, 222
  and credit card purchase of
    ticket, 90
  extra for luggage, 125
  health, travelers', 164
  homeowners and lost luggage,
    46
  for trip protection, 124
Internal Revenue Service
  business travel diary for, 17
  surviving an audit by, 318–
    19, 321–23
  travel deductions rules of,
    309–15
International Air Transport Association (IATA)
  safety complaints to, 190
  travel agents approval sys-
    tem, 53
International Association for
  Medical Assistance to
  Travelers (IAMAT)
  foreign treatment centers
    listed, 167–68
  service provided by, 162–63
International Bureau of Chambers of Commerce and ob-
    taining ATA Carnet, 241–
    42

International SOS Assistance,
Inc., 164
Intestinal gas from travel, 129,
130
    diet to prevent, 34
    foods that cause, 155–56
    overcoming, 156–57
Ireland, discount tickets to, 105
Itinerary review prior to travel,
126

Jet lag, 130–32
    and eastbound travel, 136
    factors, 136–43
    how to beat, 133–34
    and westbound travel, 135

Keys, 11, 17
    hiding set of, 29–30
Know Before You Go, U.S. Cus-
    toms Service booklet, 236

Las Vegas, information on,
    362–64
Laundry, 22
Legal rights of U.S. travelers
    outside U.S., 205–7
Liability
    of airlines for lost and dam-
        aged luggage, 45–46
    of travel agents, 65–66
    See also Insurance
Local emergency number (911),
    164, 204
Lockerbie (Scotland), 183, 186
Lodging, 1–2
    as deductible business ex-
        penses, 315
    discounts listed, 107–12
    escaping fires in, 228–33
    and hotel robbery, 224–28
    lost reservations at, 213–16
    storage of valuables at, 32
    and tax deductions, 313
    tipping, 288, 289–91
    tipping of by country, 292–98
London, discount tickets to,
    105–6
Loneliness during business
    travel, 1–2
Los Angeles, information on,
    377–80
Loss leader air fares, 70–71
Luggage, 10, 22–24
    and bomb threat, 186
    business traveler's, 20–21
    carrying on, 43–45
    correct packing of, 21–22,
        41–42
    and delayed flights, 127
    excess weight of, 44–45

extra insurance on, 125
and first-class service listed,
    76–77
lost or damaged, 45–48, 124–
    25
to phantom destinations, 101
special handling listed by air-
    lines, 84–88
traveling with minimal, 37–
    41

Malaria, 158, 161–62
Malden, Karl, travelers check
    advertisements by, 223,
    247, 250
Maps of travel destination, 27
Martin, Monica, 57–58
Mastercard travelers checks,
    257–58. *See also* Travelers
    checks
Maugham, Somerset, 5–6
Meals, 2
    in business-class listed by air-
        line, 84–88
    as deductible business travel
        expense, 312–16, 322
    service on airlines listed, 76–
        77
    and snacks while flying, 33
    special airline, 10, 12, 14–15
Medical Alert Foundation, 164
Medical emergencies, sources of
    foreign treatment listed,
    167–68. *See also* Emergen-
    cies
Medication, 11
    bracelet describing, 32
    for in-flight earache, 149–51
    for travel diarrhea, 153
    travel-related reactions to,
        130–31
Mexaform, caution against tak-
    ing, 153
Miami, information on, 364–67
Military uniforms as tip to ter-
    rorists, 188
Millward & Co. CPA, 310
Minneapolis, information on,
    347–50
Motion sickness, 130, 141
    cleaning up after, 147–49
    prevention of, 142–47
Mugging, preventing, 219–25
Mutinies of airline crews, 177–
    79

Name brands, fakes, 239
Nationwide/Worldwide Emer-
    gency Ambulance Return
    (N.E.A.R.), 164
New Orleans, information on,
    367–70

New York City, information
    on, 330–33

Orlando, information on, 370–
    72
Overseas Citizens Emergency
    Center, 163, 164–65
Oxygen starvation, 137–39

Pam Am Flight 103, 183, 186
Paramedics, 203
Paris, discount tickets to, 105
Passport
    keeping record of, 30
    help in emergencies with, 164
    procedures when you lack,
        243–45
    of pseudo-nation to fool ter-
        rorists, 188
Personal auto policy (PAP) and
    car rentals, 272–76
Phantom destinations, 96, 98–
    101
Phoenix, information on, 373–
    75
Phone numbers
    for emergencies with travelers
        checks, 257–58
    of professionals, leaving a file
        of, 17
    for weather information, 175
Photographic film, safeguarding
    while flying, 34–35
Pickpockets, avoiding, 259–62
Pittsburgh, information on,
    333–35
Planning
    benefits of, 35
    booking flights and accom-
        modation, 11–13
    for car rentals, 268, 270
    checking weather conditions,
        18–20
    checklist of items, 25–29
    to confirm reservations, 24–
        25
    expense diary usage, 18
    for file of documents at
        home, 17
    five tips for preflight, 33–35
    importance of for business
        travel, 3–4, 7
    and last-minute business
        travel, 4–5
    for luggage, 20–24
    to make a travel itinerary, 13,
        16, 18, 23
    to overcome jet lag, 133–36
    for packing correctly, 21–22
    preparation checklist, 10–11
    seven special hints for, 29–32

    to travel light, 37–48
Poison Control Center, 164
Political unrest, 191–97
Prostitution, dangers of, 159

Recreational activities, possibil-
    ity for in business travel, 6
Rental cars. See Car Rentals
Reservations, 10
    on airlines, 11–13, 24–25
    computers representation of,
        103–4
    hotel, 13
    if lost, 213–16
    overbooked flight and, 120–
        24
    by travel agents, 54–56
Restaurants
    credit card refusal by, 217–19
    tipping in, 288, 289–91
    tipping in by country, 292–98
Ricci, Robert L., 310
Rights
    of airline passengers, 117–18
    of airline passengers on over-
        booked flights, 120, 121–23
    of U.S. travelers outside U.S.,
        205–7
Robbery, preventing, 219–28

Safety
    accessibility of important
        documents for, 17
    and airline terrorism, 183–90
    and avoiding political unrest,
        191–94
    complaints to airlines about,
        190
    in-flight precautions for, 181–
        83
    keeping extra copies of airline
        tickets for, 16
    of luggage, 23–24
    tips for foreign travel, 21
    of valuables in hotel, 32
Safety box, 11
Salt Lake City, information on,
    380–82
San Francisco, information on,
    382–85
Scanlon, Lynne Waller, 133–34
Scotland, discount tickets to,
    106
Seats
    business-class, 79–88
    coach class, 82–95
    first class, 74–79
    safest airline, 181–83
    selection of airline, 114–16
Seattle, information on, 385–87
Ship

tickets as tax deductible business expense, 316
travel and motion sickness, 147, 149
Shoes, packing, 40
Sickness
  constipation, 154–55
  dehydration, 139–40
  emergency medical services listed, 163–65
  of a hostage, 196
  in-flight earaches, 149–51
  in-flight toothaches, 151–52
  intestinal gas, 155–57
  jet lag, 131–41
  from lack of rest or sleep before travel, 140
  malaria, prevention of, 161–63
  motion, 144–49
  from overeating or excessive drinking, 140–41
  from oxygen starvation (altitude), 137–39
  reaction to sudden medical emergencies, 200–204
  travel diarrhea, 152–54
  from travel-related reactions to medication, 130–31
  traveler's depression, 157–69
  from viruses, food poisoning, and other diseases, 158–59
Sinus problems, 149
Skin moisturizer, 28, 29
Sleep
  as preventive for motion sickness, 146
  prior to travel, 140
Smoking, 10, 12
Spoon, packing, 28
St. Louis, information on, 350–52
St. Paul, information on, 347–50
Super saver fares, on airlines, 83, 90–93
Swiss army knife, packing, 28

Taxes
  benefits of thorough record keeping for, 319–23
  business travel diary for, 17
  on car rentals, 265
  IRS rules on travel deductions for, 309–15
  seven common business travel expenses for, 315–17
  six frequently overlooked travel expenses, 317–18
  surviving an audit, 318–19
Taxis, tipping in, 326

Team flying, 101–3
Terrorism, 183–84
  hijacking, 184–86
  and hostage situation, 195–97
  and political unrest, 191–94
  tips to save your life, 186–90
Thieves, luggage, 23–24. See also Crime and Robbery
Thomas Cook/Mastercard travelers checks, 257–58. See also Travelers checks
Ticket agents and seat selection, 114–16
Ticket consolidators
  buying first-class seats from, 78–79
  list of, 80–81
Tickets
  advance purchase of, 78, 95
  airline discount, 83
  for business-class seats, 78, 79, 82
  for coach-class service, 82–83
  cost savings by booking beyond destination, 98–101
  confirming and checking times of, 126–27
  discount first-class, 75–78
  Europe, discount, 105–6
  higher airline prices for business travel, 67–69
  keeping copies of, 13, 16
  last minute charges, 125–26
  loss leader, 70–71
  and overbooked flights, 120–24
  prices of around-the-world fares, 96–97
  savings by crisscrossing, 90–93
  strategies for cheaper, 89–106
  for team flying, 101–3
  two for price of one, 93–94
  using nonrefundable, 94–95
Time, changes in, 24–25
Tipping
  in foreign travel, 288–98
  for taxis, 326
  in U.S., 287, 288
Toiletries, 40–41
Toothaches, 130, 151–52
Trains
  lost or damaged luggage on, 46
  tickets as tax deductible business expense, 315–16
Travel agents, 49–66
  airline bookings by, 12–13
  assignment to your account of, 58–59
  automation of services, 54–56

car rental arrangements by, 265
checking references of, 59
clear instructions for, 126
complaints to, 127
computer reservation system of, 103–5
conveniently located, 59–60
and discount airfares, 89
and discount first-class tickets, 75–78
false claims by, 1
keeping a super agent, 66
for leisure needs, 60
liability of, 65–66
owner-operated, 56
phantom destinations and, 100–101
problems with, 64–65
and purchase of tickets from consolidators, 79
selecting, 51–66
tracking effectiveness of, 63
training of, 56–58
and trip protection insurance, 124
Travel expenses, 10
and airline competition, 71–73
benefits of records for, 319–23
car rental, 269–79
as cost of doing business, 2
and discounts from travel agents, 60–62
for gifts, 298–307
higher business, 67–69
IRS rules on, 309–15
keeping diary of, 18
and loss leader fares, 70–71
savings from being bumped, 123–24
tax deductible, 315–18
and tipping, 287–98, 326
Travelers checks, 223, 248–50
acceptance of, 247–48
bank cashing of, 250–51
copy of numbers of, 16, 17
emergency contact phone numbers for, 257–58
in foreign travel, 248, 249, 250–51, 252
free for business travelers, 27
keeping records of, 30
lost and stolen, 252–55
system for keeping track of, 255–56
tips for safekeeping, 258–62

Tunnel vision as result of oxygen starvation, 137
TWA, frequent flyer upgrades on, 75
Twenty-percent rule and travel tax deductions, 312–15
Two-percent rule and travel tax deductions, 310–12

U.S. Customs Service. See Customs
U.S. Department of Transportation and airline complaints, 70, 128
U.S. Embassy, contacting for customs problems, 238
U.S. Foreign Service Offices listed by country, 165–67
U.S. State Department, 185
Overseas Citizens Emergency Center, 163, 164–65
United States Council for International Business and obtaining ATA Carnet, 242
Upgrades
airline ticket, 75, 82, 83
rental car, 278–79

Vaccination status, 161
Venereal disease, dangers of, 159
Viruses, from traveling, 130, 158–59
Visa travelers checks, 257. See also Travelers checks

Wait lists and airline travel, 73
Wallet, 11
tips for safekeeping of, 259
Warsaw Convention (1929) and lost and damaged luggage, 45, 124
Washington, D.C., information on, 336–38
Weather, 10, 19
causes airline delays, 171–74
checking destination's, 18–20
climate maps available from IAMAT, 162
delays, avoiding, 174–75
sources of information on, 175
World Immunization Chart, 163

X rays at airports and photographic film, 34–35